Attu: Birding on the Edge

A Quarter Century of Birding
the Western Reaches of North America

A publication of Charles Osgood and the American Birding Association

Edited by Christa Watters

American Birding
ASSOCIATION

Library of Congress Catalog Number 200310–304
ISBN Number: 1-878788-31-0
First Edition
1   2   3   4   5   6   7   8   9

Printed in the United States of America
American Birding Association, Colorado Springs, Colorado 80904 USA
Charles E. Osgood, Kearsarge, NH 03847

Typeset in Hoefler Text
Design and Layout by Chris Foley, Old Town Editions, Alexandria, VA 22314 USA

Distributed by ABA Sales
P.O. Box 6599
Colorado Springs, Colorado 80934-6599 USA
Tel. 719-578-0607 Fax 719-578-9705 Website http://www.americanbirding.org/

Excerpts from "The Holy Grail of North American Birding" by John Fitchen appeared in the *Atlantic Monthly*, October 2001 and in *Birding*, June 2003. "The Murrelets" was first published in *Bird Observer*, June 2001. The following poems by Macklin Smith first appeared in other publications as follows: "Airstrip at Alexai Point", *Beloit Poetry Review* 41/4, 1991; "Roger Tory Peterson and I", *Appalachia*, 194, 1992, reprinted in *Shared Sighting: An Anthology of Bird Poems,* ed. Sheila Goldburgh Johnson (John Daniel and Co., Santa Barbara, 1995); "After Storm Late May", and "And Just to Think That", *Transplant*, Shaman Drum Books (Ann Arbor, 2003)

Cover Photograph: Ed Harper, "Looking west-northwest across Massacre Bay from Alexai Point, May 1980"
Back Cover Photograph: Ed Harper, "The road to Lower Base from Murder Point, May 1988"

Acknowledgments

This book, a compilation of the writings and photos of many individuals, reflects the help and generosity of all those who shared their memories. We thank all those who contributed their writings and photographs; you can see them profiled on page 207.

While we cannot mention each contributor here, a few deserve special recognition. First of all, Larry Balch: Without his vision, drive, and perseverance, there would have been no quarter century of Attour birding to commemorate. Then, when we asked him to explain how he came to do this, he wrote a detailed look behind the scenes, explaining how the trips were planned and managed over the years. And to make clear that in the end the passion for birding was what drove him, he contributed an annotated list of the birds recorded on the trips. He and his crew made the logistics possible, building and maintaining, wiring, plumbing, patching and improvising, lugging and laboring, cooking, leading the birders.

We thank Paul J. Baicich, ABA Director of Conservation and Public Policy, for his insights, suggestions, and support; for sharing his wide network of contacts, his geographical knowledge of the birding terrain, and his willingness to read and proof the work as well as help with photographic selection and identification. Thanks to Brian Small for collecting and coordinating so many of the best photos. Paul Green and John Kricher of the ABA lent their support. Thanks to Allan Burns, ABA Director of Publications, for his support, advice, and editing help; to Cindy Lippincott for her splendid maps, her solid recommendations, help and counsel, and her willingness to be a reader. Eli Elder contributed her lovely photos of the plants of Attu, and from early on lent her support, suggestions, and enthusiasm to the project. Thanks to Jim Burns for his beautifully written contributions, and for the reminder that Attu birders are not just counters, they are passionate poets, mystics, and seekers as well. John Fitchen's story lent us further insight into birders' motivations and ethics. He was also a helpful reader, editor, and proofer along the way. Macklin Smith enriched the book with his beautiful poems, philosophical insights, and willingness to read the work. George West's bird illustrations amplify the annotated bird list. Elise Earl applied her skills to create the index. And Lyndia Terre and Roger Taylor provided not just their writings, photos, and art, but also the initial (and sustaining) enthusiasm and support for the idea of the book.

To each of you who sent a story, answered a question, or e-mailed a query prodding us onward during the long process, we say a heartfelt thank you.

We recognize that we're covering a long period of time, and that memories are sometimes unreliable. We hope we have been as accurate as possible; we acknowledge that different people sometimes remember the details differently and have allowed small variances to stand, while taking responsibility for any errors.

We wish you good reading, looking, and remembering.

Charles Osgood

Christa Watters

A name is just a name, but at times a name conjures up magical images of unrealized dreams. For birders there are many names that bring us images: Chicot Country, Holla Bend, Lake Millwood, Arizona, Everglades, The Valley. But there is one that stands above all the others. One that is spoken with awe and reverence. One that even when whispered, strikes like a bombshell:

ATTU

—*Leif Anderson*

Charles Osgood and Eli Elder birding on Attu, September 2000

Preface

Attu is the westernmost island in the Aleutians, a curving chain of volcanic islands that belong to Alaska and separate the North Pacific from the Bering Sea. Here the arctic air from the north meets the moist air of the Pacific, breeding fierce winds and frequent storms. Attu lies some 1,200 miles from the Alaskan mainland, closer by far to Asia than to North America. It is this confluence of weather and geography that makes Attu one of the most remarkable birding destinations in the world. When storms push in from the southwest and cause migrating birds to fall out of the sky to take shelter on Attu during spring and fall migrations, they are likely to be rare birds seldom seen elsewhere in North America. Attu can claim more first and second ABA-Area records than any other single birding location.

This remote island has a long and sometimes dark history. Attu's native Aleut population was exploited by Russian fur traders in the eighteenth and nineteenth century. During World War II, the Japanese removed the Attuans to Japan, and the island became the site of the Pacific theater's second bloodiest battle. After the war, the natives were not allowed to return, and though groups of scientists and other scholars visited from time to time, the only people living on the island were those manning a United States Coast Guard Station. Still, birders seeking to expand their life lists occasionally found ways to visit Attu. They noted, and reported to friends and colleagues, that the birding was spectacular.

For about the last 25 years of the twentieth century, Larry Balch, an avid birder and former ABA president, brought groups of birders to the island each year but one, under the aegis of the company he founded for the purpose, Attour, Inc. When New Hampshire birder Charles Osgood went on the very last Attour trip to Attu in the fall of 2000, he decided that this northern island birding experience, shared by more than 1,000 people over the years, was so special that it deserved to be memorialized in word and picture for all those who took part in the trips, as well as for lovers of adventure travel who may still have Attu on their wish lists. He talked about the idea with friends and enlisted fellow birders to send in contributions. His vision and support made this book a reality.

The trips to Attu meant different things to different people. For some, the birding was everything. For others, the time on this remote and often inhospitable island meant more: a chance to experience life at a more elemental level in a place little touched by civilization, except for the debris left by World War II. Living conditions, as noted by writer after writer, were uncomfortable, the weather and terrain, harsh. And yet for many, the island had an almost mystical pull that drew them back time and again, whether as paying guests or members of the Attour staff.

Attu: Birding on the Edge is a compendium of personal essays, poems, historical narratives, maps, photos, and drawings. Of particular note for all serious birders is the inclusion of an extensive annotated checklist by Larry Balch. The book is an attempt to document the Attu experience over the years, sharing the highs and the lows, the lighter side and the darker. And perhaps it will inspire someone to try once again to bring birders to this very special place.

—*Christa Watters*

Contents

INTRODUCTION

THE ISLAND

BIRDING THE ISLAND

THE RECORDS

CLOSING THE CIRCLE

CONTRIBUTORS

INDEX

The Large Quiet

It's the large quiet
and the sudden unknown
the wind calling your name
whispering your history
the histories of this place

placing your feet on solid ground
that becomes suddenly
bog, muskeg
almost swallowing you
into the stream below
not a stream but
a vast crevice
maybe miles deep
you see possible death
in the rushing, cold water

the mountains
casting green shadows
directly in your path
a glimpse of wild iris
of cottongrass
you are intoxicated
to walk on

you circle the lakes
that have been there for centuries
or only since this spring
you will never know

you are an uninvited guest
in this vast beauty
the contradictions eating at your core

suddenly
quiet
the vastness of the mountains
the forever distance of ocean
the clarity of sky

a flock of arctic geese
you feel they are familiar
then their voices speak to you
in a foreign tongue
you realize you know nothing

you surrender to the winds
they unwrap you
into the large quiet
the sudden unknown
that is Attu.

—*Lyndia Terre*

Introduction

Looking east at Siddens Valley, Lake Nicholas, Sarana Bay, Gilbert Ridge (north side)

Reflections on 25 Years of Extraordinary Birding

Paul J. Baicich

Attu, the western end of North America, officially closed for easy-access birding in early October 2000. The last birders on the last organized trip came home. Of all the things that Attu was, it stands boldly as the place where new bird species were recorded on this continent for the first time. In this book's contribution by Thede Tobish, there is a chart of "firsts" for North America since 1911 from Alaska. As he points out, 19 of those were from Attu, and a baker's dozen since 1984. Some of the birds seen just since that year are enough to take your breath away: Yellow Bittern (1989), Lesser White-front-ed Goose (1994), Oriental Pratincole (1985), Great Spotted Woodpecker (1986), Lanceolated Warbler (1984), Narcissus Flycatcher (1989), and Pine Bunting (1985). It is even more amazing when one considers that so many of the rarities of North America have been regulars nearly every spring on Attu: Common Greenshank, Common Sandpiper, Siberian Rubythroat, Sky Lark, Eyebrowed Thrush, Olive-backed Pipit, Black-backed Wagtail, Rustic Bunting, and Brambling, to name a few. (For details on these occurrences see the invaluable annotated list compiled beginning on page 149 by Larry Balch on all the species seen over the years.)

The pattern is explainable—at least in terms of access. During the early 1970s through 2000, bird-ers visited Attu almost every spring, bringing with them enthusiasm and eagerness, and taking home knowledge and substantial records. Thirty years ago we knew very little about the occurrences of such birds as Long-toed Stint, Siberian Rubythroat, and Rustic Bunting. These species were thought to be accidental in North America; now we are familiar with them as migrants in small numbers in the outer Aleutians, spillovers from a regular Asian coastal migration route—birds on a Japan–Kurile–Kamchatka flight path

Serious birders first picked up on Joe Taylor's tantalizing Attu report after his 1972 trip. Jerry and Laurette Maisel visited in the spring of 1973. Other independent birders and some small tours orga-nized by Bird Bonanzas and Northeast Birding followed in quick succession. Those were the days when honest-to-goodness scheduled air service to Attu—through Reeve Aleutian Airways—was still available. (Once a week to the Coast Guard airstrip.) Each year, more birders came to Attu, essential-ly concentrating on the southeast corner of the island where an old road network near the shore was left over from the aftermath of World War II. (Attu, of course, was the site of a bloody battle, where about 3,000 Japanese and American soldiers died in 1943. About a fifth of those who died were U.S. troops.) There, birders searched around combat ruins, old Quonset huts, and military debris, scouring the tundra, low willow scrub, miles of beaches, and what is probably the best fresh-water marsh in the Aleutians. They were looking for those birds not seen regularly anywhere else on the continent. Occasionally, they came up with birds that even they had failed to anticipate, the stuff that birding dreams are made of.

The real opening of Attu could not have been possible without the efforts of Larry Balch, and his company, Attour, Inc. Larry, enamored with Attu's beauty and birding potential in the mid-1970s, was concerned that birders might jeopardize access to the island by putting too many demands on the U.S. Coast Guard Loran station there and on the U.S. Fish and Wildlife Service. To make things easier for all concerned, he formed Attour, which started running organized trips in 1979. Attour's final trips were in 2000: a remarkable spring with such glorious birds as Far Eastern Curlew, Common and Oriental Cuckoos, Middendorff's Grasshopper-Warbler, Lanceolated Warbler, Red-breasted Flycatcher, and Rufous-tailed Robin, and a striking fall trip when Baillon's Crake, Fork-tailed Swift, Great Spotted Woodpecker, and Dusky Warbler were observed.

Over the years, Attour brought more than 1,000 birders to Attu, a significant accomplishment. Consider, if you will, the problems of planning, provisioning, and maintenance for scores of birders at a time. This was no mean feat when one realizes that Attu is some 1,500 air miles from Anchorage (about the distance between Boston and Miami). Larry Balch covers these concerns skillfully in his contribution, "How It All Started". While Larry Balch's Attour was certainly a commercial venture, it was also a service to the birding community. (Just about every one of the 70-odd ABA-Area listers with 750 birds or more has been to Attu at least once.) Because of the many risks involved (the availability of planes, the uncertainty of crumbling buildings, the maintenance of runways, the complexity of permissions from the FAA, Coast Guard, USFWS, and the expected closing of the Coast Guard Loran station on the island), Attour ceased operations. It is unlikely that access to the outer Aleutians will be as easily available for birders in the near future. Perhaps some people will be able to visit briefly by ocean-going vessel. Yes, access to Adak is also a possibility. Even Shemya might become available one of these years. These possibilities are ephemeral, though, and birding under these circumstances has its limitations, logistically and biogeographically.

In 1990, the legendary Roger Tory Peterson wrote a short article for *American Birds* (Volume 44, Number 1) on "The Attu Experience". Three of his carefully drawn and captivating plates of Alaska strays accompanied the article, illustrating mostly those Attu specialties that stir the birding sprit. The location has also figured in multiple articles in *Birding*, in Pete Dunne's *The Feather Quest*, in a number of "big year" narratives, and in tall stories whenever passionate birders gather in North America. These are among the reasons that Charles Osgood was inspired to assemble this book.

A chapter has ended, a birding frontier conquered. For those who have had the privilege of taking part in the Attu adventure, the memories and friendships are legion. The impressive bird records pile up. Memories of the haunting beauty and uniqueness of Attu remain.

Whether or not you were able to partake of the adventure of Attu, the lively stories, diverse poems, engaging photos, and birding chronicles fit between the covers of this book may be able to capture something of what it was like. 🐦

Photo: Ed Harper

The road to Lower Base from Murder Point, May 1988

The XO's Orientation

Walk the bicycles across all wood bridges.

Never venture out alone on snow or tundra
In battle areas. We've had amputated feet
From men hiking into live ordnance areas,
And incidents of temporary disappearance
Have transpired. Please exercise caution.
You might just find yourself subterranean
What with all the trenches, tunnels, etc.

Anything metal on the ground, bypass it.
Never handle bullets, bombs, ammo boxes,
Grenades, etc., don't even think about it.
We've got ten thousand unexpended rounds
Out there just itching for human contact.
Any dud you reconnoiter, we'll handle it.

Consider that you have spent over $4000
To come to Attu Island for the purpose
Of birding. Keep that priority in mind.

You are now in a designated war memorial:
Authorized historians only are permitted
To gather, move, or collect war articles.
Best let them lie. That scrap of leather
Will unearth into a government issue boot
Containing a full complement of foot bones,
Meaning soon you might could find yourself
A civilian psychological casualty, gazing
At your Bering Sea out there, dead radio,
Missing out on all that costly ornithology.

—*Macklin Smith*

Photo: Jerry Maisel

Lake Elwood from the east side of Bullfinch Pass, looking into West Massacre Valley

The Maps

The Map of Attu

It gives you ideas.

It reduces and multiplies the mountains.

It makes sea cliffs and beaches one jagged shore.

It gives you ideas to forget.

(If you gaze too long at the blank
Space east of Cape Wrangell
Where the contour lines end in
Explanation, "Obscured by Clouds,"
You might think of walking out
There. No one ever has.)

—*Macklin Smith*

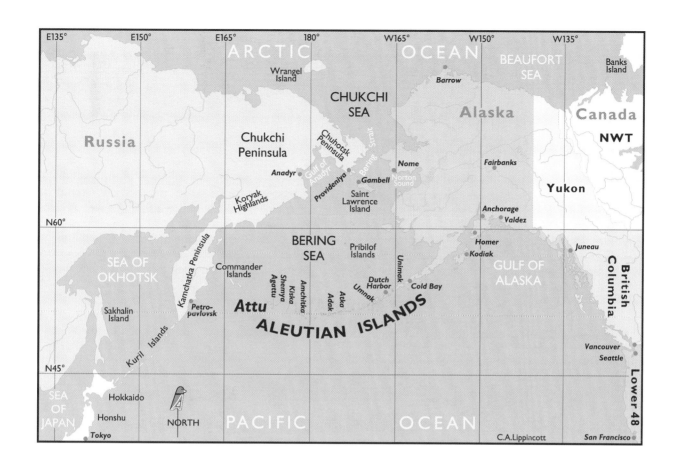

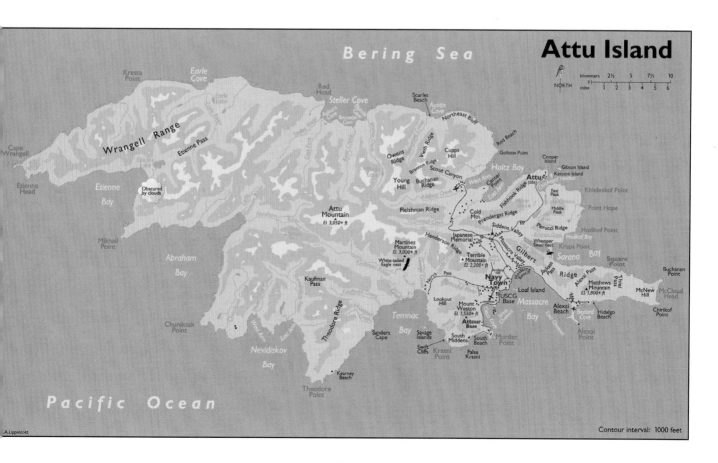

Attu Island
Eastern Half

Bering Sea

kilometers   2½   5   7½   10
miles   1   2   3   4   5   6

NORTH

Steller Cove
Blonde Cove
Brunette Cove
Scarlet Beach
Austin Cove
Northeast Bluff
Red Beach
Goltsov Point
Cooper Island
Gibson Island
Kennon Island
Attu (site)
Chichagof Harbor
Khlebnikof Point

Kent Creek
Valentine Creek
Dishn Creek
Owens Ridge
Vieth Ridge
Cupps Hill
Holtz Bay
West Arm
Center Point
East Arm
Fishhook Ridge
East Peak
Lake Nicenirco
Point Hope
Middle Peak

Brannon Ridge
Scout Canyon
Young Hill
Buchanan Ridge
Addison Creek
Fleishman Ridge
Cold Mtn
Prendergat Ridge
Mirror Lake
Hodikof Point
Hodikof Bay
Eckman Creek

Attu Mountain
El. 3,050+ ft
O'Donnell Creek
Siddens Valley
Pierucci Ridge
Whooper Swan nest
Krupa Point
Sarana Bay
Square Point

Japanese Memorial
Henderson Ridge
Gilbert
Lake Nicholas
Massacre Valley
Jackass Pass
Alexai Pass
Thiel Pass
Buchanan Point

Martinez Mountain
El. 3,000+ ft
White-tailed Eagle nest
Terrible Mountain
El. 2,200+ ft
Lake Betwood
Artillery Hill
Ridge
Matthews Mountain
El. 1,800+ ft
McNew Hill
McCloud Head

Temnac River
Leffler Creek
George River
North Norton River
Pass
Peaceful River
Navy Town
Massacre Beach
Loaf Island
Massacre Bay
Alexai Beach
Bedard Cove
Hidalgo Beach
Chirikof Point

Kaufman Creek
Lookout Hill
Mount Weston
El. 1,550+ ft
USCG Base
West Channel
Cisco Cove
East Channel

Theodore Ridge
Hoekslete Creek
Temnac Bay
Savage Islands
Attour Base
South Middens
South Beach
Murder Point
Alexai Point

Sanders Cape
Swift Cliffs
Krasni Point
False Krasni

Kearney Beach

Pacific Ocean

Cindy Lippincott

Contour interval: 1000 feet

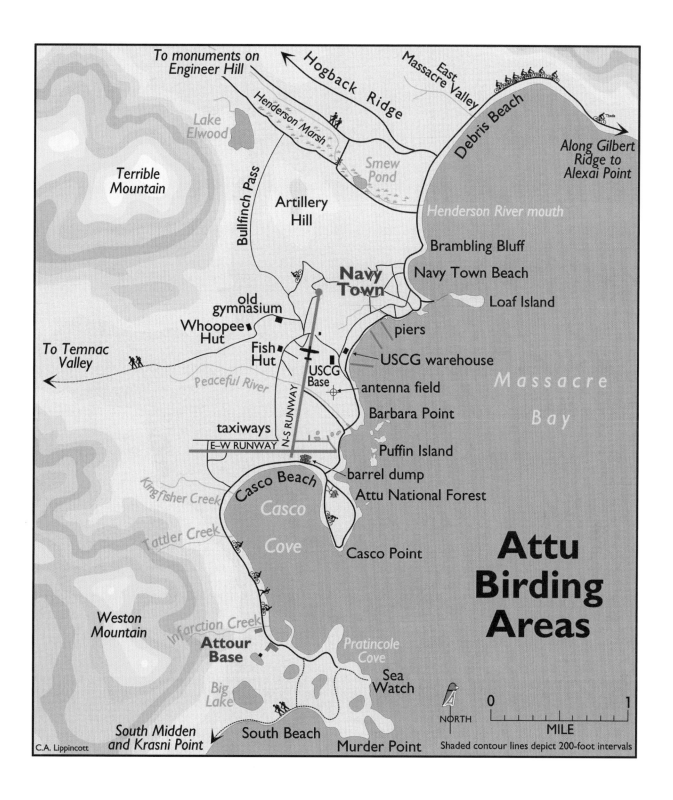

To monuments on
Engineer Hill

Hogback Ridge

East
Massacre Valley

Debris Beach

Lake Elwood

Henderson Marsh

Smew Pond

Along Gilbert
Ridge to
Alexai Point

Terrible
Mountain

Bullfinch Pass

Artillery
Hill

Henderson River mouth

Brambling Bluff

Navy Town Beach

Navy
Town

Loaf Island

old
gymnasium

Whoopee
Hut

piers

Fish
Hut

USCG warehouse

USCG
Base

Massacre

To Temnac
Valley

Peaceful River

antenna field

Bay

Barbara Point

taxiways

Puffin Island

E–W RUNWAY

N–S RUNWAY

barrel dump

Casco Beach

Attu National Forest

Kingfisher Creek

Casco
Cove

Tattler Creek

Casco Point

Attu
Birding
Areas

Weston
Mountain

Infarction Creek

Attour
Base

Pratincole
Cove

Sea
Watch

Big
Lake

0   1

NORTH   MILE

South Midden
and Krasni Point

South Beach

Murder Point

Shaded contour lines depict 200-foot intervals

C.A. Lippincott

The Island

Photo: Ed Harper

Looking down Siddens Valley to Lake Nicholas, September 1983

A Time and Place Before Birders

Jennifer Jolis

Seven Women living on Attu, most westerly of the Aleutian Islands, spent a year cutting, curing, and splitting grass from which to weave baskets. The baskets woven from that grass were taken by a Mr. Summerville to Unalaska where they were exchanged for lumber and materials. Using these supplies the people of Attu built a village church of the Russian Orthodox Faith. Now the Attu people are scattered throughout the Aleutians and the rest of Alaska. World War II destroyed their village and their church, and they themselves were taken captives of the Japanese. When it was all over and they were brought back to Alaska but were not taken to Attu we began to see that they also were destroyed—not spectacularly, but one by one, even today, in different villages where they can live. When somebody comes who was from Attu, Mom likes to speak in the Attu language. Otherwise there is nobody.[1]

The Place

Attu Island, 40 miles long, 20 miles wide, mist-enshrouded, wind-whipped, mountainous, and mysterious, lies at the western end of the Aleutian chain of islands, which curve across the top of the North Pacific like jewels in a necklace, connecting North America with its past. These volcanic islands are the crests of a submarine ridge approximately 1,400 miles long, 20–60 miles wide, and 12,000 feet high above the ocean floor to either side.[2]

The islands separate the North Pacific Ocean to the south from the Bering Sea to the north. Coming together over the islands, the weather systems of these two bodies of water clash and mingle, giving rise to climatic conditions that have earned the Aleutians the sobriquet "birthplace of the winds." At any time of year warm moist air from the Pacific, meeting the frigid arctic air of the Bering Sea, can produce gale force winds, dense fog to sea level, or brilliantly clear sunny skies followed in moments by rain squalls and more fog.

Attu is the westernmost island in this arc, indeed the westernmost point in North America. At longitude 173° East, it lies more than 1,100 miles from the mainland of Alaska and less than 550 miles from the Kamchatka Peninsula of Russia. The island's volcanic origins have produced a terrain of steep mountains rising from a deeply indented coastline with an abundance of bays and inlets.

In summer, wildflowers bloom in brilliant profusion in the alpine tundra—lovely surprises for any-one who looks closely: orchid, monkshood, lupine, rhododendron. The British botanist Isobel Hutchison collected 69 species in less than two hours at the end of the 1936 season and estimated that a complete sampling would rival the 350 species found on Unalaska, at the eastern end of the Aleutian chain.

The long beach grasses bend and sway to the earth before the winds that sweep across the hills, mimicking the waves in the coves and bays. On foggy evenings, the calls of loons and eiders sound—lonely, lost, otherworldly. The upwelling produced by the convergence of the northern and southern waters around the islands produces a marine life of great richness and variety. The sea is home to sea otters, sea lions, harbor seals, the occasional whale, migrating waterfowl and gulls, halibut, salmon, greenling, flounder. Although numbers of all species have diminished over time, the area continues to be one of the most rich and productive in the world, boasting the world's largest number of sea mammal species.[3]

The People

They call themselves Unangan, or Angagin, and on Atka Angaginas—roughly, "We, the People." They tell their children that they lived in the Aleutian Islands since time began, that they used to be many and now are few and that they are one people.[4]

The very conditions that, 4,000 years later, were to impede and harry the soldiers of the Japanese and U.S. armies made life on Attu not only possible but rich for its prehistoric peoples. An ancient people whose roots on the islands are thought to go back at least 8,000 years, the Aleuts adapted themselves superbly to their environment. Aleut prehistory is generally regarded as representing a homogeneous cultural continuity that has been traced, through examination of midden sites, along the length of the Aleutian Chain. The Aleuts of prehistory are thought to comprise two populations: a more ancient population named the Paleo-Aleuts and a much more recent group in the eastern islands known as the Neo-Aleuts, with migration in both groups from the East, from the Alaska Peninsula. Among the populations of the different island groups, physical differences were noted. Historian Lydia T. Black noted: "The people differed in physical appearance; especially the Attuans were different. To this day many people believe that the Attuan women were taller and much more beautiful than women in other islands."[5]

What united the Aleuts along the length of the islands was more significant than what separated them. The marine environment they inhabited in common, which provided them with bounty and challenges from the sea, led to a unity of material culture. The fog and gales produced by the confluence of the Bering and Pacific systems did not hinder these remarkable people, who were said to be able to nav-

View from Lower Base across Casco Cove and Massacre Bay to Gilbert Ridge, September 2000

igate by smell and by the feel of the waters beneath their boats.

"In an emergency, they could travel at night, seeing almost nothing but feeling the direction of the water beneath them and the wind above them,"[6] wrote the Smithsonian Institution's Margaret Lantis in describing the Aleuts.

Oriented almost completely to the marine environment, they were not concerned with the treacherous mountains and inland passes. Offshore waters rich in sea mammals provided not only sustenance but also light, heat, and clothing. The Aleuts used the skins of sea mammals to fabricate the light, swift, incredibly buoyant boats called bidarkas. These agile craft allowed them to hunt and fish far offshore as well as to travel between islands along the chain. The many bays and coves of the coastline provided a littoral teeming with mollusks, crustaceans, and sea urchins.

They harvested seaweed to make lines and ropes. In the stream mouths they found migrating salmon, and from inland lakes and ponds they took fish and migrating waterfowl. From the steep cliff homes of breeding birds, they could snatch eggs for food. Women gathered plants to supplement the protein-rich diet of the sea with berries and greens and to provide medicines for their extensive pharmacopoeia.

It was women also who gathered and dried the beach rye grass used to make baskets and mats of the finest weave. These mats, while serving to divide by family the areas of the large communal sod shelters known as barabaras, were greatly prized for their colorful and decorative designs. Living space was further separated into work and sleep spaces, with additional small spaces dug out behind the sleeping areas for storage. In the barabaras seal oil burned in stone lamps for light and warmth. Driftwood was difficult to come by, so it was not used for heat or for cooking, but was used to support the sod of the roof and provide the ladders for entry.

Settlements of these well-adapted people were located on headlands or promontories with easy access to the sea on either side, allowing for alternate escape routes in case of attack. Equally critical to siting were a supply of fresh water and a hill from which to guard against attack. By 1973, thirteen such sites had been identified on Attu—three large and ten small, the latter possibly summer villages.[7]

Outside Contacts

The products of the Aleutian environment were what drew Russian Traders to the area, which in turn caused the eventual decline of the Aleut population. The whole history of human activity in the Aleutian region has been of a similar nature; the environment and the people have always been entwined.[8]

Attu's geographic location protected its inhabitants from contact with Europeans until the middle of the eighteenth century. Their very isolation was sufficient to allow for the development of a dialect that was virtually unintelligible to the natives of Atka, 500 miles to the east.[9]

The community was stable, well adapted to its island home, protected by its remoteness from external influences—a world in equilibrium. That beyond this world there were other people who were not like them the Attuans would have known from the fragments of ships and artifacts that washed up on their shores.[10] They would not have had any way of knowing that events half a world away were bringing drastic change inexorably to their shores. For more than 100 years Russian fur traders had been moving eastward across Asia toward the Arctic Ocean. In the 1740s, the curiosity of Peter the Great of Russia set in motion the eastward travels of the Danish explorer Vitus Bering. For the insatiably curious czar, exploration of the unknown lands to the east offered a chance to expand his empire to a land that might be worth "more than a dozen Siberias."[11] The explorations would also allow the opportunity to test his new shipbuilding knowledge and the new science of astronomy. Bering was ordered to build two boats and mount an expedition to the lands to the east.

In the fall of 1741, two Russian ships set out from the Kamchatka Peninsula, one captained by Bering, the other by Alexei Chirikof. The ships became separated, but each made contact with the North American coast. On the return voyage, Bering's ship was wrecked and he died on the island later named after him. Enough of his crew survived to return to Kamchatka with a load of the virtually unknown sea otter pelts gleaned during their enforced stay on Bering Island.[12] This bounty marked the start of the expansion of Russian America, a move that was to change the fate of all Aleuts.

An upland vista (September 2000)

Attu's position at the western end of the chain, as part of the island group accurately named by the Russians, Blishni (Near) Islands, a group comprising Attu, Agattu, Shemya, Nizki and Alaid, placed it in the forefront of Russian exploration. On 27 September 1745, after an initial skirmish with the natives at Agattu that made overwintering there impossible, the ship *Yevdokia* hove to offshore of Attu. The following day a shore party made contact with a party of five Aleut men, their wives and children, all of whom immediately took flight. One day later, while on shore searching for a safe harbor in which to winter, the Russians came upon a group of Aleuts from whom, after a scuffle, they took a prisoner. The captive and an old woman who insisted on following him were taken aboard the ship. A severe storm forced them to put to sea, and they were unable to return until 9 October. Returning to shore, they were greeted by 34 Attuans who "danced and sang to the sound of bladder-drums, and made presents of colored clay, receiving in return handkerchiefs, needles, and thimbles."[13]

Although two Aleuts hurt in the initial scuffle died, relations between the natives and the Russians remained friendly until the end of the month. Gift giving, dancing, and singing continued. At the end of the month, Captain Chuprof sent a party of 11 men, led by Alexei Bliaief, to explore the island more thoroughly. Coming upon a village site, Bliaief "managed to pick a quarrel, in the course of which fifteen islanders were killed. There is little doubt that this encounter was willfully provoked and the male natives slaughtered for a purpose.... It is distinctly charged that Bliaief caused the men to be shot in order to secure the women."[14]

The site, named by the survivors, remains known as Massacre Bay. The year that followed "until the day when the *Yevdokia* departed, which was the 14th of September 1746, was not a time of rejoicing to the people of Attoo. To this day the cruelties committed by the first Russians are recited by the poverty-stricken remnants of a once prosperous and happy people."[15]

During the years that followed, the course of Aleut history and culture were changed irrevocably. In the eight decades that followed Russian contact, it is estimated that the Aleut population was reduced by 80 percent along the length of the Aleutian chain.[16] Causes of death included disease, suicide, punishment for resistance to the Russian domination, and exposure at sea as the men were forced to hunt sea mammals for the Russians. The Attuans were forced by the Russians to move from traditional village sites and congregate in only one site, at Chichagof Harbor. This consolidation facilitated the loading of furs onto merchant ships while at the same time affording the Russians safety from attack by the Attuans.

As sea mammal populations close to shore declined under increased hunting pressure, the men of Attu were forced to hunt at ever-greater distances from the island. Their cooperation was ensured by the taking of hostages by the Russians, usually young boys, close kin of chiefs and other important Aleuts. (Sometimes, as in the case of the chief's nephew Temnack, who was sent to Kamchatka on the *Yevdokia*, hostages were sent to Siberia to be educated and later returned to the islands to act as interpreters.)[17]

These protracted absences from the island resulted not only in an increasingly high mortality rate among the hunters but also in the breakdown of social and kinship ties. While the hunters were absent from the island for increasingly long periods of time, Attuan women served not only as cooks and servants to the Russians but as sexual partners as well. Lines of respect and lineage became blurred, undermining the social system, kinship ties, and traditional beliefs. This was unacceptable to the Attuans who, by 1811, had sent two chiefs and one chief's representative to Okhotsk to complain that the Russians were too free with the women.[18]

By the 1760s, as the sea mammal population declined, the brunt of the Russian invasion had moved on past Attu, with ships calling only at "intervals as great as five years." The Attuans had "been baptized, had learned the Russian language and had adopted part of the clothing and customs of the Russians." By 1811, only two Russians lived on Attu, and "they lived like Aleuts."[19]

Sixty-one years later there were only 130 natives and 25 people of mixed blood, and a few years later still, there were but 100 people living on Attu.[20]

Behind the fur traders came the Russian America Company and the Russian Orthodox Church. The Company established schools and by the end of the 1820s, Aleuts employed by the Company received salaries, were entitled to hold managerial positions, to serve as ship captains, and to be ordained as ministers. Father Veniaminov, the first resident Russian Orthodox priest, devised, with the assistance of two Aleuts, an alphabet and began to translate liturgical works into Aleut.[21] It was at this time that the deep and abiding faith in the Russian Orthodox Church took root among the Aleuts, a faith that replaced their own religious practices. That this took on deep significance for the Attuans, as it did for all the Aleuts, became abundantly clear in the wake of the dislocations of the Second World War.

In 1867, when the "Great Land" was bought by the United States, the Aleut population had returned to a stable level. Aleuts had civil rights, an intellectual tradition combining both traditional and Russian ways, and the persistence of the old ways in material culture. Classes were taught in Aleut as well as in

Russian, and vaccinations against smallpox were common. Positive though these indicators were, it is valuable to remember that it was only the presence of the Russians that made such changes necessary in the first place.

Though remote and isolated, the Attuans of the twentieth century were not cocooned from the events of the world as their ancestors had been in the eighteenth. When they saw evidence of outsiders in their islands, they not only took note, they were aware of the implications. When they saw that Japanese had landed on the island and set stakes in the ground, they sent the evidence to U.S. authorities in Juneau but received no response.

U.S. military authorities knew that a Japanese invasion of the Aleutians was likely and considered evacuating the native population, but bureaucratic conflicts over which agency of civilian or military government had jurisdiction delayed a decision. In the end, Territorial Governor Ernest Gruening said that the final decision should be made by the Attuans themselves, but security prevented his decision from being relayed by radio. In the meantime, the Japanese invaded, reaching Attu on 7 June 1942. At the time, 44 people were living on Attu, 42 of them Aleuts. In skirmishes around the time of the Japanese arrival, one Attuan was killed. The American schoolteacher died after being beaten and kicked by the Japanese, who forced him and his wife from their home. By August, the Japanese had decided to evacuate the remaining 41 Aleuts to Japan. They arrived on the island of Hokkaido on 27 September 1942. They were quartered in the city of Otaru, where they stayed for almost exactly three years. The Attuans were treated as internees, allowed to stay together as families with civilian rather than military guards, and allowed to keep the possessions, including food that they had brought with them. The Japanese required them to work in clay pits, digging bentonite, work that was unpleasant but not dangerous.

But something was wrong. They began to suffer and die almost from the time they arrived. Like their Japanese captors, they were living on a diet of mostly rice, and not much of that. Striving to give the foreigners the best of their scant food supply, the Japanese offered them only polished rice, while they themselves ate brown rice and other grains. In any case, the Attuans suffered from malnutrition; the most common cause of death was beriberi, a disease caused by a lack of Vitamin B_I.

By the time they were released on 27 September 1945, only 25 Attuans remained alive. Five children were born in Otaru; only one of them survived.[22]

The Attuans were returned to the Aleutians, but not to their home island. Instead, they were resettled on the island of Atka. In November 1945, General Superintendent Donald Foster of the Alaska Native Service (ANS) received word that "The survivors [from Attu] are so few that it will be difficult if not impossible to justify the assignment of a teacher or other employee to Attu." On 13 November 1945, the Interior Department, Washington D.C., parent agency of the ANS, was notified that Attu was not off limits or restricted in any way and that the Attuans were welcome to return. On 7 December 1945, Mr. J. Lichtenwalner, the Interior Department's liaison to the Attuans was so informed. However, a list of the survivors and their "desired" disposition, dated 27 November 1945, records that eight of the surviving adults "desired to return to Atka".

The facts were that no school or medical care would be available to them on Attu. According to Foster, who presented the facts to the Attuans in early December, each of them agreed that it was best for them to be resettled at Atka village. Foster also noted, in a letter to William Brophy, Commission of Indian Affairs, Washington, D.C., in January 1946, that "settling the Attu people at Atka has saved the government an enormous amount."[23]

In 1985, Attu was designated a National Historic Landmark. For the time being it is inhabited by about 24 Coast Guardsmen who attend the Loran Station there, a mission that is likely to end in the next few years. It has no scheduled air flights and is accessible only by chartered plane or by boat. Periodically the island is visited by fishermen or by interested naturalists, biologists and archaeologists, usually in the employ of the U.S. Fish and Wildlife Service. The buildings and bridges built by the Navy are disappearing; each year the wind and waves take back some of the land. Each spring the grasses continue to wave, the eiders to sound their lonely calls. A lone eagle flies over the Temnac Valley. The people are gone. The island remains.

NOTES

[1]Shapsnikof, Anfesia E., & Raymond L. Hudson: *Aleut Basketry*, Anthropological Papers of the University of Alaska, vol. 16, No. 2 (Fairbanks: University of Alaska Press, 1974), 41.

[2]U.S. Fish and Wildlife Service, *Aleutian Islands National Wildlife Refuge Wilderness Study Report* (Anchorage, Alaska: US Fish and Wildlife Service, n.p. 1973), 4.

[3]Hutchison, Isobel Wylie, *Stepping Stones from Alaska to Asia* (London and Glasgow: Blackie & Son Limited, 1937), 175; Allen P. McCartney, "Prehistory of the Aleutian Region," in *Handbook of North American Indians*, vol.5, ed. William C. Sturtevant (Washington, DC: Smithsonian Institution, 1984), 134; Robert A. Henning, Barbara Olds, and Penny Rennick, eds, "A Photographic Geography of Alaska," *Alaska Geographic*, vol. 7, no. 2 (Anchorage: Alaska Geographic Society, 1980), 77.

[4]Black, Lydia T., "Early History," in *The Aleutians*, in Alaska Geographic vol. 7, no. 3, ed. Lael Morgan. (Anchorage: The Alaska Geographic Society, 1980), 82.

[5]Black, "Early History," 84.

[6]Lantis, Margaret, "Aleut," in *Handbook of North American Indians*, vol. 5, ed. William C. Sturtevant, (Washington, DC.: Smithsonian Institution 1984, 173.

[7]McCartney, *Prehistory*, pp. 121 and 133; Black, *Early History*, 84 & 87; Margaret Lantis, "The Aleut Social System," in *Ethnohistory in Southwestern Alaska and the Southern Yukon, Method and Content*, ed. Margaret Lantis (Lexington, Kentucky: University of Kentucky Press, 1970), 87; U.S. Fish and Wildlife Service, 116.

[8]Stein, Gary C., *Cultural Resources of the Aleutian Region*, vol. 1, Occasional Papers No. 6 (Fairbanks, Alaska: Anthropology and Historic Preservation, Cooperative Park Studies Unit, University of Alaska, 1977) 6.

[9]Black, *Early History*, 84.

[10]Stein, *Cultural Resources*, 88; Black, Early History, 89.

[11]Bancroft, Hubert Howe, "History of Alaska, 1730-1885", in *The Works of Hubert Howe Bancroft*, vol. XXXIII (San Francisco: A.L. Bancroft and Company, 1886), 35.

[12]Ibid, 103–105.

[13]Ibid, 105

[14]Ibid.

[15]Ibid.

[16]Lantis, "The Aleut Social System," 179.

[17]Bancroft, *History of Alaska*, 118.

[18]Black, *Early History*, 100.

[19]Ibid

[20]Bergsland, *Aleut Dialects*, 15.

[21]Black, *Early History*, 103-105; Stein, *Cultural Resources*, 52-53.

[22]Steward, in Kirtland, vol.1, 125-127; Prokopeuff, *An Account*, 53 and 53; Golodoff, Last Days, 9.

[23]Donald Foster letter quoted in Kirtland, vol. IV, 239

Photo: Ed Harper

Looking at Gilbert Ridge from Navy Cove, May 1980

The Plants

Nootka lupine (*Lupinus nootkatensis*)

The Flora of Attu—
A Brief Overview

Randy Meyers

Attu, open to the winds and wild Aleutian weather, is classified by Amundsen (1977) as maritime tundra. There are no native tree species. Instead, grasses and forbs (herbaceous perennial plants), nurtured by a long, cool, moist growing season, and often somewhat sheltered by terrain, attain impressive heights. Woody plants do occur, among them occasional dense stands of medium to tall willows, which take hold in protected lowland pockets. An informal listing of the primary plant communities found on Attu includes: upper beach strand, coastal meadow, tall forb meadow, medium to tall shrub, alpine meadow, and exposed alpine heath.

The upper beach strand plant community forms a narrow fringe around the island and can provide food and cover for a variety of passerine, shorebird, and waterfowl species. In September, dense mats of low-growing beach greens (*Honckenya peploides*) can shelter birds such as a roosting juvenile Ruff on blustery days. Beach pea (*Lathyrus maritimus*) forms loose mats, sports rose-purple blossoms in the spring, and forms abundant seedpods in the summer. The often muted grays, blacks, browns, and greens of an ocean beach on an overcast day come alive when forming a backdrop to beach fleabane (*Senecio pseudoarnica*), with its robust stature and bright yellow, sunflower-sized flower heads.

One of the most common plants in the coastal meadow is beach rye grass (*Elymus arenarius* ssp. *mollis*). Often seen in dense stands 5 to 6 feet tall, vast fields of it glow green, constantly rippling and flowing like ocean waves in the wind. For birds foraging along the coast it provides immediate shelter and cover; the birds frequently drop or swoop into its depths and disappear, resisting all attempts to flush them out.

The tall forb meadow community, an Aleutian trademark, is often found on slopes in sheltered valleys. Plants such as Nootka lupine (*Lupinus nootkatensis*), with its stout, hairy seed pods and dark blue and white flowers, or cow parsnip (*Heracleum lanatum*), with tall, upright, umbrella-like umbels, are normally 2 to 3 feet high in more northern, mainland parts of Alaska. On Attu they grow to 5 and 7 feet tall, respectively. Song Sparrows are a characteristic sight, perched and singing in gigantic tree-like umbels of cow parsnip. Kamchatka thistle (*Cirsium kamtschaticum*), an Asian species found in Alaska only on Attu, Agattu, and Alaid Islands, can grow over 6 feet tall in Attu meadows. Kamchatka thistle has pink-purple flowers that wither to brown fairly quickly, and the tips of its sharply lobed leaves attenuate into weak spines. Robust ferns, such as lady fern (*Athyrium filix-femina*), grow thick, reaching 3 to 4 feet tall in this habitat, providing visual variety with their lacy fans of dark green leaves.

The medium to tall shrub community is much less extensive on Attu than the tall forb meadow. Stands of medium to tall shrubs occur along mountain stream courses, in bands along sheltered hillsides, and in protected pockets in coastal lowlands. One of the most unusual members is arctic willow (*Salix arctica*). Throughout Alaska arctic willow is a prostrate or trailing shrub, occasionally reaching 12 to 20 inches high in protected habitats. However, in some of Attu's protected habitats it reaches heights of 4 to 6 feet, and in some cases sends up branches as high as 9 feet. One of the most striking members of the medium to tall shrub community is Siberian mountain ash (*Sorbus sambucifolia*). The islands of Attu, Agattu, Alaid, and Buldir represent this Siberian species' easternmost range in North America. On Attu, it is usually a medium-sized shrub, 2 to 3 feet tall. It flowers in July, and by September the berries are a rich orange. Early September leaves are a mix of green and orange-gold, with graceful pinnately compound sprays of sharply toothed leaves. Some berries persist until spring, making this season a good time to watch for interesting passerines, especially thrushes, in patches of Siberian mountain ash. This shrub grows on sheltered ridges and mountain slopes and is quite luxuriant in the revegetated depressions in Navy Town, which are scattered along low-angle, east-facing slopes.

Alpine meadows, characteristically fairly moist and somewhat protected from prevailing winds, host a diverse array of colorful flowering forbs. Species with blue blossoms include the sky-blue tones of wild geranium (*Geranium erianthum*), the dark blue hues of Kamchatka aconite (*Aconitum maximum*), and the pale blue of Alaska violet (*Viola langsdorffii*). Pockets of dark brown chocolate lily (*Fritillaria camschatcensis*), rose-purple Fischer's Orchis (*Dactylorhiza aristata*), and pink wedge-leaf primrose (*Primula cunefolia*) provide ample contrast to the sparkling white of bog candle (*Platanthera dilatata*) and narcissus-flowered anemone (*Anemone narcissiflora*). Growing among flowering perennials in high alpine meadows are also many species of dwarf shrubs, such as Kamchatka rhododendron (*Rhododendron camtschaticum*), with its striking dark magenta blossoms, plus numerous grasses, sedges, rushes, mosses, and lichens.

The alpine heath community occupies exposed windswept ridges, summits, fellfields, and scree slopes; it is a sparsely vegetated zone, harboring mat and cushion plants, wind-pruned diminutive forms of prostrate shrubs and hardy forbs, and a few grasses, sedges, rushes, and mosses. Tiny patches of many different lichen types (crustose, fruticose, and foliose) and species are found adhering to rocks and woody stems, as well as in pockets of soil and rocky crevices. Heath family members, such as Aleutian mountain heather (*Phyllodoce aleutica*), alpine azalea (*Loiseleuria procumbens*), and club-moss mountain heather (*Cassiope lycopodioides*), are common in this habitat. Several hardy members of the saxifrage family, such as purple mountain saxifrage (*Saxifraga oppositifolia*), spotted saxifrage (*Saxifraga bronchialis*), and Aleutian saxifrage (*Saxifraga aleutica*), can successfully compete and persist in these rugged sites.

The thick, lush vegetation of Attu provides birds with abundant food, cover, and perches, plus nesting materials and nest sites. Varying combinations of buds, berries, and seeds are available throughout most of the year. Plants producing berries include Siberian mountain ash, bunchberry (*Cornus suecica*), crowberry (*Empetrum nigrum*), nagoonberry (*Rubus arcticus*), alpine blueberry (*Vaccinium uliginosum* ssp. *microphyllum*), low bush cranberry (*Vaccinium vitis-idaea*), and twisted stalk (*Streptopus amplexifolius*). Among plant species producing conspicuous amounts of seed attractive to birds are cow parsnip, wild celery (*Angelica lucida*), Nootka lupine, wormwood (five different species of Artemisia on Attu), arctic

Kamchatka thistle (*Cirsium kamtschaticum*)

Cow parsnip (*Heracleum lanatum*)

Wooly hawkweed (*Hieracium triste*)

Wormwood (*Artemisia unalaskensis*)

Beach pea (*Lathyrus maritimus*)

Siberian mountain ash berries (*Sorbus sambucifolia*)

Oysterleaf (*Mertensia maritima*)

Aleutian Mountain Heather (*Phyllodoce aleutica*), September 1993

24

willow, bluejoint (*Calamagrostis canadensis*), large-flower speargrass (*Poa eminens*), alkali grass (*Puccinellia langeana*), and beach rye grass.

Birders on Attu have found that the vegetation affects birdfinding differently in early spring than in fall. In some ways, spring hiking on Attu is easier, as winter wind, rain, sleet, and snow have flattened the mostly dead aboveground parts of once-tall grasses, sedges, and forbs. Overall visibility is better when shrubs are bare-branched and plants are withered and dormant. When snow still lies at higher elevations, birds tend to be more concentrated in the lowlands. Generally, birds are more easily seen, tracked, and relocated in the spring. The late spring/early summer birder on Attu can enjoy the emerging green sprouts and leaves and be dazzled by colorful wildflowers initiating their blooming cycles. By fall, vegetation on Attu has become tall and dense in the stream valleys, in meadows above the beaches, and along the slopes of coastal ridges, making hiking in these areas fairly difficult and finding birds challenging. Spring birds are singing and breeding; fall birds are more silent and less conspicuous. However, September on Attu is usually warmer than early spring, and the vegetation is at peak variety, biomass, and fruit production, plus there is the potential for strong bird-bringing storms. As elsewhere, seasonal variations have their own beauty and value, and each adds its unique interest and challenges for birders.

References for further study concerning the flora of Attu:

Amundsen, Clifford C. (1977). *Terrestrial Plant Ecology*, pp. 203-226. In M.L. Merritt and R.G. Fuller (eds.), The Environment of Amchitka Island, Alaska. Energy, Research, and Development Administration TID-26712. Washington, D.C., Technical Information Center.

Hultén, Eric. (1960). *Flora of the Aleutian Islands and Westernmost Alaska Peninsula With Notes on the Flora of the Commander Islands*. (2nd ed., revised). Weinheim, Germany: J. Cramer.

Hultén, Eric. (1968). *Flora of Alaska and Neighboring Territories*. Stanford, CA: Stanford University Press.

Rennick, Penny (ed.). (1995). *The Aleutian Islands*. Vol. 22, No. 2, Anchorage, AK: Alaska Geographic Society.

Talbot, Stephen S., Sandra L. Talbot, & John W. Thompson (1991). "Lichens of Attu Island, Alaska," *The Bryologist*: 94 (4), 421–426.

Viereck, Leslie A. and Elbert L. Little, Jr. (1972). *Alaska Trees and Shrubs, Agriculture Handbook No. 410*. Washington, D.C.: Forest Service, U.S. Department of Agriculture.

Airstrip at Alexai Point

Filling the circles in the runway matting
Like done muffins in a battalion kitchen
Sit hundreds of clumps, thousands: purple

Flowers so minuscule you crouch to see,
The beauty of them fathoms future warmth.
Interspersed, the fat Siberian dandelions

High as your calf, anemone and saxifrage,
And the nearly hidden stands of moonwort,
Thought rare in America till we found it

Abundant. They laid this Marsden Matting
Working twenty-four-hour shifts, fitting
Tooth to tooth the serious puzzle pieces,

Iron, three-men-long. The snow had stopped.
They had hot coffee, cigarettes, and songs.
Only the few oldtimers feared the Japanese

Survivors regrouping up in Abraham Valley.
Conversations started up about elsewhere,
The girls back home, the range of bombers,

And could Intrepid Airmen taking off from
Here find Tokyo? How soon? Who can see
Through brass, a Corporal Schoenfeld said,

But this airstrip is, repeat is, priority
Urgent from what I've been receiving today:
And they took six days, an Aleutian record.

Today the Golden and the Mongolian Plovers
Appreciate it. We do also in our own way.
And these endless formations of flowerpots.

Here and there rises a forty-year willow,
Thick-stemmed, less than three inches high;
Branches cling onto the matting like roots,

The way summer snakes dart from an egg-berm
Or how a mandala will swirl. The willows
Speak about tenacity, a recovering of time,

The experience of winter and spring winds.

—*Macklin Smith*

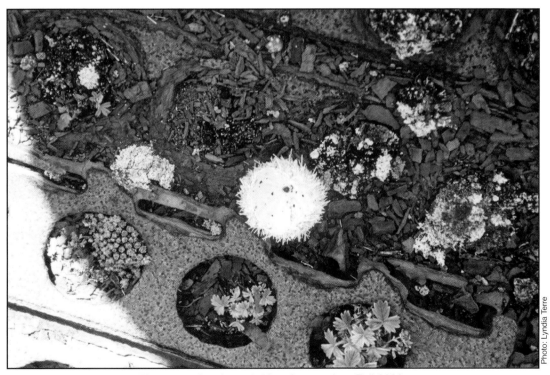

Plants growing through Marsden matting, Fall 2002

Photo: Lyndia Terre

Birding the Island

Photo: John Fitchen

Lunch at the first stacks, May 2000

28

How It All Started
(and Kept Going for a While)

Larry Balch

Most of the other material in this book is what a birding trip to Attu was like for the participants, what birding conditions were like, and how our leaders dealt with the challenges afield. I would like to tell you what it was like behind the scenes, so to speak. That is, how the trips started, and what was involved in operating them. I hope this will answer many of the questions people have asked me about our trips, and for those who went with us, maybe it will clear up a few mysteries.

Larry Balch, June 1979

It started with a computer conference in Atlantic City and a pelagic trip to North Carolina. In May 1971, I took a break from the conference to visit Tuckerton, touted in a *Birding* insert as a place to search for Curlew Sandpipers. I had been birding for five years, and was getting really caught up in it. At Tuckerton, I notched lifer number 468—Glossy Ibis—but had no luck finding the sandpiper, so I headed back in late afternoon to the road head where I was parked. A Jeep Wagoneer was also there, with its tailgate down, and a distinguished-looking couple was relaxing in lawn chairs with Scotch and sodas. Their binoculars betrayed them as fellow birders, so we talked, and eventually introduced ourselves. They were Joe and Helen Taylor, well known to me because Joe was an officer of the American Birding Association, and was the country's top lister, the first to reach the magic total of 700. Yet, Joe recognized my name, since I had just finished writing a Checklist Bibliography for the ABA. (Little did either of us know at the time how intertwined our birding careers and the future of the ABA would become.)

Joe was looking for his lifer Black Rail at Tuckerton. Naturally, I was curious what else was left for America's most-traveled birder. "Whiskered Auklet" was the answer. Joe was about to leave on a trip to Alaska. There he would travel all the way out the Aleutians to Attu, in search of the auklet and whatever else might come his way. I'd never heard of Attu, but Joe's stories of his past visits to Alaska made me determined to go there someday.

The October 1976 pelagic trip was organized by Paul DuMont and Bob Ake. The night before, Paul invited me to dinner, where he regaled me with the results of an Alaskan bird trip Paul Sykes had arranged for Paul, Benton Basham, and himself. What impressed me the most was the Aleutian

Overlooking the mouth of Casco Cove, 1973

part of the trip. They went to Adak to bird with Commanding Officer Tony White, then to Shemya, and then via U.S. Fish & Wildlife boat to Attu. I knew that Joe Taylor had seen not only his Whiskered Auklet (at Adak), but had also seen things hardly anyone else had on their ABA lists, such as Spotted Redshank and Gray-spotted Flycatcher. (In fact, the latter species put Joe up to 700 again, after lumps had dropped him below.) Nevertheless, the list of birds Paul rattled off was mind-boggling to me, and I was particularly captivated by his account of their sighting of a flock of six Oriental Greenfinches, the first for North America. Now I knew where I had to go first when I got to Alaska.

The opportunity came quickly. The next spring, I would finish a two-year consulting project that would leave me with a free summer and a stream of disposable income that would continue for years. Serendipitously, my school had just switched to a new schedule on which the spring semester ended after the first week of May. So I began by calling Paul Sykes, whom I did not know, to get some information on traveling in the Aleutians. As a biologist for the federal government, he had no trouble making the necessary arrangements, but he didn't think I would be able to. He was only partly right, fortunately. Shemya Island, with its Air Force base and many top-secret missions would, of course, be off limits. Joe Taylor and (later) a small Bird Bonanzas tour group had birded Adak, where they stayed in officer's quarters. I found that birders were no longer welcome there, and not even the help of the admiral in charge

44 Charlie, Reeve Aleutian Airways on the runway, 1973

of the Great Lakes Naval Center could get my party permission to stay there. On Attu, Paul's group, Joe, and Jerry and Laurette Maisel, in 1973, had all stayed at the Coast Guard Loran Station. That wouldn't be possible for us, but the Coast Guard had no objection to us visiting Attu, as long as we were completely self-sufficient.

Transportation would be no problem. Reeve Aleutian Airways had scheduled service to Attu every Tuesday and Friday, and they even had an "excursion" fare on the books! (At about $430, it was more than my fare from Chicago to Anchorage, I think, but quite a bit less than the regular fare to Attu.) I had already overcome one problem: when I couldn't find anyone to accompany me on what would be a rather expensive trip, I made an offer that they couldn't refuse to Jerry Rosenband and Charlie Clark, my friends and favorite birding companions from the Chicago area. They agreed to go. We got together a tent and other camping gear for our Attu stay. (Benton had suggested we might camp in one of the many abandoned buildings left from the post-World War II occupation of Attu, when the Navy stationed 10,000 men there.) Off we went to Alaska—first stop Anchorage, then Attu.

We stepped off the Reever on 20 May. After walking less than 50 yards, we spotted a male Brambling. What a piece of cake this is going to be, I thought! I thus became the first of many birders to have a mistaken idea of how easy it would be to find birds on Attu. We set off to find a place to stay. I had a start when I saw a dark, almost thrush-sized bird. Instead of being some Asian rarity, though, it was just Attu's version of a Song Sparrow. We saw nothing exciting in several miles of walking, and found no suitable place to pitch our tent. So we went back to our gear at the airport and carried it to the nearby gymnasium.

That cavernous building no longer had doors, and the bowling lane along its side had collapsed, but it offered good protection from the wind and the rain. We pitched our tent, broke out our Svea stove and freeze-dried food, and Jerry hung his wet socks over the basketball hoop.

They never dried. Not until we got back to Anchorage two weeks later. The stagnant air in that big gym didn't warm up during the day, the way the weather did outside. It was pretty much 35 degrees all day long in there, so basically, we lived in a refrigerator for two weeks. At least it was warmer outside, and that's where the birds were. There were also other birders. Thede Tobish and Karl Haflinger were young biologists hired to study Rock Ptarmigan. They were staying a couple of miles away. When the Coast Guard told them of our arrival, they came over to see what kind of weirdos would come out to Attu to bird. Thede made the ptarmigans his second priority and began to bird with us. Karl came along frequently, too. Later, a Coast Guard C-130 brought in Lynn Hamilton, an orthopedic surgeon and birder from New Orleans with Coast Guard connections.

The birding was slow, especially for me, because I was having trouble walking after I slipped stepping up from a creek bed and hit both knees on the edge of the bank. The Coast Guard kindly suggested I could rest in their library during the day until I got better. It was hard to sit there thinking the others might finally be finding some birds, so I went out to hobble around close to the station as best I could, and there I saw my first Eyebrowed Thrush. Or so I thought—on closer examination, it turned out to be an American Robin! Back to the station—my knees would have to get better before my list would.

The next day was our first nice, sunny day. At about 4 in the afternoon, Jerry, Thede, and Lynn stopped by the station and announced they were going to West Massacre Valley. Charlie decided it was too late in the day to start a new hike. I was worried that the guys just might get lucky and finally find something really good, and my knee was a bit better, so I went along. But I couldn't keep up—two and a half miles later, as the others headed up the north side of the Henderson River in the valley, I was already a couple of hundred yards behind. I was therefore pretty much by myself when one of the two or three most exciting experiences of my birding life took place.

Gulls making a big commotion attracted our attention. We all looked up and saw an eagle heading into the valley from what would later be known as Bullfinch Pass. Another eagle was following it, and clearly, they were White-tailed Eagles, not Bald Eagles! They flew around over the heads of the other guys (lucky them!) and then headed down the valley toward me. Suddenly, they came together, locked talons, and began tumbling out of the sky, as if to fall onto my head. They separated not far above me, and then headed out the valley toward the bay. We were dumbfounded, and I was hooked on Attu.

The next day we made the long hike to Alexai Point—I could walk OK again—where we found a male Reed Bunting poking around at the edge of a snow bank. We were the first birders to see this species in the ABA Area. Now I was really hooked. In the next week, the birding picked up, and we added Siberian Rubythroat, Olive-backed Pipit, Yellow Wagtail, Gray-spotted Flycatcher, Black-backed Wagtail, and finally, some shorebirds: Red-necked Stint, Long-toed Stint, and Wood Sandpiper. We left the island happy and headed for Gambell, where there were a lot of birders. I had already figured out just where I'd stay when I returned next spring to Attu.

The Gambell birders had seen some really good birds. The news of what we had seen on Attu—especially the eagle—got them even more excited. Two bird tour companies began making plans to visit Attu in 1978, and I was happy to give them advice on how to do it and where to stay.

Attu saw its first flood of birders in 1978. There were 29: Davis Finch, Rich Stallcup, and Noble Proctor brought ten people for Northeast Birding; Ben King brought seven people for Bird Bonanzas, and the eight birders not with a tour group were a couple from Colorado, my girlfriend Barbara and I, Terry Savaloja, Joe and Helen Taylor, and Jim Tucker, founder of the ABA. (Noble and Terry would later become leaders for Attour, Inc.) I went to Adak for three days to see Whiskered Auklet (I was already learning how to arrange things in the Aleutians) and then Davis and Barbara and I headed to Attu. Plane problems delayed us for two days on Shemya (Common Pochard!), but we got to Attu five days ahead of everyone else. Davis started setting up camp for his group in the gym. Meanwhile, Barbara and I uncrated the ATV I had shipped out in advance, and drove to the old Loran station at the south end of Casco Cove. We would be very comfortable staying in its old pantry, which was perhaps the only room in the building with an intact window and no leaks. We had brought along a small heater, and Barbara was able to charm some Coasties, who hadn't seen women in a while, into bringing us a bunk bed with real, thick innerspring mattresses.

We birded with Davis, saw the eagle, and the day before everyone else arrived, we found the bullfinch after which the pass was named. We also located a Bean Goose for the group. So they were chasing after birds as soon as they arrived. Later, Bird Bonanzas moved into one of two small metal huts (the "red quonset" and the "green quonset") not far from the runway. The large doors on their fronts were falling off. The other six independent birders stayed in different rooms in the old Loran station. This abandoned building was reinforced concrete, and since almost all the windows were gone, the wind blew through the rooms. Barbara and I were the only birders with a heater.

Weather conditions were much the same as the previous years—broken snow cover, temperatures ranging down to freezing at night, and 35°–50° in the day, wind speed from calm to 20 mph or so (except when storms came), and almost constant cloud cover. It never rained very hard in the spring, but we often got drizzle. People were not comfortable birding in these conditions, especially with no warm, dry quarters to return to at night. Five of Ben King's people and the couple from Colorado left the island a week early. Other people began hanging around at the Coast Guard station. One of them even snuck in and slept overnight. The CO (Commanding Officer) was, as usual, a very young guy straight out of the CG Academy and on his first tour of duty. Dealing with this situation was not something they had trained him for, so I saw trouble coming. We birders were supposed to be completely self-sufficient and independent of the Coast Guard, but now some of us were treating the station like home. I thought it was only a matter of time before Attu became like Adak—off limits to birders.

Attu was clearly a special place, and it wasn't only the birds. (Our highlights in 1978, in addition to the bullfinch, were Dusky Thrush and White-throated Needletail.) It is a wildly beautiful and majestic island that is peacefully remote. I wanted to continue to return, and I thought the key to being able to do that was for birders to have such comfortable quarters that we would, indeed, be independent of the Coast Guard. So I conceived of starting a tour company that would provide such quarters, and I named it Attour. There were two insulated buildings not far from the runway that birders did not use. One— the Whoopee Hut—was where Coasties went to kick up their heels on off-hours. The other one belonged to the Air Force, we were told. It was called the Fish Hut because Air Force people from

Shemya would use it when they came to Attu on R&R to fish. They didn't need it until later in June, however.

I obtained permission to use the Fish Hut from the Air Force Commanding Officer on Shemya. The hut had two rooms—one with bunk beds for twelve people, and one with a couple of picnic tables, a cooking area, and a non-functioning coal stove. I hired Thede and Jerry as leaders, and sent them out early with a new (and rather heavy) stove that they installed. They also installed a stovepipe oven, so that we could bake cakes. Jerry and I packed dozens of boxes with real (i.e., not freeze-dried) food in Chicago and mailed them to Attu. At that time, Attu mail had an Anchorage zip code, because Reeve had the contract to take all mail to Attu. We paid 35 cents extra per carton to send everything Special Handling. That way, postal regulations mandated Reeve to take them immediately, rather than fit them in with their other cargo when it was convenient. We also mailed bicycles.

Fuel was a big problem (and would remain so until the very end of our trips). There were coal piles on Attu from which we could fuel our new stove. But that was a heating stove, not one for cooking. White gas for cook stoves was a hazardous material, requiring packaging in many small special containers, individually boxed with special absorbent material, then combined into a special carton accompanied by proper paperwork. We did that the first year, but for our second trip, I bought kerosene cook stoves in Pennsylvania Amish country. Kerosene and heating oil are not volatile, hazardous materials, and we could simply slap a mailing label on a 5-gallon pail and mail it to Attu. The cost to mail that pail from Anchorage to another zip code in Anchorage, Special Handling? Less than $2. The cost of sending that pail by the alternative method, Reeve Air Cargo at $1 per pound for the 1,500-mile flight? $40.

Perhaps it was these amenities that allowed Attour to operate its first trip to Attu in 1979 with three leaders and 13 participants. Or perhaps it was the lower price—I had objectives other than turning a profit. The other two tour groups had nine and four people, including leaders. The Coast Guard had declared the gym structurally unsound, so the two other tours had to stay in the Red and Green Quonsets, again without heat. A group of four independent birders with a military connection were able to stay at the Coast Guard station.

I will never forget the first "good bird" of this first Attour trip. On arrival, all of us went immediately to our respective quarters. While unpacking, one of our participants stepped outside, looked up, and yelled. We all piled out and saw Attour's logo bird, the White-tailed Eagle.

All the 33 birders on the island cooperated to make a very successful two-week trip. Our best birds were probably the Spotted Redshank, the third North American Pechora Pipit, and the first confirmed record of Green Sandpiper for North America. We all saw the same birds, but Attour was the only tour company with beds, bikes, and bread, not to mention warm, comfortable quarters. There was room for improvement, of course—every morning, we all grabbed a collapsible water jug and went down to the nearby creek to get our daily water supply. We had no showers or laundry, and we ran out of toilet paper three days early. But the contrast between the tours was noticed. One tour company did not return in 1980. The other tour company was challenged, however, and in August its head told me, over a cocktail on the Bluenose Ferry, that they were going to "put you out of business". At that moment, however, I knew something he didn't: in about six weeks, scheduled air service to Attu would end.

Shum Suffel in bunkhouse of the Fish Hut, June 1979

Reeve suggested to me (and, I am sure, to the other company) that we charter flights to Attu and back. This had certain advantages. We could go and come when we wanted, we could design a trip that went straight from Attu to Gambell instead of going back to Anchorage first, and we could take a lot of cargo. Chartering also had a very serious disadvantage—cost. Instead of buying just the right number of seats, we had to buy the whole plane, and it would fly empty one way between Anchorage and Attu. We would need a lot of customers. It was a risk greater than Northeast Birding wanted to take, but since my consulting royalties were strong and getting stronger, I took the risk. Northeast and any independent birders would have to buy seats on our plane. Still, we would have to double the size of our own group. The Fish Hut was full. Where would we put them where they could be warm and comfortable?

I concocted a plan. The Coast Guard chartered a Reever from Shemya (32 miles away) once every two weeks to rotate personnel and bring the mail. We would send Thede and Jerry well ahead of the group on the day the Reever was scheduled to run its Coast Guard flight to Attu. They would take some rolls of fiberglass insulation, and pre-drilled aluminum struts that could be fastened together and bent into giant semicircular hoops to press the insulation against the interior of the red Quonset. When our plane arrived, we'd bring kerosene heaters and material to repair the doors. The result? The red Quonset would be warm, and we would house our additional people there.

Our travel plan was a major gamble. The Reeve pilots didn't always want to go over to Attu on the scheduled day, so they would declare "unsuitable weather conditions" for the VFR (Visual Flight Rules) trip, and head back to Anchorage instead. We couldn't have our guys go back there—we'd have to buy them tickets out to Shemya all over again. So we had another scheme, too, one that we successfully implemented for several years. For a reasonable sum, I arranged with the Coast Guard's Seventeenth District headquarters in Juneau for permission for our guys to ride over on the next C-130 that might come along on its regular patrol flight ("log flight"). (In retrospect, I'm surprised they went for this. I can't remember or imagine what I could have told them to get them to agree to it.) Then if the Reever didn't interrupt its scheduled Adak to Shemya to Anchorage flight to jump over to Attu, Thede and Jerry would stay on Shemya until a C-130 came by in a few days. Of course, we couldn't get permission for them to stay there. So when Reeve unloaded all its passengers to the Shemya terminal building while it refueled and/or decided what it was going to do, Thede and Jerry would go into the john. If an announcement were made soon asking people to re-board to go back to Anchorage, they just wouldn't come out until the Reever left. Believe it or not, they always got to Attu this way.

Here's how it worked one year. The Reever went back to Anchorage without going over to Attu. Thede and Jerry came out of the john after the plane left, and were immediately picked up by the military police, who confined them to the main building, which had quarters for visitors. While they were standing in line at the cafeteria, they heard a voice. "Thede, what are you doing here?" It was a high-ranking officer whom Thede had met the previous fall when he spent a couple of months on Shemya as part of a government-sanctioned research program. "Confined to the building? Forget it. Come with me, I'll get you a car and you can go where you want," he said. "But let me show you around first." That he did, and one of the places he took them was the control room for what was arguably Shemya's most top-secret mission. At night, they flew one of two large planes loaded with sophisticated electronic surveillance equipment over to the coast of the Soviet Union, to monitor what they were doing near their secret bases on Kamchatka. The planes were called "Snoopy" and "Red Baron". (It was one of these planes the Soviets thought they were shooting at when they shot down Korean Air 007 in 1983.) While they were in the control room, the officer suddenly got a call, and he asked Jerry and Thede to wait there until he got back. So there were Thede and Jerry, all alone in one of the most secret rooms in America, with mission maps, communications equipment, operations manuals, etc. all about! Maybe I shouldn't be telling this story.

Well, back to 1980. When Thede and Jerry arrived on Attu, they found the whole front of the red Quonset had been blown off during the winter, and the building was unusable. The Coast Guard CO took pity on them, and said we could use their Whoopee Hut. Our first charter arrived carrying 48 birders. Northeast's 8 people went off to the Green Quonset, and 4 well-connected people went to the CG station. Attour was now 39 strong, including its 5 leaders (we had added Ben King and Dan Gibson). The Whoopee Hut was so crammed with the 22 extra people that at night it was hard to get out without stepping on someone. At the Fish Hut, we started doing what we would do every year from then on— make improvements. This year, we added a water system in which a tiny pump worked all day to fill our water barrel. (There were electric lights in the Fish Hut.) No more carrying water from the stream. (One wit once maintained that the history of birding Attu was that of moving water: drinking water in and rain water out.) We also installed our first water heater.

Unknown at that time, the elimination of scheduled service was only the first installment in what was to become an unwelcome aspect of conducting trips to Attu—the Annual Crisis.

We birded Attu for two weeks in 1980. We found our first Falcated Teal, enjoyed a flock of 21 Terek Sandpipers, and argued fruitlessly for a week whether a reed bunting was a Common or a Pallas's. Unfortunately, what were arguably the best birds—Black-tailed Gull and Gray Bunting—were each seen

Approaching the Attu landing strip over Casco Cove, with Casco Point in the center, September 1983

by only a small group. This would not be typical of the birding in future years. The best birds would almost always be seen by almost everyone.

At the end of the two weeks, our charter flight was to pick us up and fly straight to Gambell, where it would let off the Attour people and continue on to Anchorage with everyone else. That was the plan. As we passed over the Pribilofs, however, Al Driscoll, a retired aircraft maintenance officer for the Air Force, noticed that the flaps on the Reever were not in the right position, and we didn't seem to be making the speed we should. We flew over Gambell, where we could see the runway below, but the pilot said conditions were not right for landing, and we would head to Nome. When we arrived at Nome, the runway was cleared, fire trucks were on alert, and we made what must be described as a high-speed landing that rather excited the airport personnel. Flight attendants and everyone else were put off the plane, and it took off for Anchorage. Clearly, there had been a mechanical problem. Reeve made no arrangements for people to continue to Anchorage, or for us to get people to Gambell. It was an inauspicious start to our chartering business with Reeve.

When the trips were finished, it was time to deal with the Reeve problem. I spent a day in Anchorage researching the State of Alaska air charter regulations. They clearly indicated that we were due compensation for the failure to provide the planned service. I took copies with me when Jerry and I met with President Dick Reeve about the situation. After a brilliant presentation based on the written Alaska regulations, Dick said, "You're a year too late, Larry. We've just had not only federal airline deregulation, but also state, and nothing you have there still applies." So we negotiated, and eventually Reeve refunded about half of the extra expense we had incurred. It would not be the only bone of contention over the years.

Reeve Aleutian Airways was a family business founded by Bob Reeve, one of the most famous Alaska bush pilots. It was one of the oldest established airlines in the country, and had one of the best safety records. As Dick tells it, when Bob retired, he decided the airline should go to the winner of a fistfight between his two sons. Dick won. His sister Janice Reeve Ogle was head of Passenger Services. There was not a lot of formality involved in our business with Reeve. We'd agree on price in advance and set the dates, and they'd get the job done. In the beginning, we'd give them a check in advance, but later, they'd just bill us after the flights were complete. There was never any written contract until the late 1990s.

We would have our problems with RAA, the most serious being in 1987–1988, 1995, and 2000 (more on those later), but almost all the problems were related to the difficult operating environment: a remote area with frequent bad weather and few public facilities, subject to military control. I'm sure we were not the easiest customers to accommodate, either. We were, in a sense, high-risk customers because we were located farthest from Anchorage. There was always the possibility that a plane sent to pick us up would arrive to find an unexpected local weather condition that forced the plane all the way back to Anchorage. The result would be 3,000 miles wasted, a schedule disrupted, and they would have to start all over. Reeve bore the risk itself in the early years, until the first time they had to fly an extra 900 miles from Attu back to Adak to wait, then return to Attu. After that, we had to pay for any extra flying, although at a negotiated reduced rate.

It is clear in retrospect that in the beginning, we were very lucky in our travels for a long time. Up to 1992, we had only one delay, two days long, when leaving Attu. After 1992, the frequency of delays seemed to be constantly increasing, and we had ten delays totaling 21 days. Whether one factor was that in our early years the pilots had much more experience in the region is hard to say. In any case, they were all highly skilled and we had complete confidence in them. They had to fly us using visual flight rules into a downhill airstrip with a hill at one end, water at the other end, a 600-foot antenna on one side, and a high mountain on the other side. We had our share of "white-knuckle" landings. On more than one occasion, we passed low over the highly instrumented airfield at Shemya, barely glimpsing it through fog and low clouds. Then we headed at less than 500 feet over to Attu, seeing hardly anything out the windows except intermittent glimpses of the ocean close below. Remember, there are big mountains on Attu. After 15 minutes of what must have been building tension for many people, we would start circling. Suddenly, a quick break in the low clouds would reveal something familiar below us, the plane would alter its course, and we would break out into a successful approach and landing. Loud applause inevitably followed.

Leaving was only slightly less anxiety-producing. When it was time to leave, people wanted to go. Just go. I don't remember that anyone really wished to be delayed in the hope of seeing even more birds. We would walk to the airport and wait for the plane, critically evaluating the weather all the while. "If the Reever came now, it could make it" became a mantra. Our most unforgettable experience waiting for the plane was in 1990, when a former leader and his wife were supposed to be riding on the plane that was coming to pick us up. We were all waiting along the unused west runway, and the CO was there, in contact with his radio room. The cloud cover was very, very low. We didn't think there was any hope of the plane making a landing, but it was on its way. Then we heard it. It was somewhere right above us. We began to catch glimpses of it flying very low, parallel to the runway, on the ocean side, east of the tower. The CO was commenting that the pilot was crazy, and he instructed the radio room to tell the pilot not to attempt a landing. People were scared. Some were taking cover in ditches, or moving far away. Our cook was crying, thinking her friends were on board. I remarked, "Well, if he makes it, we know he'll have to come from the south, because Artillery Hill is to the north". Shortly, we heard the Reever again, but now it was taxiing down the runway from the north. All of us were stunned and relieved, and also happy to discover that Buzz and Kerry were not on the plane, after all.

Our increased tour size meant we would not be able to use the Whoopee Hut in 1981. Before I had a chance to think much about it, the next Annual Crisis appeared—we would not be able to use the Fish Hut, either. It seems that Bird Bonanzas decided that the reason they no longer had customers for their Attu tour was because our use of the Fish Hut gave us an unfair advantage. They complained to the Coast Guard, and asked that they be allowed to use it, instead. That was when I learned that the Air Force didn't really own it. The Coast Guard promptly decided nobody was going to use it. I flew to Juneau to talk to the legal department of the Seventeenth District, but they explained that for any of us to use the Fish Hut, they would have to put it up for bid to any interested party, which would require a large book of bidding regulations, etc, and it would not be worth their time and effort. So that was it.

As would happen so many times to come, what appeared to be a real problem at first, ultimately turned out to be for the best. The Fish and Wildlife Service told us we could use the two buildings at the south end of Casco Cove. These weren't under the control of the Coast Guard, and potentially had much more room for us. I say potentially, because at the time, there were piles of debris in both build-

The old Loran station, Lower Base, 1988

ings, and many windows were missing. Jerry and Thede would be very busy before the tour came. They had to start by shoveling out all that debris. Despite yeoman efforts, there was a limit to how much two guys could accomplish. In 1981, we packed more people into a smaller space than ever before or since: 23 people in a 15 x 30 room at the upper building.

Thus began a long process of continually rehabilitating and upgrading these two abandoned buildings. The concrete lower building was the old Loran station. It had 14 rooms (some unusable) in 1981. Eventually, it would have 20 rooms, all used. Just 700 feet up the road was the frame-construction former transmitter building. It would eventually house no more than four people, serving primarily as our dining hall and kitchen. From the two buildings, over the years, we would remove several tons of transformers, floor tiles that trapped water, slate sheets from showers, and years of accumulated debris. Jerry and I spent a good part of our 1983 fall trip building window frames at the lower building and sealing its roof (as best we could). Over the years, we replaced windows with unbreakable Lexan for protection from winter winds. We removed walls and built others. We brought in kerosene room heaters, then propane radiant heaters (normally used by farmers to keep pigs warm), and finally electric heaters. We installed a water pump, but then replaced it with a 1000-foot water pipeline coming down the mountain behind the upper building. We dug ditches and installed drainpipes. We installed real showers, a washing machine, and dryers. We built five outhouses. We brought out gasoline-powered generators, and eventually installed 12 KW and 20 KW diesel generators. We installed a commercial restaurant range and oven, and brought out freezers and refrigerators. We bought spring cots with mattresses and had special bunk frames manufactured to hold them. Over the years, we brought out several ATVs, two eight-foot carts, and more than two hundred bicycles. (Over the years our bicycle-use evolved from simple one-speed work-horses to three-speed models, finally to elegant but sturdy 18-speed mountain bikes. The bicycle was the essential mainstay of access to parts of the island for our birders. Conditions were always brutal on the equipment; maintenance was always challenging.) All this was done in keeping with the original goal Attour had when it was founded—to make sure Attu birders were as comfortable as possible. All this work was performed by our advance party, by leaders, by me and staff hired for the purpose, and with the help of many, many participants.

One shouldn't think all of this resulted in plush quarters. With two bunk beds in a 10 x 10 room, space was tight. Our social room could seat 30–35, but at the nightly bird count, there were sometimes 60 or more people present. We never succeeded in making the lower building leak-proof. On clear, cold nights, our water line would freeze and we wouldn't have water for showers first thing in the morning. (I was always coming up with various schemes for preventing those freeze-ups, but Al Driscoll, the head of Attu Power and Light, would always persuade me they weren't worth the cost and trouble.) There was always something to repair, it seems. Bikes broke, engines stopped running, pipes burst, and sometimes really serious repairs were needed. For example, once we arrived to find some windows, frames and all, missing from the Day Room (lounge) in the lower building, and once we found a section of roof collapsed. On arrival in 2000, we discovered the worst situation of all. Sometime after we left in 1999, someone broke into both buildings and stole tools and radios. At the upper building, they broke into the rat-proof rooms where we washed dishes, stored dry food over the winter, and where four leaders lived. The intruders left the doors open, so rats got in. Instead of mostly dying out in the winter snows, they

Navy Town with buildings still standing in June 1973

had found a protected space full of food. There they bred like crazy, and eliminated like crazy. We had to seal the area off and improvise substitute facilities. We also went after the rats, and got more than 100 of them. (When people saw our cook, Walter Chuck, our champion rat-killer, roasting one of them on a spit in the yard, I had to assure people he did not use them in our recipes.) We were a long time returning to some semblance of normality. Fortunately, we always had resourceful, hard-working, and clever staff—and knowledgeable, helpful participants—who never failed to cope with problems.

Our 1981 birders, 46 strong, (including a small number of birders with what was now WINGS) didn't have quarters to match those of later years, but at least that Annual Crisis, where to stay, was over. Unfortunately, that year was also the worst birding we ever had. We saw only 93 species, even though it was our first three-week long trip. Fortunately, 26 of them were Asian species.

From 1982 on, Attour was the sole company operating on Attu. That year, 43 of us, including Roger Tory Peterson, headed off to Attu with everything going smoothly, and no Annual Crisis. Not until we landed, that is. Trying to improve all aspects of our operation, we had started in 1979 with all canned and dry food that we could mail to Attu, but by 1982 we were also bringing more and more fresh and frozen food. We stored it in snowbanks, which worked OK for a while. In 1982, we planned to build a frozen food locker immediately on arrival in order to store the larger quantity that we would use that year. We unloaded the plane, which contained the locker materials, but where was the frozen food? Reeve had forgotten to load it. Needless to say, our menus required immediate adjustment. A week later, Reeve made a special trip over from Shemya to deliver our food. What people remembered from that year, however, is not the food, but that it was our best year ever, and remained so until 16 years later.

More and more people wanted to go to Attu. From 1983 through 1987, the size of our groups increased from 45 to 78. That meant we needed more food, more fuel, more building supplies, more equipment, more of everything. Our planes could carry a lot. They were Lockheed L-188 Electras, "the least successful commercial aircraft of the 1950s", as one wag once said. It's true that the wings on the early ones tended to fall off, but that problem was corrected—it was the arrival of jet aircraft that did them in. Reeve's Electras were really the only planes available in Alaska that could meet our needs. (That's why I always felt we needed them more than they needed us.) They were long-range; they could carry 84 people, the equivalent in cargo, or various combinations of both; and they were four-engine turboprops that could fly with only two engines in an emergency. Turboprops are what you want where there are a lot of mountains, or bad weather, or VFR (as at Attu). When you change the pitch on their propellers, they bite the air differently and the plane reacts immediately. The reaction of a jet when you punch the throttle isn't as quick, because there is a lag while the inertia of the turbines is overcome.

We would load everything in Anchorage and fly non-stop to Attu. The empty plane would hop over to Shemya, refuel, and return to Anchorage. The plane picking us up would refuel first at Shemya and then pick us up and return to Anchorage. (Notice that in both cases there would be no one but crew on the plane. That's the way Shemya liked it.) The plane would have to carry enough additional fuel to fly the 441 miles from Attu to Adak in case we couldn't land on Attu. Once the amount of fuel needed was loaded, there was usually a payload of 20,000 pounds left for passengers, baggage, and cargo. As the trips grew in size, that wasn't enough. You can do the math—one person with 45 pounds of baggage and three weeks of fresh and frozen food weighs 290 pounds, on average. So we could take 68 people if the weather was good, and if we didn't need any additional supplies. (We needed another 70 pounds of dry food per person for a three-week trip, but we found other ways to get that to Attu.) In any case, we could not carry volatile fuels like propane or gasoline on the plane (except in minute quantities).

We met our transport needs in two ways. One was to load a lot of dry food and other supplies onto the empty plane that came to pick us up, for use by the following year's tour. Of course, that meant we had to keep the plane on the ground while we unloaded the cargo, transported it to a storage location, put away our vehicles and carts, and came back to the plane. It also required good advance planning for the following year.

The second way was to ship supplies on the barge that visited Attu annually. This was essential for getting our gasoline and propane, and it also required good advance planning. The COOL barge, as it was called (Container On Ocean Liner) was chartered by the Bureau of Indian Affairs to bring supplies to remote villages in some parts of Alaska. It carried Conexes (containers) above board, and large quantities of fuel below. The supplies could be loaded on lighters and brought to shore, while the fuel was simply pumped to shore through pipes. In this fashion, 250,000 gallons of fuel oil were delivered to the Coast Guard every year, along with equipment they might need, such as trucks. It usually arrived just after we left the island in June. It took nothing but money for us to arrange to ship anything we wanted on the barge, even hazardous materials. The Coast Guard would sign for its receipt, and bring it to our base to await our arrival the following year. We would ship bicycles, bunk frames, pallets of lumber, 55-gallon fuel drums, propane cylinders, food, and so on. One year there were three 1,200-pound wooden crates of food. When we arrived the next year, we were surprised to find there had been a glitch in the order, and one crate contained nothing but cartons of cookies. Luckily, they were really good Pepperidge Farm cookies packed by twos in Mylar packages. We ate them for five years, and they were still fresh! I used to go on pelagic trips and see Attuvians snacking on them.

The very serious Asbestos Crisis hit us in 1985. We were all set for 69 of us to go that year, when I got a call in mid-February from the Fish & Wildlife Service Refuge Manager. "Larry," he said, "I'm afraid we can't let you use the old Loran A station any more." He went on to explain that in December, the Coast Guard had sent an asbestos inspector to Attu, and he had found a lot of it on pipes in the lower building. (The Coast Guard leasehold ends at Kingfisher Creek, over a mile away, so he must have run out of things to do while he waited for the next plane!) He sent a report to the F&WS telling them the building was not habitable. When I asked the Refuge Manager for more details, he didn't know much else. "We don't know where or how long or what size the pipes are," he said.

I knew. I had a three-ring binder containing nothing but photos of both buildings—every room, every wall, every floor, and every ceiling. I got it out, and sure enough, there they were, asbestos-covered pipes running through the washroom, day room, corridor, and so on. With a little interpolation from known objects, I could even determine their diameter. I also had, long ago, measured the building and made floor plans. Now I knew the extent of the problem.

Research told me that the standard solution to this problem was to remove the asbestos. This required the building openings to be covered so that a fan could duct air from outside to create a positive pressure inside the building. Then workers wearing protective clothing and respirators would remove the asbestos. The filters from the respirators had to be sent each day to an approved laboratory for measurement of exposure levels. The removed material had to be packaged in a specified way and sent to a special dump approved to receive it. Of course the nearest lab and dump were in Anchorage. This obviously would not work. I discovered, however, that there was a second method—encapsulation with a gooey polymer substance that hardened on exposure to air. Some contractors I talked to didn't even know about this. I found the material was made by a chemical company in West Virginia, and determined that we would need several hundred pounds of it.

Attour, Inc. (name change) would have to become an asbestos contractor, and we'd have to get both the material and a crew of workers to Attu in time to have the work inspected before the group got there. I began by preparing a formal plan for submission to the USF&WS engineering office in Anchorage. It required engineering drawings, material specifications, OSHA documents, etc, etc, etc. I hired a consulting service near Chicago to check over the plan to make sure I was doing things right. The plan was approved in Anchorage, and since it was their building (in a sense, being on their property, but it was officially listed as abandoned and no longer on the asset roster), if I got the pails of polymer to Kodiak, they would get the Coast Guard to bring it to Attu on one of their C-130 log flights. Now all I had to do was hire a small jet to take part of our staff, protective clothing, and painting mitts to Attu. The Refuge Manager himself would drop by Attu on a C-130 to check that the work was done.

This was all very expensive, needless to say, but now there were empty seats on the Reever, and we had a waiting list. So we could add some customers to provide extra revenue to help with the cost.

Everything went well, and the staff even got to do a little birding on its own. The group arrived, and settled in. After dinner, someone wandered down the road a ways past the lower building to a small cove. Our leader Terry Savaloja got word that he had found something good, and went to check it out. Terry identified North America's first Oriental Pratincole on the beach, and suddenly, at 9:30–10 in the evening, everyone was racing to see it. Al Driscoll wanted to make sure everyone knew about it, so he walked down the corridor of the lower building shouting "Oriental Pratincole on the beach!" A voice came back from one of the rooms: "Quiet please, some of us are trying to sleep."

Soon after the 1985 trip, I heard that Dick Reeve was thinking of selling the Electras. I asked him to give me as much advance notice as possible if he did, and I put out the word that it might happen. I knew that some people planned trips to Attu years in advance, so I thought the fairest thing to do was to let everyone know what might happen, rather than to suddenly hear, "The planes are gone. Sorry." For the same reason, I would continue to put out the word when I learned of other possible trip-ending developments, such as the Coast Guard moving to Shemya, and Loran shutting down altogether. Unfortunately, many people interpreted these efforts to keep people informed as really an effort to scare people into signing up right away for our trips. As it turned out, Reeve never sold the Electras, and in 1999, Dick told me that it was the worst mistake he had ever made. He said he thought the communities they served would be growing significantly, and that they would need the capacity the planes had. But the communities didn't grow, and he got stuck with fuel-hungry, high-maintenance, excess-capacity planes. Reeve would go bankrupt the next year, two months after we ended our trips.

Thank goodness the Reevers were not gone in 1986, when we saw the all-time favorite Attu bird, Spoonbill Sandpipers.

After the Asbestos Crisis, I thought we had seen it all. What more could possibly happen (other than a roof collapsing)? Things would actually get worse, yet I continued to think each crisis would be the last.

In 1987, we chartered two small planes to carry an advance party and extra passengers to Attu. The company contacted the Department of Defense for permission to land at Shemya and refuel. When it was denied, they protested that Reeve could stop there, and like Reeve, they were also transporting bird watchers. Well, that was news to the DOD (although not to Shemya base commanders, who didn't much care). We knew none of this at the time. The DOD immediately cancelled Reeve's permission. Each year, Reeve had simply let the DOD assume that our flights, like all of Reeve's other flights, were simply the usual military business. This cancellation happened the night before our tour's get-together dinner in Anchorage. Reeve informed us we would have to leave 5,000 pounds of passengers and other stuff in Anchorage because now they had to refuel at Adak, 450 miles from Attu. When they left Adak, they had to have (FAA requirement) enough fuel to return not only to Adak if weather were bad at Attu, but to an alternate airport. That would be Cold Bay, 625 miles east of Adak, and it would require 5,000 more pounds of fuel.

Reeve and I hatched a plan whereby everything would be taken to Adak, but then only the passengers and 20 pounds of baggage per person would continue on to Attu. The plane would make an extra 900-mile round trip back to Adak to pick up the remaining supplies and baggage and bring them to us. That's what happened. We got there on Sunday, and the rest of our stuff arrived Monday morning. We had some great birds, and when we left Attu, the Reever stopped at the Pribilofs on the way back to Anchorage, so that 32 people could get off for a couple of days birding there.

A couple of weeks later, I got a bill from Reeve for the extra flying involved. I pointed out that the flying was necessary only because a gamble they alone made had failed; we didn't even know about it. If we had, and therefore had at least implicitly accepted the risk, we would expect to pay. I told Dick he should "sharpen his pencil and figure it out again". I didn't hear from him again. With that, and for some other reasons, I thought that they had written us off as people they wanted to deal with. I wasn't that worried, because I thought that we now had an alternative.

One day on the trip we had just finished, I saw a Mark Air 737 jet on Attu's runway. I found out that the Coast Guard was again chartering flights every two weeks, but now they were with Mark Air, not Reeve. That would be a great way to go to Attu—a shorter trip, a little bigger payload, and the price, I found, wasn't that much more. I assumed that Mark Air couldn't land at Shemya, either. I ran some figures and decided that to accommodate the number of people who wanted to take our 1988 trip, and their supplies, two planes would be needed. I planned an additional one-week trip to help cover the cost.

As it happened, 1988 had enough Annual Crises to last several years. Beginning in February, until I had a laminectomy in July after the ABA Convention in Duluth, I had severe back pain. The doctors ordered several months of bed rest. The staff suspended a laptop computer over my cot on Attu, and I spent most of my time there. (However, I managed to get up long enough to see the Yellow-breasted Bunting.)

A week or so before the first scheduled Mark Air flight, I got a call from them telling me that they could not fly us to Attu. Their contract with the Coast Guard was over, which meant that the CG no longer supplied the certified weather observer who, by FAA regulations, had to be on the ground 24 hours before any plane with at least 30 seats could land. This wasn't a problem for Reeve—they could come down within sight of the ground at Shemya, which had a weather observer, and then fly at very low altitude for 32 miles across to Attu without ever losing sight of the ground. That's possible in a turboprop, but the FAA won't allow it in a jet.

I started scrambling, if you can do that flat on your back. The first thing to check, clearly, was this weather observer situation. I called the Loran Station on Attu, and before I even asked a question, they told me Reeve had just called them to check on the airport and touch base for our usual spring flights. So my next call was to Dick Reeve. He didn't seem surprised to hear from me so late, nor at the situation we were in. He just expressed his dislike for Mark Air and penciled us onto the flight schedule. We had to make a few adjustments because the payloads did not match: a couple of people had to be cancelled and given refunds and discounts on future trips, and the one-week group on the first plane had to go through the Adak baggage shuttle routine again. So a disaster had been averted once again, although not through any cleverness on my part.

Perhaps the gods decided I really did have enough in 1988—everything seemed to go quite smoothly for the next few years. In 1990, we were able to offer some alternatives to the usual three-week trip by bringing some small planes in, at one-week intervals. We had some great birds, of course. In 1989, for example, when we operated successive one- and three-week trips, the earlier group found the first North American records of Yellow Bittern and the gorgeous little Narcissus Flycatcher, not to mention an Oriental Turtle-Dove. The neat thing was, they were all still there when the second group arrived! In 1991, Pin-tailed Snipe, Oriental Cuckoo, Pechora Pipit, and all four stints were enough to make birders drool.

In 1992, things started getting significantly more difficult, operationally. We had a mini-crisis that didn't last very long. The plan was to have successive two-week trips. On a Sunday, a Reever brought the second group to Attu, and intended to take the first group back. But before it could take off, the pilots discovered that a fuel transfer pump was not working properly. That pump moves fuel between the wing tanks in such a way as to keep the plane balanced. The only thing to do was to put everyone off the plane, including the flight attendants, and fly the plane back to Anchorage. The Coast Guard offered to house the flight attendants for the night (what a surprise!). We were faced with providing dinner, a place to sleep, and breakfast for 110 people. The food was no problem—we always had extra food, in case we were delayed leaving the island. Luckily, we had a lot of old cots, and found space in the day room, the dining room, and even the runway helicopter quonset of the top-secret Operation Queen Match. (Funny, we never had any trouble finding out or figuring out what these secret things were about.) The plane returned the next morning, so we were quickly back to normal.

That was the year we got the disturbing news that the 1992 COOL barge would be the last. This would greatly complicate our logistics, especially when it came to fuel. We used a lot of propane and gasoline for heaters, water heaters, cooking, and generating electricity for power and light. If we switched as many of those to diesel fuel and heating oil, and used our existing stockpile of propane cylinders and gasoline drums only for cooking and our ATVs, we would be able to operate satisfactorily for several years. We began making plans to do just that—replace water heaters with five-times-as-expensive oil-fired units, and replace gasoline-fueled generators with big diesel generators. Then the fuel we needed could always be brought in by plane. It wouldn't be cheap, but we could keep operating.

The worst news in 1992 was that our long-time leader Terry Savaloja was too ill to be with us. Terry—known to many as "Mr. Yellow Rail" for his skill in finding the bird for birders who visited Minnesota—was the first birder to get stuck on Attu. That was for 10 (!) extra days in 1978. He compensated for the fact that we were all running around Gambell by single-handedly finding the first North American records of Green Sandpiper and Eurasian Siskin. All of us, and all our participants, loved Terry. He was quiet and unassuming, but always with something perceptive and witty to say at an appropriate moment. We hoped against hope that he might return some day, but that summer he died. In spring, 1993, we honored his last wishes by scattering his ashes at a spot on the side of Weston Mountain, behind the upper building.

Sadly, we would lose another leader the next year. Malcolm E. "Pete" Isleib was a biologist and commercial fisherman whose energy and cheerfulness knew no bounds. No one could keep up with Pete.

You could depend on him totally—there seemed to be nothing he wasn't able and eager to do. Pete's drive was exemplified by his Alaska list, which was significantly larger than anyone else's. Just after our spring trip, as he prepared for a season of fishing in Bristol Bay, he was killed in an accident. Pete has ashes scattered at Alexai Point.

The most somber time we had in all our years on Attu was not at these ceremonies, however. It was on our final trip to Attu, when John LaVia succumbed almost immediately to a heart attack while going up to the Japanese monument with more than half the people on the tour. John's two sons were also on the trip, and one was nearby. Like me, John was a teacher who had recently retired. My impression was that he was probably many students' favorite teacher. The Coast Guard had a full-dress ceremony the next day, just before the LaVia family left Attu on a chartered business jet.

Perhaps this is a good point to mention the matters of health and safety that we had to address. (We never had to address any psychological problems, nor did we ever have any truly difficult or disruptive personalities.) By jet air ambulance, Attu is three to four hours from Anchorage. If there were a life-threatening emergency, especially one in the field, we would need to be prepared to deal with it ourselves as much as possible. It takes time to radio for help, mobilize the help, and get the person back to our quarters or the Coast Guard's medical ward. Once, for example, there was a party on Alexai Point, and one person suddenly collapsed. (The joke later—you can tell it did not turn out to be serious—was that four doctors were there before he hit the ground.) We were ten miles from our base, and for only half of that distance were there roads on which we could operate our ATV with trailer. Fortunately, the man came to right away, and showed no symptoms of any lingering distress or illness. We were able to bring our Zodiac five miles across the bay and then return him to quarters for rest. But this illustrates the kind of serious logistic situation we could potentially face.

Early on, we depended on an extensive medical kit prepared and maintained by Dr. Norman Mellor, who, many of you will recall, wrote many articles for *Birding* about precautions and treatment in remote areas, and who was on one of our trips. In later years, an even more complete kit was provided by a major hospital in Anchorage, and used by Dr. Dave Sonneborn, one of our leaders. Once we depended on the medical expertise of Dr. Craig Roberts. Dr. Bill Rydell, a surgeon and many times a participant, used the kit on at least three occasions for stitching minor wounds. One of our staff was a surgical nurse. The Coast Guard's ward had equipment (such as a defibrillator) and medicines we did not have, but they had only a medic, while we always had several doctors among our participants. (The consensus was that it would be best if we always had an emergency-room physician, an orthopedic surgeon, and a psychiatrist.) I believe we provided the Coast Guard more advice over the years than they provided help to us. If more medical assistance were required, it would be eight hours at the very best before a small jet air ambulance could get someone back to a hospital in Anchorage.

John's death, on our very last trip to Attu, was the only truly serious health crisis that we had. I am sure we helped ourselves by informing everyone, both in advance and again on the island, of what the hazards and risks were, and by having our leaders constantly alert to unsafe behavior. In 23 other trips, there were only a few minor injuries, mostly from biking accidents (in a couple of cases from, shall we say, "bottling" accidents?)—sprained ankles or knees, a few cuts. We had two precautionary evacuations of staff members by C-130s, which had arrived on log flights. One required a cystoscopy, and the other spent time in an Anchorage hospital with pneumonia. In all those years, the only emergency evacuations—all by Coast Guard medical staff on C-130s sent from Kodiak—were for non-birders: a woman from a Russian transport ship who had appendicitis, a construction worker who caught his hand in a rock crusher, and a fisherman who had injured himself. We strongly recommended to participants that they make sure their own medical policies covered evacuation, and to purchase such coverage if not, because our insurance did not cover it. These $25,000–35,000 medical flights were covered for our staff by our worker's compensation policies, but our liability insurance didn't specifically address such situations.

Attour was required to have not only worker's compensation insurance, but also, beginning in 1993, to specifically provide $1,000,000 of coverage for the Coast Guard runway. We also had to meet other Coast Guard requirements (more on that later), to obtain an annual Special Use Permit (basically just for being on the island) from the USF&WS, and to pay a daily use fee for each person. (There was no fee for using the abandoned buildings, for obvious reasons, but one of the 15–20 conditions of our permit stated that we did not have exclusive use of them.) We were far too remote to be visited by inspectors for regulatory agencies, but we checked things like food preparation regulations, and tried to adhere to them as closely as we could. Naturally, we failed in places. I know, for example, that we failed to meet federal standards for homeless shelters requiring one shower for every 14 people.

In the course of our operations on Attu, we had dealings with the Coast Guard, the USF&WS, the Navy, the Air Force, the U.S. Senate, the FAA, and even the Army. Contrary to popular belief, we never were encumbered by red tape, we never had unreasonable regulations imposed on us, and we never met difficult bureaucrats. On the contrary, all of these agencies of the government were very fair to us in their actions, and often (except for the Navy, which was always strictly go-by-the-book) were flexible and accommodating to us. We often benefited from things they did for us that they didn't really have to do. The Coast Guard Loran Station Attu was especially helpful: assisting with plane loading and unloading (actually, we usually assisted them!), with transport, providing communications facilities until we got our satellite phone in 1999, loaning us material in emergencies (remember the toilet paper shortage in 1979?), generally looking after us, and inviting us to social affairs. In turn, we mostly tried to stay out of their way, but we were able to provide help to them several times, especially with our planes. Every year we dealt with a different CO on Attu, and just what that individual would be willing to do, and to let us do, was always unpredictable.

Although we had better facilities every year than the year before, our trips began to get more difficult in the early 1990s. Some things we had feared never actually happened—Reeve still had the Electras, and nothing had come of all the talk we heard several years before that the Loran Station was going to move to Shemya. The loss of the COOL barge was real, though, and clearly caused difficulties for us after 1993. Too long-range to worry about was the obvious fact that Loran could not hold a candle to the Global Positioning System, so its days were probably numbered. In any case, starting in February 1993, we were presented with our most serious Annual Crisis ever: the potential loss of access to Attu. The Seventeenth Coast Guard District in Juneau called me that month. Usually in March, I would send them a letter requesting permission to use the runway, and they would respond with a one-page letter

The Coast Guard Station, 1973

granting permission, with a few requirements about flight notice, submission of participant liability releases, and being self-sufficient while we were there, as well as a Hold Harmless Agreement to sign. The caller said, "Larry, don't bother asking us to use the Attu runway this year. The Pacific area headquarters in Alameda have taken over control, and I don't think they will be receptive to any request."

I got on the phone immediately to the office of Commander, Maintenance & Logistics Command Pacific and over the next few days, I talked to officers there and in the legal department about the situation. They emphasized that the CG is not, for obvious reasons, set up to support the commercial operations of private companies. I pointed out that not only were we requesting a continuation of a long-term practice, but also that we had tons of supplies already on the island waiting for our return. The latter point seemed persuasive. Late in March, they granted us a Revocable License, "neither assignable or transferable", to use the landing strip for 1993. (I had already decided to run a fall trip that year, even though I could not get leave for it. I didn't want Attu birding to end without another attempt to discover what fall migration was really like.) MLCP said they would consider future use later.

I wouldn't have to worry about the barge for a while, either. I had learned that the Loran station was going to replace its huge generators. The company with the contract for the job had its own business jet that they flew to Attu several times. They were barging generators, heavy equipment, and supplies from Seattle and Anchorage, and they needed air support, too. I traded payload on our empty Reeve flights for space on their barge. Since I was assured most emphatically that their barge would arrive "the first week of May", in order to meet their project deadlines, I saw some wonderful ways to take advantage of this almost unlimited free shipping opportunity. First of all, we could load up on propane, gasoline, and fuel oil. To induce my wife Donna to return every year to Attu, I could send all the materials needed to build a relatively large and comfortable room and bath under the balcony in the big generator room at the back of the lower building. We could ship cases and cases of beer, wine, and soft drinks that were too heavy to take by plane. Any participants who chafed at our 45-pound weight restriction could send all the baggage they wanted via the barge. (And many did.) Those were all good ideas except the last.

People sent at least 50 boxes of baggage to the barge at Tacoma. Toward the end of April, the barge had missed its departure date, and it was clear that it would not make it to Attu by the promised date. We had to hire a freight-forwarder to retrieve all the mailed packages from the barge and ship them to Anchorage. The only fair thing to do was also to refund everyone's mailing costs. Of course, now our Reever didn't have a tight payload—it would have a too-large payload for sure. So we had to charter a $20,000 small cargo plane. At least we knew we could get the most for our money by taking up any extra payload with oil drums.

The barge? A week late? Two? Hah! We caught sight of it approaching Massacre Bay as we flew off the island in June. At least we had a fall trip coming up soon to make use of the liquid refreshments.

We had taken a gamble by loading the barge with fuel and supplies for future years, because our future had not yet been decided by Alameda. I had begun gathering material from various sources to use in presenting our case to the MLCP. As ever, I had broadcast the news of what was happening. Many former participants sent me ideas and letters of support. Dan Gibson, of the University of Alaska Museum, lent his prestige to the effort by writing the Coast Guard attesting to the value of our trips for Alaskan ornithology, and attaching relevant published papers. In the end, I never had to present our case to the MLCP. Winnie Conway, who had visited Attu in 1990 with her husband, was upset that we might not be allowed to return after 1993. Winnie is well connected, and wrote her senator, who wrote the Washington headquarters of the Coast Guard. The result was a letter in August from headquarters to Senator Philip Gramm, telling about the "pleasant relationship" the Coast Guard had with us, how glad the island personnel were to see us every year, what good care we took while we were there, and so on. It said, "We expect to continue this working relationship with Attour into the future."

When we got to Attu in 1994, I found out what had taken place behind the scenes. When Washington got the senator's inquiry, they were, of course, in the dark not only about Attour, but probably Attu as well (Alameda didn't even know Attu had a paved runway). Anxious calls went from them to Alameda, to Juneau, and finally to Attu. As luck would have it, the CO who fielded the calls knew us well. He had enjoyed our visit when he was stationed on Attu several years before. (Very few Coasties return to Attu, and few of them become CO!) He told me this story with a great deal of relish, chuckling at how anxious the higher-ups were to avoid Congressional inquiries.

Our biggest-yet Annual Crisis was over. I stashed the letter in a safe-deposit box. Our Attu future was secured, at least as far as the runway was concerned. Basically, the result was that the rather loose policy that Juneau had followed was tightened up by the MLCP in Alameda. Requests to use the runway for non-government business were not granted, but Attour, Inc. was grandfathered in. Landing fees increased markedly, and the one- or two-page letter of permission that Juneau used to send me was replaced by a 22-page license with environmental checklist. These were nothing, now that we had what we wanted. I loaded the fall trip's October pickup plane with more oil drums for 1994.

Loading planes was a continuing and serious problem, ever since Reeve could no longer use Shemya for our flights. We needed lots of fuel on Attu, and cutting down the number of participants didn't lower our needs much. Without barges, we needed more planes to carry that fuel, and that meant more people to pay for them. Those people wanted to take a lot of gear to such a remote area. (It took me a long time to realize how much of that gear was liquid.) We wanted to limit the personal baggage to make room for food and fuel. It was a constant tug-of-war, especially since a few people always seemed to think that anything carried on shouldn't count against their weight allowance. It was also a constant tug-of-war between Reeve and me. The allowable payload figures they would give me just before flight time kept decreasing throughout the 1990s, and I could never get a consistent, logical explanation why.

Clearly, the easy solution to all this was to regain the ability to land at Shemya. I know Reeve made efforts to do so, and so did we, independently. The Air Force was winding down its operations on Shemya, as was the Navy on Adak. Some activities would remain, but the islands' facilities would be operated by civilian contractors. The time seemed ripe for a change, and we went through Senator Stevens' office. We even met with one of his staff members who took a trip out to the Aleutians. If anyone could gain us access, it figured to be Alaska's Senator Stevens, Chairman of the Armed Services Committee, who worked tirelessly to bring new business and development to Alaska. His office pursued this all the way up to the Secretary of the Air Force. She said OK, under certain conditions. Unfortunately, those conditions involved the State of Alaska taking responsibility for certain services, and other things that were not really going to happen. (Ironically, when it finally became possible to use Shemya, that was of no value because the fuel supply was contaminated.)

We were just going to have to struggle with supplies, making use of every opportunity to get material to Attu. And we would have to finagle here, deal there. Typical of that activity was what we did one year (before we converted to mostly fuel oil), when we saw that we would run out of gasoline before the trip ended. The Coast Guard had gasoline, but we couldn't buy it. However, the summer before, a F&WS-sponsored biologist worked on Attu. We left the water turned on for him, and arranged for him to use our equipment at the upper building. He brought propane for the range, on the F&WS boat. Afterwards, he called and said they owed me a propane cylinder, since he had run short and borrowed one of ours. So I went over to the Loran Station and called the F&WS to propose that they buy a drum of gasoline from the Coast Guard and give it to us as repayment for the propane. The biologist's research account was still open, so all the necessary paperwork was possible, and we got our gas.

On 1 April 1995, the Air Force base on Shemya was converted to contractor operation. The military's role in the Aleutians (but not its control) was undergoing significant change. By this date, the Adak airport was also under contractor operation. This had consequences for us, we were to learn, when airport operating hours became M-F, 9-5. Another event in Alaska would also have repercussions for us: Mark Air stopped flying 14 April 1995 when it filed for bankruptcy.

We left Anchorage to go to Attu on Monday morning, 15 May. Reeve's Dispatch office consults the latest weather maps and draws on its vast experience when making the go/no-go decision. (If the situation were not clear-cut, they would explain the situation to us and ask for our input.) When we left

Anchorage, Attu had a 3,000-foot ceiling and several miles of visibility to the southeast, our approach direction. When we got to Attu, we could not see the runway. Fog shrouded the entire island. We returned to Adak to wait as long as we could for a break in the weather at Attu (pilots cannot exceed the 14 hours allowed for their duty day, which time begins when they report, not when the plane takes off). It did not clear, so we flew back east to Cold Bay, where there were overnight facilities: the Flying Tiger Hotel and restaurant, a USF&WS bunkhouse, and a few private homes.

I once heard Cold Bay described as "the armpit of the universe." The most exciting thing that many of us find to do here is to leave. Second-most might be sighting a Brown Bear. Actually, there have been reports of Steller's Sea-Eagle at the nearby Izembek NWR, but they were in winter. Anyway, I am glad that no one told us on landing that we would spend the next four days there. (At least I finally got to see the beautiful snow-capped Pavlov Volcano. On several previous stops, the weather was too bad.)

On Tuesday, conditions were 50-50. If we did not make it, we would eventually have to charter a total of 7,000 miles to get to Attu, instead of the usual 3,000. We needed better odds than that. We might have made it on Wednesday, but Reeve, which nearly always had a spare Electra, no longer did. They were helping to cover the scheduled routes that Mark Air had abandoned, and scheduled service always has priority. Also, airport construction along their own routes limited the use of Reeve's jets, so the Electras were needed to cover for them. No Electra was available on Wednesday.

Late Wednesday, one of the largest spring storms in years developed, and knocked out flying from Thursday through the following Monday. (An Alaska Air military charter couldn't even make it into Adak on Friday.) After a meeting of all their top personnel, searching for some way to carry out our charter, but failing, Reeve called me and gave me the bad news. It was as if the building had collapsed around me—this was one Annual Crisis that was completely inconceivable. I called a meeting, and I'm sure people could sense from my demeanor that bad news was coming. It was certainly the most difficult announcement I have ever had to make, and I was upset almost beyond words. We arranged for a number of people to go to the Pribilofs from Cold Bay, and helped some to make other arrangements. Then RAA sent their big jet to take us back to Anchorage.

We spent the time we should have been on Attu mopping up this worst of all Annual Crises. Well over half the revenues had already been spent, and little except fuel could be reused. When you charter, the rule is "When you fly, you pay", and that's whether you get where you're going or not, so half our charter costs were eaten up. We donated all the food to an outreach program in Anchorage (no, you don't get a tax deduction—it's already a business expense). We paid no wages and refunded everything we could, plus a bit more. We offered a slight discount on future trips, and turned to planning them. Could it happen again? Would the M-F, 9-5 hours at Adak airport exacerbate our difficulties? Would our material that was already on Attu be OK when it was two years old instead of one?

The whole operation was getting more difficult and more expensive. I had long worried about the lower building. I would not have been surprised to arrive some year and find that the winter freeze-thaw cycle had done in its concrete roof, and that some of it had therefore collapsed into our quarters. (I had devised more than one cockamamie plan to protect it, but with the barge gone, none were feasible.) Now we were hearing that the entire Loran system would be superseded by GPS, and the Loran station would be closed on 31 December 2000. If the decision to think seriously about ending operations had not yet been made, the seed had surely been planted.

Our return to Attu in 1996 was not auspicious. We had to send a big Electra a week ahead of the main group, because we had not delivered any supplies for the trip in 1995, and we didn't know what shape things would be in after two years. We sold places on a one-week trip to help finance it. Again, weather was bad, and the trip left Anchorage four days late, leaving a trip of only three days duration. Whereas on our first 18 trips, there had been only one departure delay, of one day, suddenly, in the last four trips we once didn't make it, and were delayed on the other trips for a total of eight days.

At least the birds were auspicious. On the first day of the three-day early trip, two participants found Whooper Swans apparently nesting (later confirmed). On the longer trip, Oriental Turtle-Dove, Great Spotted Woodpecker, and Yellow-breasted Bunting were all top-quality. That's the kind of stuff that makes you want to keep going forever; tempting also was the fact that in 1996 and 1997, we had few problems beyond the usual anguish from weather and payloads.

At the end of 1997's trip, our stockpile of extra fuel from 1993 was almost gone. From now on, we would have to send an additional plane, probably an Electra, loaded with a few people—like an advance crew—and lots of cargo. When we got to Attu in 1998 (on time!), the advance party found our roof had collapsed, not on the lower building, but on the upper building. One hundred square feet of roof was missing. We closed off the space below, made some temporary cover, and called Anchorage to get needed lumber and roofing supplies put on the plane that was coming four days later. What we saw when we peered into the rafters of the remaining roof did not fill us with a lot of confidence for the building's long-term survival. Consequently, we decided that was it. We would stop our trips by the end of 2000, even though we had learned that Loran would get a reprieve until at least 2008. In August, our web site laid out the final schedule: spring trips in 1999 and 2000, and a fall trip in 2000.

If the gods could have conceived of something that might make us reconsider, it would have been the kind of birding we had in 1998, which far, far exceeded not only any previous experiences, but anything we could even dream of. (Nevertheless, we held fast to our decision.) It was the equivalent of a 500-year storm. Perhaps it should be called The Perfect Year. Both two-week trips cleaned up big time. You can read all about it in Steve Heinl's excellent article elsewhere in this book.

The announcement was there in black and white. Our staff was telling people, "No, Larry's not crying wolf—it really is the end." So the demand to bird Attu was greater than ever. We scheduled 2-week, 2-week, and 1-week trips in the spring, and two 2-week trips in the fall. We would take 290 people to Attu in our final year. We needed all those people, because we were planning to charter ten Electra flights—six more than we chartered in the spring and fall of 1993. We had already started removing old bikes, empty propane cylinders, and other things from Attu in 1999. We would need all those planes to get everything else off.

Bird-wise, 2000 would be a very good year: in the spring, we saw Great Knot, Black-tailed Gull, Oriental Cuckoo, Middendorff's Grasshopper-Warbler, Lanceolated Warbler, the first recorded North

American occurrence of Rufous-tailed Robin, and Eurasian Bullfinch; in the fall, we saw Dusky Warbler, Great Spotted Woodpecker, Baillon's Crake (for the first time in North America), and what was almost surely a Eurasian Sparrowhawk.

Operationally and logistically, in all the years we went to Attu, 2000 was the worst of them all. It started the first week of March, when I got a phone call from Alameda. "Mr. Balch, we decided not to do the FAA airport certification process. It would be too costly and take at least six months, and we don't need it for our planes." I asked her what that had to do with us. She told me they had received a letter from the FAA in December saying our flights could no longer land at their airport unless they obtained a certain type of certificate. (Planes with more than 30 seats may use only airports with a Limited Airport Operating Certificate, except "in emergencies and special circumstances, such as the operation of air carrier aircraft transporting forest firefighters", the regulation reads.) She agreed to fax the letter to me. When I read it, I was shocked to see that the previous certificate was surrendered in April 1995, and that RAA had been exercising the exception for "emergencies and special circumstances" ever since. The FAA had decided that, after four years, our bird-watching flights were routine business. I was further shocked to see that RAA had received a carbon copy.

I called Reeve to check on the planning for our first flight in May, without letting on that I knew about the FAA letter. They said there might be a problem getting permission to land, but they would check with the Coast Guard in Juneau. Then I faxed a letter to the FAA in Anchorage and called them to make an appointment to talk to the appropriate officials on the following Monday. RAA called me on Friday with the news that "It doesn't look good." I made an appointment with Dick Reeve for Tuesday.

The meeting with the FAA went well. One of them reminded me that he was the FAA official we were transporting to Attu on our ill-fated flight in 1995, so he also had spent four days at Cold Bay! They listened carefully to my presentation, and seemed to be most impressed by our need to remove, as per our USF&WS permit, all of our accumulated material and equipment from Attu. They said, "Having given you this exception four times, we'd look pretty foolish not doing so again under these circumstances." I thought they flinched when I told them we would have ten flights, but they didn't back down. The FAA agreed to notify the Coast Guard, and they in turn agreed to certain requests by the FAA as to how to handle our flights.

At my meeting with RAA, I greeted everyone, then said, "I've just come from a meeting with the FAA, and we have permission to use the Attu airport this year." I could almost see their jaws drop, and I did not ask them about the December letter.

On the second Tuesday in May, 25 people—staff and some veteran participants—would fly to Attu, and 66 would follow on Saturday, four days later. That was the plan. As background for the disaster that would follow, let me explain that RAA had two jets and three Electras. Two Electras had cargo doors and compartments and could be put in various configurations to carry between 28 and 73 passengers; the other had no cargo compartment, but carried 84 passengers. One jet was used on a continuing charter for the Air Force, to fly passengers and cargo to Shemya every Tuesday and Friday. When we arrived in early May, one jet and one cargo-door Electra were going to be in the hangar for at least a week, under-

Photo: Dixie Coleman

Looking for Baillon's Crake, September 2000

going mandated periodic scheduled maintenance. That left only two planes—one without a cargo door—that we might use (we couldn't fly jets to Attu).

The night before our Tuesday flight was to leave (all our flights left at 7 a.m.), we were told they need-ed our cargo-door plane for the Air Force charter, because their lone available jet had developed a mechanical problem; we would have to go on Thursday. But just after leaving for Shemya, "our" Electra developed a windshield problem, and had to return for its replacement. (If you're counting, RAA is now down to only one plane.) Late Wednesday night, we got a phone call. "The Electra's window popped out, and we don't have another one. We're looking for one."

We were in deep trouble—we needed to move tons of cargo and 90 people and only the wrong Electra was available. We moved fast Thursday morning. I called a company whose web site I had been checking a month earlier, to see if we could charter their C-130 (actually, the civilian version is called L-382). We could. On the way over to their offices, we spotted a disused Electra in their yard with an intact windshield! (No go—the plane was the object of a court suit and could not be touched.)

The C-130 has huge capacity: 35,000 pounds, as compared to 14,000 on the Electra we lost. Our plan was to make maximum use of this capacity: all our cargo, anything else we wanted to splurge on, propane cylinders that we couldn't send on RAA (they can go only on all-cargo flights), and most of our baggage. We'd send two staff members on the C-130 as loadmasters, leave one person in Anchorage, put 83 people (we were at maximum weight) on the available Electra, and charter a small jet to take the five heaviest people to Attu. We had enough extra capacity on the C-130 to also take some of RAA's cargo to Adak.

55

At our get-together dinner Friday night, we explained all this to the participants, and gave them plastic trash bags to help them split up their baggage—they could take only a sleeping bag and little else. The rest of their baggage would go on the C-130. We told them we had rented a truck, would pick up their baggage the next morning, drive it to the airport and onto the C-130, fly 1500 miles to Attu, drive the truck to our base and unload, fly the truck back 1500 miles to Anchorage, and turn it in with ten miles on it. That was fantasy, of course—we weren't going to put the truck on the plane.

All three planes left on Saturday. Two made it. The C-130 couldn't land because of weather, so it returned to Adak and came the next morning.

One would hope that would be enough "adventure" for one trip. However, as I've already described, we were immediately confronted by the rat calamity. Then when it was time for the second group to come, bad weather and plane availability alternated to delay the departure of most of our first group and the arrival of most of our second group by five days. (We managed to move ten of them with only one day's delay by chartering a small turboprop.) Finally, our one-week group was delayed one day in arriving, and two days in leaving. Thus ended The Spring When We Couldn't Go Anywhere On Time. If ever I had any doubts about the decision to end our trips, I no longer did.

Our second fall group also suffered a delay, of three days departure, but they were handsomely rewarded by seeing Dusky Thrush, Fork-tailed Swift, and Rustic Bunting in those three extra days.

Every Electra that left Attu that year (except the first) carried away things we had accumulated over the years. We removed more than 200 bicycles, bunk frames, beds, generators large and small, tools, heaters, laundry machines, water heaters, refrigerators, freezers, empty oil drums, empty propane cylinders (hint: Clorox kills their smell), and assorted other stuff. Anything of any value went to an auction house in Anchorage. After the last group left, we made large bonfires of mattresses, tables, and everything plastic (including lots of our water pipes).

One hour before the last plane arrived, the final six tons of material was sitting at the edge of the runway, waiting to be stuffed into every spare nook and cranny of the Electra. We were still at base, tying up the loose ends, when something happened that was a fitting reminder of where we were, and of the kind of birding we had done for 25 years. Near our quarters, a Great Spotted Woodpecker flew in! It was a male (our 10 September bird was a female) and it gave great looks to at least one person who had not been there for the earlier bird. We left on a happy note.

If all of this has seemed to dwell too much on the problems we encountered, rest assured that for every problem, there was, first of all, the satisfaction of solving it. Secondly, there were scores of wonderful and rewarding things that happened. We also had a lot of fun trying to make the Attu visit more comfortable and more fun for people. I remember:
- The outdoor hot tub that Al Driscoll so faithfully tended.
- The fancy dinner that Jennifer Jolis produced in 1987, where the leaders served as waiters dressed in tuxedo T-shirts, and we set the tables with white tablecloths, candles, and flowers. I can still remember that the menu included veal breast stuffed with hazelnuts, and chocolate mousse in bittersweet chocolate shells with raspberry coulis.

Relaxing in the hot tub, May 2000

- Noble Proctor's once-a-trip "room inspections" and his botany excursions searching for the rare moonwort.
- Our "barbeque nights" where the leaders grilled hot dogs and hamburgers for everyone.
- The padded outhouse seats that felt oh, so warm.

Our trips produced many, many days of great birding, thousands of lifers for 1,076 birders, many first North American records, and, especially, good companionship. They provided lasting memories that we will always treasure. 🕊

Bonfire before final departure, Fall 2000

Instructions

They were told to pack in plastic
labeling socks
underwear, towels

they were told to bring
artificial fabrics
to wick away sweat
and keep out the cold

they recommended over-boots
waterproofs
cushions for the bikes
waterbottles, batteries
flashlights for inside and out

they were told to pack in plastic
and they were told right
the roof had small leaks
the floor flooded slowly
the molding walls shed
lead-based paint

they were told to pack in plastic
but they could never
have brought
enough.

—*Lyndia Terre*

View of the Tank Farm, by Navy Town 1981

Low Ceiling

As we taxi on in,
The tundra browner
Than old tea bags,
A thin rain falling
White on the mountains,
And Navy Town junkier
Than I had remembered,
The oldtimers compare
This year's snow cover
To last year's: a mild
Winter. The new ones
Remain almost speechless
Till the Electra stops.
We squirm into rainpants
And parkas, grab packs
From the overhead bins;
Finally, the binoculars.
Will I see a new bird?
I wonder just how bad
The rats will be again.
Another year. Another
Walk up to the monuments.
Could be in the Smokies
Now, ferns and trillium,
Or watching Morris pitch,
But no: this brown tundra,
Condensation in the rooms,
The inevitable mildew.

—Macklin Smith

59

The Manifest

Who were those who undertook the journey?
Mostly men past thirty-five, Americans
Professional, successful, middle-of-the-road
And white, the single-minded and the polytropic,
People with quirks and complex personalities.
I name the leaders, staff, those famous
Here or in the Lower Forty-Eight.

Pete Isleib: millionaire, a former U-2 pilot,
Captain of five trawlers in Bristol Bay,
Indifferent to ice or squall. Swiftest afoot
And farthest walker, he found on his own
The Asian Brown Flycatcher.

Dan Gibson: museum man and ornithologist,
The world's only expert on Aleutian avifauna.

Roger Tory Peterson: that writer and artist
Who taught us, first and best, our field skills.

His ample comrade from Connecticut, quickest
On the uptake, Noble Proctor. Finest
Tour-guide on five continents, a finder
Of birds and rare plants, he documented
Moonwort on Attu.

With him Thede Tobish: he of tamoshantered
Grit and fitness, heart-stopper of women
And, one imagines, men, and if I say
He's Alaska's premier birder, will Dan Gibson
Pause to snuff-and-stuff a specimen?
Yet it was Thede, not Dan, who found
And keyed the Hobby and the Pintail Snipe,
And who identified the Siberian Blue Robin.

Also Terry Savaloja, the Minnesota kid
Birdwatcher ("Little Terry") who in his youth
Chose as his profession corporate travel agent
So that he could chase rare birds for free.
Who discovered nesting White-tailed Eagles
On Attu, and kept his own company out there,
Sardonic, considerate. None of us knew
Of his personal life till he began dying
At age 39, and told us all,
His friends, his family, others.

The faxer of these leaders, Larry Balch,
Chicago math instructor and computer whiz,
Our manciple and reeve, hydrologist and roofer,
Refurbisher of ruins, breaker of Hondas
And sole stockholder. Balch colonized Attu.

With him flew Cindy Lippincott, ex-hippy,
Ex-yogini, and our cook's assistant.

And Al Driscoll, man of Bacchus, of oiled
Hands and lost tools, most enigmatic
Man of discourse. "Dyslexics of the world,
Untie!" his T-shirt said. He had commanded
Flight maintenance crews, and could himself repair
Any aircraft they'd let out of Thailand. Al told
How his father's ancestral father in Salem,
Massachusetts, being pressed as a witch, spoke
Last words of wrath and pleading: "More rocks."

Benton Basham followed, first on the manifest,
A Tennessee anesthetist whose ABA life list
Has ranked and ranks and will rank highest.

An anesthesiologist as well, Jerry Maisel
Of Tarzana, California. It was he who packed
And carried in the field the most equipment.

Other Californians came with Guy McCaskie,
Compiler for the Southern California Region,
A wizard of immediate and accurate ID,
Versed in tertials, secondaries, primaries.

Our eldest, Thompson Marsh, was able at eighty,
This Colorado man of law, to shoulder
A long oak bench over a half mile of tundra.

One of us, a destroyer gunnery officer,
Had lobbed 16-inch rounds onto the island.
Three had fought in Asia.

One had waited months to cast her wedding ring
Into the Bering Sea. This she did in June, 1985,
Walking all day over to Holtz Bay and back.

Another came to honor the Japanese dead,
Her two great-uncles.

In 1979, Jim Vardaman, doing his ABA Big Year.
In 1980, a distinguished Western novelist.
In 1981, the painter John Pitcher.
Until 1983, H. Granville Smith.

And many others joined the tour
Repeatedly or once, possessed
And questing birders, lovers and contemplatives, people
Trying to kill time: teachers, priests, oncologists,
A midwife, a widow, an astrophysicist,
A psychoanalyst, a baggage handler,
Historians and housewives,
A father and a daughter,
A father and a son,
A cook, a poet, and myself,
There were no more.

—*Macklin Smith*

King Eiders, May 1989

Photo: Jim Burns

Photo: Ed Harper

Upper and lower base from the side of Weston Mountain, September 1983

The Holy Grail of North American Birding

John Fitchen

We stood huddled on the soggy tundra beside the remote airstrip, our backs to the 35-knot wind and horizontal sleet. Driven by internal engines hard to explain to those we left behind, we had come to this stark and distant place in search of birds. As the sleet pelted Gore-Tex and penetrated cracks in our clothing, I found myself wondering, *"Why am I here? Why do we do this?"*

Sitting on the tarmac in front of us was the plane that had brought us, a 1950s vintage Lockheed Electra 188 turboprop operated by Reeve Aleutian Airways. The Electra looked old-fashioned but seasoned, as well it might since it is a close relative of the planes used by the Weather Service to fly into hurricanes. The trusty Electra had carried us 1,492 miles west of Anchorage, past the 180th meridian, to the outermost of the Aleutian Islands: to Attu, the Holy Grail of North American birding.

The location of Attu is not well depicted on most maps. Attu is so far west, so distant from the Alaskan mainland, that it is usually shown in an inset on maps of that state, or perhaps as a speck off the coast of Asia on maps of eastern Siberia. Either way, the key geographical feature of Attu is lost in the presentation. The crucial fact, at least to birders, is that although the island is part of Alaska, it is much closer to Asia than it is to North America. A surprisingly informative view of the Aleutian geography, of Attu's place in the world, is shown in the route map printed on the paper place mats used by Reeve during in-flight food service:

Paper place mats used by Reeve during in-flight food service

In bucket-brigade fashion we off-loaded our luggage and a few boxes of supplies from the cargo bay, and stowed them under a tarp at the side of the runway. It was noon ABT (Attu Birding Time). We turned to watch the Electra taxi for takeoff. With a vague sense of foreboding, I realized the plane would not soon return. Like it or not, we were going to spend the next two weeks on this desolate island, uninhabited except for us birders and a handful of U.S. Coast Guard personnel operating a Loran navigation station. As we stood shivering by the runway, the leaders explained that they needed some time to get our quarters set up. In the meantime, we were all going birding! For the next five hours, in what became whimsically known as "The Death March", we trudged around in the general vicinity of the runway and along the shores of Massacre Bay. The weather was so foul that birding was essentially impossible. Eyeglasses, binoculars, and spotting scopes were either fogged up, water-splattered, or both. Finally, we returned to the tarp by the runway to pick up our stuff and lug it the two miles to "Lower Base". As I bent into the howling wind and dermabrasive sleet, the thought came again, *"Why am I here? Why do we do this?"*

Things in Anchorage had not gone smoothly. Plans for an advance party to fly to Attu to lay in provisions and prepare for the arrival of the main body had evaporated when Reeve encountered a series of equipment problems, most importantly a cracked windshield that had to be replaced with a part flown in from Sweden. As a result, the advance party and main body would have to fly together and our individual luggage weight limit, originally set at 45 pounds, would be reduced to 12 pounds. A C-130 cargo plane, arranged at the eleventh hour, would fly in the balance of our luggage, as well as food and other supplies. The C-130 would follow a few hours behind the Electra after loading was completed. Given the vagaries of weather and antiquated equipment, this sort of last-minute improvisation was apparently "normal" for trips to Attu.

While we had been on the Death March, the weather had deteriorated, and the C-130, trailing our flight by some three hours, was unable to land. We fretted about the balance of our luggage; the organizers fretted about other things like food and toilet paper. Backup provisions had been stored in the upper building ("Upper Base", as it was called) at the end of the previous season, but over the winter the building had been broken into by persons unknown. Only a few things had been stolen, most notably some large cans of WD-40, but the door had been left ajar and rats had gained access to the stored food. When the leaders entered the building, there were rats everywhere. One room that previously had been used as sleeping quarters for the leaders and other staff was so badly infested that it had to be sealed off for the duration of our stay. Most of the packaged goods had been completely devoured by the rats, but apparently some canned goods had survived.

A recent convert to serious birding, I had been unaware of Attu except as a distant battle site in World War II. Then, in September of 1998, while bouncing around in a fishing boat on a pelagic birding trip off the coast of Monterey, California, I listened intently as one of the guides described his trip to Attu that spring. He spoke with awe and excitement about the unbelievable birds he had seen, about the fact that he had gotten lots of lifers, even though he already had a list of more than 700 species before going on the trip. When I got home, I called Larry Balch, the director of Attour, Inc., the outfit that had organized birding trips to Attu since the late 1970s. He told me that the three trips offered in

2000 would be the last. The Coast Guard station was scheduled to close in the next few years, and when the station closed, there would be no one to maintain the airstrip, the only viable access to the island. I sent in deposits for my wife, Ellen, and me for the May 2000 trip, the first of the final year.

Over the ensuing months, as we received a steady stream of information from Attour, Ellen began to waver. There were descriptions of the Attuvian weather and the primitive living conditions; lists of recommended clothing, of footwear appropriate for walking the soggy tundra, and of sources for water-tight gloves; admonitions about the remoteness from medical facilities and warnings that fickle weather could delay arrival or postpone departure; exhortations to show up in good shape as all travel on the island would be by foot or mountain bike on rough terrain, and that we would need to move quickly when a good bird was discovered. Ellen is a lover of nature who delights in looking at birds, but she is not obsessed like me. Ultimately, she demurred, reasoning that if she didn't like Attu she couldn't just take the next plane home—there is no scheduled commercial air service to the island. When you're there, you're there until the plane comes to get you two weeks hence, if then.

Now, some 18 months after I had signed up, here I was (minus my favorite birding companion) in the wind and sleet with a bunch of people I'd never met, all of whom I presumed to be deranged because, like me, they had chosen to come to Attu. There were 86 of us in all, 63 men and 23 women—74 paying customers and 12 leaders/staff. We had shelled out nearly $5,000 each, not including travel to and from Anchorage, to fly to Attu and spend two weeks living in marginal circumstances searching for rare birds on this cold, remote island.

Why is Attu so special, such a storied place in the lore of North American birding? Less than 250 miles from the Commander Islands (Russia) and almost 1,500 miles from Anchorage, Attu is still part of the state of Alaska, and therefore part of North America. This means that Attu is also part of the so-called ABA Area, a territory defined by the American Birding Association as North America north of Mexico, excluding the Caribbean, Hawaii, and Greenland. This matters to birders because they keep lists of birds seen in specific geographical regions. For many, the list of birds they have seen in the ABA Area is the most important, the primary yardstick of their skill and achievement. Because Attu is close to the Orient, Asian birds are more likely to show up there than on the North American mainland. And if these Asian birds are seen on Attu, they count as ABA birds. Attu is special because it delivers Asian birds within the ABA Area—lifers, birds to add to one's life list, birds to build one's ABA total.

As we approached the aging building at the south end of Casco Cove, it was hard to believe that this decrepit structure could possibly house 86 people for the coming two weeks. Our "hotel", erected just after World War II, had been abandoned in the 1960s and left unmaintained since. Exhausted, soaked, and curious, we went inside. Despite ongoing mopping and the use of "salamanders", kerosene-powered fans that blew hot air onto the surface, the concrete floors were soaked throughout the building. In most places, the cement walls were crumbling. As I walked down the dank hallway and peered into the rooms, I noticed some writing on the few places where the walls were smooth—summaries of previous trips with names and life totals for the ABA Area. Some of the totals were *over 800*, and nearly all of the rest were in the 600s and 700s. A few months before departing for Attu, I had taken considerable pride in

Lower Base, May 2000

reaching the 500-bird milestone for the ABA Area. I stared at the big numbers on the wall and thought *I'd better keep my mouth shut.*

I was assigned to Room 9, a 12-by-18-foot space that I would share with nine other men. A cardboard sign on the wall, left by the previous year's occupants, read "Home Swamp Home". The room was furnished with five bunk beds. Since all ten of us were essentially middle-aged men, protestations of the need for a lower bunk because of "prostate problems" fell on deaf ears. Storage was another problem. Nothing could be left on the floor—it was a quarter inch deep in water—and the concrete walls wouldn't accept nails from which to hang things. Over the years, ingenious but rickety rope and wire contraptions had been rigged for drying wet clothes, which dripped onto the wet floor in the room; out in the hallway there were hooks for heavy stuff like parkas, which dripped onto the wet floor in the hallway. Eventually, we got ourselves settled.

That night we were served canned chili with stale crackers. Coming, as it did, after the Death March and our uneasy introduction to Base, it was one of the best meals I've ever had. Larry Balch told us that he was hopeful the C-130 would be able to get in the next morning, but the situation was day-to-day. Meanwhile, running water was in place, piped in through rubber hoses from a stream a quarter mile up the mountain behind Base. As gas generators and diesel heaters kicked in, there would even be hot water. Old-timers, veterans of previous trips to Attu, assured us we were in great shape with far more amenities than they'd had in the early years.

After lights out at 11 p.m., which coincided approximately with the setting of the sun almost due north of us, I lay in my bunk trying to determine how many of my roommates were snoring. With sound waves bouncing off the concrete walls, I could be sure of only one thing; there were multiple sources of the sonorous reverberations. Two? Three? Six? Hard to tell. Then I began to perceive that there was a soloist in this nocturnal orchestra, a virtuoso who not only snored with great profundity, but who also spoke in his sleep and evidently suffered from sleep apnea as well. His cadenzas would begin quietly, with

68

SPRING 1996   ABA   AK
SANDY KOMITO .... 800+ 281
GIL EWING 756 240
CHARLES DIETSCH .700+ 200
J. B. HAYES 631 180

SPRIN   ABA AK
                   237
SANDY KOMITO 785 216
BILL EVANS   690 190
MIKE ORD   550
BILL MUELLER 756 266

SPRING 1993
              ABA AK
                  134
GEORGE ALAPAS 631 79
ROBIN SCHWARTZ 562 79
MARGIE+Bob SOKOL 676 100+

FALL 1993   ABA AK.
             819 301
BENTON BASHAM 799 277
SANDY KOMITO 780 262
PAUL SYKES JR. 738 253
DAN CANTEBURY

SPRING 1992
                  ABA AK
BENTON BASHAM   809 296
SANDY KOMITO   790 261
JERRY McCONVILLE 711 150
Gil EWING   698 106

SPRING
1994
James Huntington 780+ 215   FALL 97

Life totals on a wall at Lower Base, May 2000

an even measure, an almost soothing quality. But gradually, the volume and the tempo would increase, rising into a great crescendo at the peak of which he would cry out, "Oh my God!" His breathing would then abruptly cease, leaving only the accompaniment of the rest of the orchestra. The first few times I heard this, I was ready to spring from my bunk to check his pulse, but in a minute or two he would take a sudden deep and sighing breath and the solo sequence would start anew. As I lay awake pondering the social implications of initiating cardiopulmonary resuscitation on a man who had simply paused in the course of his nightly routine, the thought came again, *"Why am I here? Why do we do this?"*

When you start out, birding is simple. The fundamentals of birding are straightforward. I tell beginners to think about *music*, *motion*, and *anomaly*. Music, because we often hear birds before we see them. Motion, because our eyes are more likely to notice something that is moving than something that is not. Anomaly, because a motionless bird may stand out in some other way; for example, there shouldn't be a lump in the middle of a telephone wire, so if you see a lump on a telephone wire, it's probably a bird. Each of these fundamentals has a deeper, richer meaning as well. Really good birders can hear a single "chip" note and tell you what bird produced it, or at least provide a short list of two or three possibilities. In fact, a "good ear" is probably the most prevalent attribute of top birders. Over time you learn that motion has to do with more than simple movement. It has to do with the *kind* of movement, the frequency and depth of wingbeats, flicking of the tail, bobbing of the head. British birders adopted a term used by RAF plane spotters during World War II—*jizz* (from G.I.S.— "general impression and shape")—to describe the overall gestalt of a bird, an impression that is often based on the way it moves. Top birders are able to make amazing identifications at great distances from jizz alone. Anomaly becomes a more and more powerful tool as knowledge increases: gulls don't perch in trees but kites do, so look carefully at a gull-sized white bird perched in a tree—it might be a White-tailed Kite.

In the morning after oatmeal and canned fruit, we walked in the general vicinity of Base. The scores of bicycles, most of which had been left on Attu over the winter, would not be ready for a day or two, another casualty of the aborted early arrival of the advance party. The slow pace of the walking on spongy and uneven tundra was useful for getting a clear picture of the background avifauna of the island, especially for an Attu rookie like me. The more clearly you imprint what is common, the more likely you are to perceive the unusual. Lapland Longspurs were everywhere. Rock Ptarmigans and Gray-crowned Rosy-Finches were easy to find along Casco Bluff, a couple hundred yards from Base. Common Eiders and Ancient Murrelets drifted by in the nearby cove, and Tufted Ducks were located on Pump House Pond, just over the ridge behind Base. All of these birds are difficult to find in the Lower 48 states (Ancient Murrelet and Tufted Duck were lifers for me), but here on Attu they were just part of the standard background. At around noon, we broke to have lunch—canned spaghetti.

Just as we settled in at the long tables, one of the leaders, who had stepped behind the building to relieve his bladder, burst into the dining room. "EURASIAN BULLFINCH BEHIND UPPER BASE!" Bowls of spaghetti were abandoned *en masse* as we all tried to cram through the door at the same time. Walter, the cook, stood by the door with a bemused look on his face, assessing the stampede with knowing eyes. In the confusion and flurry of questions that followed ("Did it land?" "Exactly where?" "Did it fly?" "Which direction?"), nobody was quite sure what had happened or where the bird had gone. Apparently, while the leader had stood quietly minding his business, the bright red songbird had dropped in on a gust of wind and landed in the scruffy grass, not 15 feet from the tip of his nose. As his heart pounded, he considered the options. Should he stay put and keep an eye on the bird, hoping that someone else would venture out behind the building? Or should he alert the rest of us immediately before the bird took off? Either decision was likely to be the subject of endless second-guessing. "How could you just stand there and not let us know?" vs. "How could you leave the scene and lose track of the bird?"

Sweeps of the hillside were organized in an effort to flush the bird. All afternoon we fanned out across the tundra, combing the area downwind from Upper Base. Nothing. The search extended into the next day. It was reasoned that the bird might have moved on to Kingfisher Creek, about a mile down the road along Casco Cove. A massive sweep with more than 80 birders spaced at 10- to 20-yard intervals inched up the valley defined by the creek. Everyone was there, with the top birders leading the way. This was a much-desired bird, a Code-5 bird in the parlance of the ABA (Code-1 = easy to find: Code 6 = extinct). Everyone needed the bullfinch, everyone wanted to be the hero who rediscovered the bird. Nothing. Late that day, as they pedaled home, a handful of lucky souls got a brief fly-over glimpse of the bird near the mouth of Kingfisher Creek. This sighting prompted a whole new round of excitement and sweeps. Nothing. The bullfinch was never seen again.

To understand why people go to Attu, why they subject themselves to the rigors of living in a crumbling, dank, abandoned Loran station, and of biking and hiking across uneven tundra and treacherous snow banks, it is necessary to understand the phenomenon of *listing*. Each year, as a supplement to its flagship publication, *Birding*, the ABA publishes a List Report. In this report, birders are given an opportunity to make public the number of birds they have seen in the ABA Area (or their state, or the world, and so forth). If you send in your name and your numbers, you are a "lister". Listing means more than just keeping lists, it means that you are willing, even eager, to have the size of your list known publicly. Some birders keep track of life lists but choose to keep that information private. Even though they do not choose to have their information published, many still scrutinize the Supplement, and derive satisfaction in discovering that they are "ahead" of birder X or birder Y, that their life list is longer. In the latest issue of the Supplement, only 23 birders have ABA totals of 800 or more. The actual number of birders with ABA totals above 800 is unknown. One veteran of Attu told me that for every birder with 800 "who wants to brag about it, there are probably five who don't." But even if the 23 who choose to go public represent a substantial underestimate of birders with 800 or more ABA birds, this is an elite group. A recent report compiled by the U.S. Fish and Wildlife Service indicates that more than 60,000,000 Americans are "watchers of birds". The majority of these people watch birds at backyard feeders, but more than a third of them (23,500,000) watch birds "away from home". Birders with 800 ABA birds occupy a lofty place on a very large pyramid. They have amazing drive and persistence. I asked one of them what he did when he got lifer No. 800. He looked me in the eye and said in an even tone, "I started looking for No. 801."

Birders like being outdoors, in touch with the biological world, informed about living things. But they tend to have a special affinity for avian life that transcends the rest of nature. One day, as we were riding our bikes along the shores of Massacre Bay, an orca appeared close to land. We stopped and gathered to check out the whale. A straggler, seeing a focused group, sped to catch up, screeched to a halt in our midst, and blurted out, "What've you got?" We pointed toward the water: "There's an orca close in." He paused to process this information. "Does it have feathers?" he asked. Such is the preoccupation of birders.

By day three, the situation had improved considerably: the bikes were operational, the wind had abated, the temperature was now in the high 30s, and the precipitation had ceased. There were even some brief periods of sunshine. Life on Attu began to take on a natural rhythm. You get up, throw on some clothes, walk the 200 yards to Upper Base, eat breakfast, make your lunch, return to Lower Base to add more layers of clothing, mill around in the "Courtyard" discussing the weather and what birds it might bring, check your bike, join up with one of the leaders, and head to the venue you are guessing might have something interesting that day.

Birding on Attu is carried out in a great arc centered on Massacre Bay: to the north is the Gilbert Ridge, a range of mountains hugging the northern shore of the bay, with Alexai Point at its eastern end; to the south is Casco Cove, where Base is located, and farther south is Murder Point, a promontory looking out over the open expanse of the Pacific Ocean. [Note: The place-name references to mayhem (Murder Point, Massacre Bay) date to the eighteenth and nineteenth century, when native Aleuts were indentured and maltreated by Russian fur traders, not to the bloody battle of World War II.] Along the western side of Massacre Bay is a series of spots known as the runway ponds, Puffin Island, Debris Beach, Navy Town, Henderson Marsh, and the Pyramid. Base is near the southern end of the arc, a 1.2-mile walk from Murder Point to the south and a 12-mile bike ride/walk from the tip of Alexai Point to the north and east.

Groups of 10 to 15 birders fan out around the bay, maintaining contact by radio. If a rarity is sighted at Alexai Point, you hope you aren't at Murder Point, 14 miles away. But even if you are, the wisdom of the old timers is, "Go now, because if you wait till tomorrow, it will probably be gone." At the end of one particularly peripatetic day, I called home on the intermittently functional satellite phone and told Ellen, "It's been one of those days. Go here, drag in, get the bird; call goes up, next place, hop on your bike, pedal your guts out, walk through the tundra, get to the next place—whoops!—there's a bird somewhere else, go there, get the bird." After a while, you begin to realize that it's a good idea to stay "central", that is, to position yourself in a location from which you can make a dash in any direction to get an important bird.

When I'm at home, I rarely eat breakfast, but on Attu, I ate breakfast every day. And when the C-130 delivered all its goodies, I ate a *big* breakfast every day—cold cereal, oatmeal, scrambled eggs, sausage, fruit, milk, coffee, more cereal. Immediately following breakfast, we would repair to a Quonset-shaped tent just outside Upper Base where we would make lunch to carry into the field. The first few days I was timid, thinking there might not be enough to go around. That changed quickly. By day three, I was filling my lunch bag with two sandwiches, three or four candy bars, two bags of pretzels, cheese, yogurt, cookies. Thus armed, I would basically eat all day in the field, return with appetite for Walter's hearty dinner offering, then continue to munch on whatever was left in my lunch bag until bedtime. Despite this profligate caloric consumption, I lost 12 pounds during my time on Attu.

The Japanese Army occupied Attu and Kiska in June of 1942. Although the strategic significance of this maneuver was debatable, the effect on American morale was tangible. In the wake of the disaster at Pearl Harbor, it was unthinkable for President Roosevelt to accept foreign occupation of American soil. The Japanese garrison on Attu, a force of some 2,650 men, was commanded by Col. Yasugo Yamasaki. Unable to cover the whole 20-by-40-mile island with this modest complement of troops, he ordered his men to build fortifications on the ridges above Massacre Bay in the south and Holtz Bay to the north. On 11 May 1943, American soldiers landed on the beaches of Massacre Bay. Another prong of the attack had come ashore north of Holtz Bay the night before. With air and sea superiority and some 16,000 men at their disposal, the U.S. generals believed they could capture the island in a matter of days. They were wrong. The soldiers who manned the invasion had been trained for fighting the desert campaign in Africa and many were dressed in short-sleeved fatigues. The battle that ensued, the second bloodiest in the Pacific Theater, lasted almost three weeks and cost 549 American lives and more than 3,200 wounded. In a secret report, U.S. commanders conceded that "frostbite casualties exceeded battle casualties two to one." The climax came on 29 May when the remaining Japanese, by this time hopelessly outnumbered, mounted a succession of suicide charges against the American positions on the ridges at the head of the Massacre Valley. When the battle was over, only 28 Japanese had survived.

Fifty-seven years later, reminders of the Battle of Attu are still strewn across the landscape. Overgrown foxholes dent the high ground, the shore at Barbara Point is clogged with rusting heaps of abandoned materiel, and twisted piles of Marsden matting—used in the war to make roads and runways across the spongy tundra—dot the level portions of the topography. We were cautioned to watch where we stepped, but it is hard to watch your feet when you are looking for birds. Inevitably, a preoccupied birder impaled his big toe with a rusty memento of World War II. Putting pursuit over pain—he was closing in on 700—he biked and hiked more than 25 miles before returning to Base to assess the damage. With eight of us in the group being doctors, it was predictable that there would be eight different opinions on the best way to manage the wound. The only unanimous conclusion was that the man needed a tetanus shot. A call was made to the Coast Guard station three miles away, a runner was dispatched, an ampoule of tetanus toxoid was delivered, and the shot was given. Patient and doctors were doing fine.

As the days passed, there was growing concern about the weather. It had become too nice. The wind abated, the rain stopped, and the sun came out. Ultimately, we had nine straight days without precipitation, an Attour record. At first this was a welcome change, a chance to dry out and warm up. But the respite from bad weather came at a high price—no new birds. The sentiment shifted from "We need a break" to "We need a storm." We would later be reminded of the aphorism, "Be careful what you wish for."

At 54, I figured I would be one of the oldest people on Attu. Given the pre-trip descriptions of the rigors of life on the island, I thought that most of the participants would be in their 20s or 30s. I could-

Checking out the Siberian Rubythroat (Gilbert Ridge), May 2000

n't have been more wrong. Most of us were in our 50s, 60s, or 70s, and I'm pretty sure we were graced by the presence of an octogenarian or two. On reflection, this makes sense, I suppose, given the duration of the trip. People who have retired would be more likely to have the requisite amount of time and perhaps the requisite amount of money. The age of the participants was incongruous, however, with the physical demands of birding on Attu, at odds with the hours of walking, the miles of biking, the climbing of snow banks, the fording of rivers. It was remarkable how fit everyone was, and how game. One woman in her 60s fractured two ribs when she fell from her bike onto a rocky escarpment on the way

Attu Birders

Attu birders
are like no other travelers
I have ever met

They wait for storms
and then they rush out
in changing weather
to see vagrants

hard-wired in the wrong direction
or blown off course
by the storm
or birds that just turned
east instead of west
lost forever

Attu birders
are unlike any other travelers
I have met
to them it's a vacation
if it rains.

—*Lyndia Terre*

to Alexai Point. She recuperated at Base for a single day, then gritted her teeth, climbed back on her bike, and set forth into the field once again.

In the interest of staying central, I was with a group walking the beaches of Casco Cove when the call came in from the Pyramid. Siberian Rubythroat! We piled onto our bikes for the four-mile dash, praying that the bird would stay put. When we arrived, a row of birders was stationed along the rutted track, scopes and binoculars trained on the willow shrubs at the base of the ridge. The bird, they said, was just behind a small rise and might pop up at any time. I focused my binoculars on the little clump of dwarf willows, staring at a tan leaf that seemed larger than the leaves typical of these small shrubs. Then suddenly, Wham! The "leaf" turned toward me with a dazzling flash of its fiery red throat. Over the course of the next hour, we worked our way to a small embankment above the dwarf willows where the bird was foraging. From this vantage point, we could get nearly continuous looks at the bird through spotting scopes from close range. As I looked down at this extraordinary creature, at this small bird with great impact, a birder behind me spoke in a hushed voice. "Jeeezuss!" he said, "What a bird!"

Birders usually don't say "I *saw* the bird," they say "I *got* the bird" or "I *have* the bird." And when they have gotten it, they *take* it ("tick" it on their life list). The choice of verbs is revealing, suggesting possession, ownership. "Getting," "having" and "taking" evoke emotions that hark back to our hunter-gath-

Photo: John Fitchen

Fording the Peaceful River, May 2000

Written in an Outhouse

Need, want, get, and tick—
That's the birders' nervous tic:
As steady as a tick-tock-tick,
Tenacious as a tiny tick!

—*Macklin Smith*

erer ancestry. But there is a level even deeper than "get" or "have" or "take". There is a point at which you *know* the bird, the bird is in your brain—you know its form, its behavior, its seasonal timing, its preferred habitat, its silhouette, its call, its song, its jizz—you can identify it at great distance in fading light because you *know that bird and you know where to find it*. The combination of certain identification and reliable location of an unusual bird is a highly valuable commodity in the world of birding.

All birds are not gotten equally. Sometimes the light is perfect, the bird is close, and lingers, and sings, and the angle of observation is such that key field marks are readily observed. And then there are times when everything is marginal: the light is poor, the angle is wrong, the bird is silent, and distant, and uncooperative in displaying the necessary parts to the observer. One may *see* a small form flit by, but to *get* it, to know what it is beyond a reasonable doubt, to *have* it, to *take* it, you must see (or hear) specific things—field signs that make the identification solid. Not all of the birds on one's life list are perfectly observed. Every serious birder knows there is "bomb-proof identification" at one end of the spectrum and "definitely didn't get it" at the other. In between are shades of gray, shades of uncertainty. Where, one might ask, is the threshold and how is it defined?

Certainty of identification is a topic one approaches gingerly, for it may touch a tender nerve; integrity, a birder's value—it may threaten the number, the *life total*. But at some point, all true birders must come to grips with the reality of the identification threshold. How many field marks are enough? How much do you have to see or hear to be certain? When do you *have* the bird? If you are too liberal

"Tick"er

There's a photograph
of a classic birder-ticker
who year after year
would come up to Attu
staying fully dressed
indoors
bundled with fleece-lined jacket
high waterproof boots
heavy gloves

he would sit by the radio
all day monitoring
until someone would announce
a bird he needed
for his life list
a bird he had not seen
and then he would move
biking at full speed
to the spot of bird

"tick"
he'd seen it

and pedal back
to his chair.

—Lyndia Terre

in your acceptance of life birds, you run the risk of losing the respect of your fellow birders, who may question your integrity, to your face, or worse, behind your back. But if you nitpick, if you insist on seeing every minor detail, and take only those birds that you have seen under ideal conditions, you will cheat yourself out of perfectly acceptable ticks. Where do you draw the line? When do you *have* the bird? I asked this question of a fellow Attuvian, a retired nephrologist from New Jersey, who told me the key is to get the *essence of the bird*. That essence could be a diagnostic field mark, a distinctive call, jizz.

He offered further that he always knew when he had a bird's essence because at that instant he got an adrenaline rush. I asked him how this had been validated: "What is the Gold Standard, the confirmation that your adrenaline rush is a valid indicator?" As a diagnostician, a physician-scientist, he stopped to ponder. "You have a point there," he said with a tilt of his head. The notion of the essence of the bird is right on. I'm still thinking about the adrenaline theory. It has some merit, and may be part of why we do what we do.

Another aspect of listing that birders tend not to talk about is *how* one gets a bird. What if you have paid a lot of money to go on a guided tour, the guide finds the bird, frames it in a spotting scope, and then you step up and take a very quick look because there are others behind you waiting for their chance? Have you got the bird? Would you know the bird if you encountered it again on your own? Maybe not. Does it still count? For some birders it does; for some it doesn't; for others it is, well, a shaky lifer, a dubious tick, a "BVD" (better view desired), a bird with a nagging mental footnote. In the end, the decision to take a bird is an individual choice predicated on a personal honor system with no official referees.

I was sitting at Murder Point, hunched against the wind, in a hole between two tundral hummocks, thinking, "This sea-watch is a waste of time. I don't have a scope with me, and even if I did, what the leaders are calling is near the gloomy margin of the optics—a zone where they are comfortable and confident because of years of local experience, but a zone beyond my personal sense of internally comfortable identification. I need to go somewhere else." The timing of the radio report was perfect—a Mongolian Plover had just been sighted at the tip of Alexai Point. "I'm as far away as I can be, but nothing's happening here, I'm in shape, the old-timers say to go now—don't wait, I need this bird, I'm gonna go for it!" So I fast-walk the two miles to Base, climb on my bike and pedal 6.5 miles to the beginning of the Gilbert Ridge, then on and off the bike to push it through the snow banks that lie across the track every couple hundred yards for four miles along the ridge, and finally two more miles on foot to arrive at Alexai Point. It has taken me over two hours to travel the 14 miles from Murder Point to Alexai Point. "Is it still here?" I ask the people at the stakeout, gasping for breath. "Haven't seen it for at least half an hour," they tell me, "but we're about to go out on the tidal rocks—that's where it flew." The kelp on the rocks is wet and slippery, the tide is coming in and we need to hurry before our exit route is submerged. And then, "Oh my God there it is!"

With chest heaving, I get great looks at this beautiful bird—a fragile, sweet, innocent being on the kelp and rocks in the middle of this huge expanse. The old-timers are right. Go for it now! This is a special bird, worth the 14 miles, worth the ruts, and snow, and slippery rocks, worth every bit of the effort.

A few months before I left for Attu, a good friend asked me why I was going, what it was about birding that drove me to go to such a place. He had made the effort to locate Attu in an atlas, and even to read about the role it played in World War II, so I took his question seriously. As my departure for Attu drew nearer, and as my sense of anticipation grew, I was surprised by the intensity of my excitement and by what it might reveal about birding and birders, and about me. Why, I wondered, do we do it? What are the motivations and the rewards, the drivers of our unusual behavior? Why are we willing to pay sub-

Mongolian Plover, June 1988

stantial amounts of money to live in marginal circumstances in order to spend day after day searching for birds? My wonderment was intensified by the reality of being on the island, by the actual events of the Attuvian experience.

The allure is hard to explain, I told my friend, but I'd try. It has to do with the confluence of nature, curiosity, discovery and satisfaction. Although interesting birds can and do show up anywhere, they tend to congregate in remote, wild places. My dad had an abiding love of nature. When I was a boy, we took long walks together in the fields and woods around Hamilton, New York (usually, at that time, in search of butterflies). Just before he died, I wrote him a poem recalling those times together. "*I wrapped my whole hand around a single finger of the tall man who walked beside me,*" the poem began. "*We walked the dirt roads together, wordless but at one,/ And in Quiet Corner listened to the silenc*e," it went on. The last stanza spoke of reverence for nature passing from one generation to the next:

> *Now the single finger's mine and the hand my son's,*
> *In easy step we walk the paths that show us Nature's ways.*
> *I see again through boyish eyes the simple and the wondrous,*
> *And pass to mine what came from you and ever is among us.*

Add to a basic love of nature the extraordinary diversity of avifauna, the subtleties of morphology, behavior and habitat, the fact that birds brighten our lives with song and color, the joy of an unequivo-cal sighting after an arduous trek, the realization that "chance favors the prepared mind", the shared experiences etched in memory because a certain special bird recalls the time and the place and the people—and you begin to understand what drives birders to go where we go and do what we do.

I asked my questions of some of the people I met on Attu. Not right away, not before I had a sense of the pecking order, of the personalities, of the relative amplitude of the drive. I had the sense that people were reluctant to talk about what birding meant to them. There was a careful dance, for example, about numbers, life numbers. We didn't ask and we didn't tell. But gradually (through one mechanism or another), the numbers became known. When I finally did ask *Why?* the reluctance to talk about numbers paled in comparison to the reluctance to talk about motivation. Too personal? Too self-revelatory? Never pondered or articulated? I found then, and continue to find, that why we bird is not an easy question to answer, and not a question that birders seem ready to discuss. Maybe they have never thought about it. (Is that possible, given the commitment of time, energy and money; the complexities of orchestrating and justifying frequent absences from family and career to pursue feathered creatures?) Or maybe there's a sense that talking about it will ruin it—that trying to define the genesis of our passion will trivialize the feelings that underlie it.

One of my favorite people on Attu was honest enough to admit that for her, birding is an obsession, maybe even an addiction. In an effort to explain her obsession, she invoked words and phrases like "freedom of flight", "gift of song", "adventure", "stillness", and (my favorite) "It keeps me looking upward." These "reasons" speak to the spiritual aspects of birding, but I'm not sure they account for the obsession. One senses there is more. There's something in our guts, something visceral, something so powerful that we speak in terms of obsession, even addiction; and more important than our words are our actions—we do things like going to Attu.

I haven't figured out the visceral part, but I have some ideas. It may have something to do with feeling cool, smart, sophisticated. We know that in many ways birding is viewed as a nerdy activity—we even go along with this, sort of, making jokes among ourselves about our bizarre behavior, our seemingly absurd preoccupation. But inside we feel cool, cool because beneath the nerdy exterior is a serious intellectual endeavor, a science, a passion attuned with nature. We feel smart, more enlightened than those who walk through the park oblivious to the glories that surround them. We feel sophisticated because we know what it takes; the fund of knowledge, the nimbleness of mind and focus necessary to sort and apply a huge amount of information to arrive at the identification of a bird whose essence may have been no more than a fleeting glimpse. Or better still, we have the moxie to identify a bird we've never seen before because we are well prepared. We've studied the books and paid attention in the field. We know the subtle hues and the rich texture of the standard canvas. We've contemplated the possible. And when a rarity occurs, it stands out. *We know what it is and call out its name!* Birders admire this moxie, perhaps above all else.

Another candidate for the visceral part is competition. Attu was my first real introduction to listing, and in the process of trying to understand that phenomenon, it dawned on me that some people (even I?) might be intensely competitive about this activity. Is it a competitive act, for example, to call out the name of a rare bird while other mere mortal birders stand around you, transfixed by your bril-

80

liance and bravado? If you're right, you must be a savvy birder. More than that, you must occupy a lofty place on the ABA pyramid. Imagine if you could preface the bird's name with "First North American sighting of a…" That would be the big time! Of course, if you're wrong, well, you don't measure up. Birders dream of finding something rare, something out of place, of making certain identification, and of bringing their discovery to the attention of other birders. There is other evidence of competition that I don't fully understand but I know I don't like, competition that seems to suspend human decorum. Competition that can forget common decency and make otherwise likable humans knock you to the ground in the stampede to get a new bird.

One of my heroes on Attu is a retired furniture designer who lives in New Jersey. He is an elegant man, an intense birder, and a sensitive human being. His proudest achievement as a birder is his New Jersey state list. State lists are revealing because they are more likely to have resulted from personal knowledge and experience than from guided tours. Extensive state lists reflect a profound awareness of a group of birds, of seasons and habitats, of what is regular and what is unusual. He had been to Attu before, and was returning with modest but hopeful expectations. To his chagrin, he got only two lifers on Attu, and while he was away from home, what would have been three exceptional state birds showed up in New Jersey. Birding takes persistence and equanimity. He has both. Another of my Attu heroes is a mail carrier from Iowa. He is inspiring because he is simultaneously a mail carrier, a world-class birder, and a philosopher. He asked me quietly one day as we were sweeping the runway ponds, "So, John, have you gone over to the Dark Side yet?" I have pondered that question ever since, and I don't yet know the answer.

The storm we had wished for came the day before we were scheduled to leave. In a matter of hours the weather turned from sunshine and warmth to cold, rain, and most relevant to air travel, 80-knot winds. Between the high winds and scheduling problems at Reeve, it was uncertain when the Electra would be able to make it back to Attu—one day late, two, three, five? Nobody knew. Worse, the weather was so bad that birding was nearly impossible. Each morning a few intrepid souls would venture forth into the gale, only to return an hour or two later soaked, shivering, and empty-handed. Most of us milled around the dayroom reading, making jigsaw puzzles, or playing chess, Scrabble or bridge. As the days crept by, these activities were less and less effective at filling the time. We were restless: anxious about families and jobs, worried about travel connections, running low on prescription medicines, eager to leave. Finally, after five days of waiting out the storm, word came one morning that we should be by the runway with our gear at noon, ready for the 1 p.m. arrival of the Electra. With the prospect of release, spirits improved, and when, at 11:30 a.m., a Gray-tailed Tattler was sighted east of the runway, spirits improved even more. We raced to get the bird before the runway lights went on; once they did, we would be prohibited from pedaling back across the tarmac to the appointed gathering place.

The ability of the plane to land would depend on the ceiling. The wisdom was that if we could see the top of the nearby Loran tower, the plane could land; if we couldn't, it couldn't. One o'clock came and went. No plane. The clouds thickened, but the top of the radio tower was still visible. Two o'clock. No plane; and the top of the radio tower was now only intermittently visible. Two-thirty. No plane. Then at

2:45 someone saw a speck on the eastern horizon. A battery of high-performance optics zoned in on that speck. It was moving. It had wings. The wings weren't flapping. It was a plane! A four-engine turboprop! The Electra!

People from the second group, stuck in Anchorage for the past five days, bounced off the airplane full of excitement and anticipation. Hurried accounts of what we had seen passed up and down the human conveyor as we off-loaded their luggage and on-loaded ours. As it turned out, their excitement was justified. The storm that had pinned us down brought in its wake a spate of fantastic birds including a first North American record, a Rufous-tailed Robin. In their first two days on the island, the second group saw more Asian vagrants and rarities than we had seen in our entire 19-day stay. Birding on Attu has much to do with the weather. The bad weather that kept the C-130 out brought good birds in. The fine weather that let us warm up and dry out meant no new birds for almost a week. And the horrendous weather that kept us on the island an extra five days was a bonanza for the group that followed.

Birding makes us feel good. It brings about the union of imagination and reality, of expectation and fruition. With study and anticipation, an image of a rare bird forms in our minds; we imagine what it will sound like, look like, move like. Over time, often over many years, we revisit that image, mold it, refine it; we are ready. And then one day, all of a sudden, there it is, unexpected despite all of the expectation: the bird *happens*—imagination and reality fuse, adrenaline flows, we are alive. Birding is deeply felt and personal. It connects human beings to nature, and to imagination. We are moved by a new bird at our feeder, an old friend reappearing at the local park with the coming of spring, a lifer on Attu. Birds keep us looking upward, learning, feeling, improving.

The day before we finally left the island, the weather eased enough for us to bike to the runway ponds for close looks at Aleutian Terns gathering to stake out breeding territories. As we walked the hummocks around the ponds, one of the leaders thought he heard a Wood Sandpiper, the Eurasian version of our Lesser Yellowlegs and a Code-4 bird. A gray form that flew like a shorebird whizzed over our heads and dropped in behind a small ridge. We sprinted to the ridge, then crept to the top. A fleeting look, then the bird was gone. "Damn," I thought to myself, "I saw it, but I didn't get it." Over the course of the next hour the bird was briefly sighted two more times. Then, suddenly, it landed less than 100 feet away. It was looking right at us, almost as if it knew why we were there. "Sure would be nice if we could see the back," I whispered to no one in particular. The bird turned 180 degrees revealing its "spangled" back, sprinkled with white and gold. "Wish it would give us a side view so we could see the subtle barring on the flanks and lateral aspect of the tail," said another birder. The sandpiper shifted a bit and turned sideways. "Doesn't it like to bob its tail?" someone asked. The bird bobbed its tail. "Aren't the wing linings key, paler than in the Green Sandpiper?" The bird shook itself and raised its wings. "It would be great to hear the call." A soft, rolling *tweadle, tweadle, tweadle* emanated from the bird. "Isn't the call louder and harsher when the bird is in display flight?" The bird soared into the air repeating its call, loud and sharp. As the Wood Sandpiper flew out of sight, there was a brief, stunned silence, then the crowd of bedazzled observers erupted into spontaneous applause—a standing ovation on the windswept tundra.

There is a special feeling about Attu, a feeling that you can let it all hang out, unfettered, unabashedly in pursuit of a collective grand passion, no need to explain or apologize. Birding on Attu is magical, in part because of the extraordinary birds and in part because of Attu itself. When I returned to civilization I told Ellen that life didn't seem complete without searching for rare birds in great sweeps across treeless Aleutian tundra peppered with hummocks, pitfalls, and the rusting relics of a distant war. Attu touches the soul.

Barrel dump along the Peaceful River

Leaders

every morning they line up
and get a group of birders
to follow them.

they share what they know
and where the best spots are

they can almost always guarantee
some sighting
even in the wettest weather
and the little troops of birders
follow right behind

each of them leads
with his own history
making old destinations
new

how often have they wanted to be solo
to flush out birds
and photograph and study
and observe

how often have they
craved
bird solitudes
waiting for their troops of new birders
to mature

—*Lyndia Terre*

Paul Sykes, James Huntington, Jerry Rosenband, Paul Baicich, Steve Heinl, and Dave Sonneborn

Birders on lunch break, including Jerry Maisel, Macklin Smith, Thede Tobish, and Noble Proctor

Roger Tory Peterson and I

We had a chat today about how illustration
Sometimes outmaneuvers the effects of sunlight.

Before I met Roger, I could not correctly identify
The second- and third-year gull plumages.

Did I tell you he is not much of a conversationalist?
When he does speak, people crick. Listen—

He imitates the calls of the eiders.
On this trip he hopes to learn more about pipits.

Though Chinet bowls are set out for the apricots,
He requests his on top of his oatmeal.

As if we weren't already fortunate to have had
This chance, Roger, as it happens, is

An avid lister. He says the only other
Feathered beings are angels, rare but regular.

What other field confers such fame from writing
One book? Roger's art with words

Endows with flight-song, habitat and range
The field marks he discovered first.

Secure in style and current accomplishment,
He still hears acutely as ever.

—Macklin Smith

The Murrelets

Brooke Stevens

Postcard from Attu: "Arrived. Infested with rats, vandalized, snowing. Having a wonderful time."

The Murrelets in front of "The Manor", May 2000. From left: Linda Ferraresso, Sandra Escala, Lynn Barber, Anna Scarborough, Betty Hardesty, Carol Ralph, Brooke Stevens, Lena Galitano

In April of 2000, three New Englanders—Carol Ralph, Linda Ferraresso, and I—were sorting through our accumulated stash of Gore-Tex, fleece, Japanese fisherman's gloves, "Xtra-Tuffs" and pacboots, waterproof optics, and the like in preparation for the last spring trip to Attu. We traveled to this "island at the end of time" in search of Asian vagrants that were countable on our North American life lists. Organized by Attour's Larry and Donna Balch, Trip A from 12 May (unintentionally extended) to 1 June 2000, was one of the last birding trips to this remote outpost in the Near Islands of the Aleutian chain, 1500 miles west of Anchorage.

Attu is part of the Aleutian Islands Unit of the Alaska Maritime National Wildlife Refuge. The island, which is located in the eastern hemisphere, its longitude about that of New Zealand, is the back door to two continents, and one can find Asian lilies and thistles pushing up through the rusted wartime Marsden matting and brown rye grass. Paralleling the period of our adventure, the island was the bleak site of the Battle of Attu in World War II. Today, the sole military presence is the U.S. Coast Guard, which tends the Loran Navigation Station. Because of the island's location, 200 miles from the Russian

Komandorskie Islands and 700 miles from Siberia's Kamchatka Peninsula, we were hoping for storms with strong west winds that would bring migrating Asian birds, blown off course, to the island.

The southeastern corner, where we hiked over tundra and rode bikes in pursuit of birds, is a national battlefield park. It provided the infrastructure for our tour: an airstrip, dirt roads, and concrete bunkers set amid the detritus of war in a landscape of astonishing beauty. We explored the same sites regularly, often seeing the same birds but sometimes finding one that was different, which was when the radios sizzled and we chased. On our daily excursions, groups led by Paul Baicich, Steve Heinl, Mike Toochin, James Huntington, or Paul Sykes set out by foot or by bicycle to various destinations: Murder Point and South Beach; Kingfisher Creek, Casco Beach, and Puffin Island; Coast Guard and Navy Town Beaches; Henderson Marsh (East and West Massacre Valley); or Gilbert Ridge and Alexai Point. Covering as many as twenty miles a day in all kinds of weather, carrying bikes over snow bridges and through rushing streams, tromping over tussocks and tundra, we became lean and fit and had no problem sleeping at night!

Local nesters were everywhere: the super-sized Aleutian races of Winter Wren belted out a harsh, raspy song from the top of the ridgeline, and dark Song Sparrows darted through the rye grass by the water's edge where they somehow survive the harshest of winters; Rock Sandpipers, so tame you could walk right up to them, trilled; Rock Ptarmigan exploded from under our feet with *grok*-like rattles; young Common Ravens fledged just as the Glaucous-winged Gulls and the western Arctic orange-billed Common Eiders were laying their eggs (an arrangement most favorable to the ravens). Add Tufted and Horned Puffins, Pelagic and Red-faced Cormorants, Mallards (imagine wild and wary puddle ducks flying against snowcapped mountains!), Harlequin Ducks, Lapland Longspurs skylarking everywhere from dawn to dusk, and Snow Buntings.

Of my companions, Carol was the instigator who saw a Brookline Bird Club presentation on Attu. It became her life's dream to go there. In 1998, a strong la Niña year, she did. Two years later, after a tour of mainland Alaska, I mustered the courage to join her before Attour's time ran out. Linda planned her own trip, and here's what I love about Linda: a group of us out on Alexai Point picked up a beautiful female Mongolian Plover in breeding plumage, and called it in. Linda was seven miles away by bike and by foot, and it would be another ten miles back to camp by the same difficult route. But when the call came over the radio while she was standing in Henderson Marsh, Paul Baicich said, "That's your bird!" and she was on her way. (Linda and her long-time birding friend, Mary Jo Murray, discovered a male Mongolian Plover on 24 July 1999 at the Charlestown, RI, Breachway, only the second occurrence of this bird in the Northeast.) On another occasion, after we had been chasing all day, Linda and I were hiking over steep tundra, trying to remember where she had left her bike; birds flushed ahead of us, and someone called "redpolls!" I was so tired I saw only fleeting shapes. "There were four of them," said Linda who turned, waved a cheery goodbye, and headed off to see a Common Sandpiper that had just been relocated. When an Olive-backed Pipit was found on South Beach, I rode like mad for six miles and hiked another two miles to find that Linda had been working the bird for several hours. She knew where it was as we arrived and what it would do when flushed. It was terribly skittish, but we got it for tour-member Mike Austin's 800th life bird. He raised both arms, then sat down abruptly on a log and smiled.

Chasing birds anywhere brings out both the best and the worst in people. It showcases the inner child in some and obsessive-compulsive tendencies in others, while the truly blessed are able to strike a Zen-like balance that is enviable. For me it is pure love-hate. What I admired on Attu was the professionalism of the leaders in handling our different chase styles and in keeping order in the field. Of course, there were instances with so many people (there were more than seventy of us in camp) when someone flushed a bird or got ahead of the group, but that was the exception, not the rule. There was also a downside to the toss of the dice each day we were on Attu. The birds that are blown off course are often exhausted and never reach their breeding grounds; some are collected for the record. Also, following early Russian rule of the area and the subsequent enslavement and slaughter of the Aleuts, the places where we find birds (Murder Point, Alexai Point, Krasni Point, Massacre Valley) have borne witness to much human suffering and death. While I don't dwell on these thoughts, they are an important layer of the Attu experience.

During the time we were on Attu, people at home were keeping track of our trip. An email correspondence between Joan Weinmayr and Michael Tarachow, who was part of the second spring group, revealed that our unbirdy weather resulted from the fact the main jet stream was parked far south of Attu, and that a split developing over China and Siberia was creating two different flows. The northern one streaming over Kamchatka and Attu fueled storms that brought a bird bonanza to Group B.

Below are excerpts from my daily record of our trip:

May 13 Carol, who is a blue-badge veteran of spring 1998 (41 life birds!), joins the volunteers going to set up camp, about a mile away. With sleet and snow blowing sideways, the rest of us white-badge first-timers head off on foot, lunches in our backpacks, to bird with Paul Baicich and Steve Heinl. The island is covered in snow. We are out for six hours.

Back at camp the buildings have been broken into and trashed. Rats have eaten stored food and destroyed mattresses on the leaders' bunks in the Fish and Wildlife building (upper base) where we take our meals. The room is walled off. Dinner is served in the former Loran station (lower base) where we sleep, shower, and hang out. We pick up our plates and eat our first Attu supper of chili, three-bean salad, and chocolate pudding while sitting on our bunk beds.

Our room is a semidetached concrete unit next to the workshop and away from the main building. It is spacious for the eight of us: Carol, Linda, and me—from Waltham, Watertown and Cambridge, MA, respectively; Anna Scarbrough and Elizabeth (Betty) Hardesty from Findlay, OH; Lena Galitano from Raleigh, NC; Lynn Barber from Forth Worth, TX; and Sandra Escala, from Bridgewater, NJ. Lena has tacked plastic sheeting to the inside top of the door to keep out the draft and fashioned a pull (there is no knob) of green nylon rope wrapped with duct tape. It is excellent. We decide to call our room Murrelet Manor, and refer to ourselves as the Murrelets. (It is a tradition at Attu to write your life list total on the wall at the end of the tour, and I notice that ours is the only group of women "listers" in the Manor.)

The author with "rat, the other white meat"

May 15 "Rat, the other white meat," says Joe Swertinski, our bike man. Our cook, Walter Chuck and staff are killing dozens of rats, sleeping with rats. Arctic Foxes were eliminated from the island last year, which is a boon for the ptarmigan, and the rats.

The laundry is set up, and the chore list is posted. I do breakfast prep, Carol is a pot scrubber, and Linda does laundry. Our walls in the Manor have been dried by Al "Attu Power & Light" Driscoll, using an industrial strength kerosene heater. Generators hum, bikes are new and easy to ride on the rough roads, food is hot and plentiful. After dinner, we have fabulous views of a Yellow-billed Loon just outside on Casco Cove.

Lena to Al: "This is just like home." Al to Lena: "Then I'll fix it."

May 16 A glorious day, clearing, calm, sun, the snow-covered mountains shining. Not what I expected on Attu! We admire five Pacific Golden-Plovers along the road and a flock of Pintail flying against the peaks. Harlequins are murmuring in the bay. We go on to Gilbert Ridge, 6.5 miles from camp, along Massacre Bay, which is calm, with a black gravel beach: Gray-crowned Rosy-Finches on the cliffs, Snow Buntings chasing and scolding, male Tufted Duck with tuft flying. As we are admiring the small Aleutian Canada Geese on the slopes, a male Rustic Bunting flies up the cliff face. Perfect views in clear light.

May 17 The bay is flat, and the pipes have frozen. Sandra has lost her toothbrush. Betty has a sore knee from falling off her bike several times. Anna is working on a crossword puzzle, and Carol is reading a romance novel.

May 18 While we are having lunch at Puffin Island, Steve Heinl reports a Smew at Alexai. Linda, Jane Kostenko, Tyler Bell, and I take off. After forty minutes of hard riding, Paul Baicich, who is coordinating arrivals, waves us on. He knows, via radio, who is coming and from where. He makes sure that we are all collected, far from the birds. Steve then forms a scope line, still far from the pond, where we get our first looks at two of these dressy little mergansers: a female and a first-year male. Steve then moves us quietly closer, calling a few at a time for scope looks. He repeats this maneuver until we have excellent views of the two birds. He and Paul have managed to get thirty birders across a field in full view of the birds without spooking them. Everyone gets good looks.

May 19 Sandra: "If I'm alive at the bunting, I'm going for the Smew."

Botanizing the Aleut middens with Paul Baicich: kakalia (leaves like plates), angelica, cow parsnip, Kamchatka thistle, Kamchatka lily, lupine, rye grass, blooming willow, false hellebore. The island is becoming greener each day.

May 20 While we are at Casco Bay, we hear that Mike Toochin's group on Gilbert Ridge has a Dusky Thrush, and he is calling for several field guides (Japan, Taiwan) to be brought from base because the bird may be the Japanese race, which has only been seen once before, on Adak in 1982. Carol and I leave for the ridge. Everyone is gathered around the foxholes and trenches. No bird. Agonizing. (This is the part of chasing that makes me crazy.) Over lunch, we discuss the bird's race. Mike takes those of us who haven't seen it to sweep along the road. No bird. Then we get a wave from the group up on the ridge, and back we trudge, up the snowfield, and get wonderful looks at the thrush feeding along the willows at the edge of a snowbank.

May 21 Birds at last. A strong west wind during the night chilled us in our concrete bunkroom and was measured at up to 80 knots at the Coast Guard Station. At Navy Town Beach an excited radio message comes in from Brad Carlson: "curlew, curlew, flying your way!" And indeed it was—a Far-eastern Curlew calling *curleeee, curleee*. Right past our heads, landing on the beach in front of a *Vega* Herring Gull. Brown bird on black sand, with an impossibly long decurved bill, foraging.

While we are sweeping Henderson Marsh, things start to pick up. We get calls: Yellow Wagtails are flying all around Brad in the Coast Guard area; Mike is looking at a Bar-tailed

Godwit at Casco; James is on a Common Greenshank in a pond near Murder Point; others have spotted a Common Sandpiper on South Beach where an Eyebrowed Thrush has just flown in off the ocean. I ride from Henderson at full throttle to base, by Pratincole Cove, and up the hill to see the greenshank, bypassing a breeding-plumaged godwit (hard to believe!). Walked over to South Beach to see the tired and spooked thrush, a male.

In the evening a Snowy Owl lands on the slope above upper base, harassed by Glaucous-winged Gulls, which are nesting on the mountain. Ravens are carrying gull eggs over camp (and carrying rats away from camp).

May 23 Northeast wind, 38 degrees. Dolly Varden (trout, a char) for breakfast. Bill Grossi has caught 26 pounds of fish at the mouth of the Peaceful River. Sweet and firm, the fish is wonderful with pancakes and bacon.

Six of us ride to Gilbert Ridge. We start out in sleet and snow, but it's dry by the time we reach the end of the runway. At the Pyramid we turn up a gorgeous male Siberian Rubythroat in the willows. He pops up and sings. Whimbrels are reported from Navy Town Beach, a Wandering Tattler at Casco. We go on to Alexai after Paul takes over the incoming crowd at the rubythroat. Out on the east tip of Alexai three plovers fly by, calling. Two are Pacific Golden-Plovers, but the other is a Mongolian Plover, which Mike picks out instantly by its call. A Common Greenshank flies over. The ride home is tiring. Carol falls in the mud. I am on breakfast prep after dinner: crack 120 eggs and make two gallons of orange juice.

May 24 Rode to Pratincole Cove after breakfast and was surprised to see two orcas fill my scope as they slid by. An adult and a calf. A long, slow day, but nice looks at the five *variegatus* Whimbrels, whose rumps are paler and browner than our *hudsonicus* race.

May 25 Six hours of walking, no new birds.

May 26 Weather from the west. Colder, windier, wetter. Dramatic red and pink sunrise mixed with gray and white tumbled low clouds. We ride to Gilbert Ridge in blowing rain. No new birds. I have long ago adjusted my expectations, taking out all the tabs I had put in my National Geo. My revised goal is now ten new birds, which seems reasonable for a second Alaskan trip. Species always seen but notably absent this time are Wood Sandpiper and Long-toed Stint. A Whooper Swan was found dead on the beach. Mike radios that he is seeing Laysan Albatrosses near shore, and I head back, riding in first gear most of the way against a formidable wind. I am almost blown to a standstill on the runway, where Aleutian Terns have been seen occasionally, flying around. They nest near the runway and land when the ceiling is low and weather wet. At Murder Point I have excellent looks at the albatross, plus Pomarine Jaegers in a large flock. Cold and wet, we ride back to camp for a hot shower and tea. After dinner, The Murrelets surprise the camp with a musical performance orchestrated by Linda, with lyrics to the tune of *Camp Granada*:

> Every day we go biking
> Otherwise its tundra hiking
> Every night we yearn to turn in
> After all day sloggin' birdin.'
>
> We have wagtails, we have pipits
> Should we chase or should we skip it?
>
> And the weather, it's been sunny
> Each bird's costing lots of money
> But they tell us "Stop complaining"
> And they say we'll have more birds when it starts raining!

May 27 Departure day. We had champagne last night and toasted Larry. Today the weather has closed in. Rain, fog, cold. Our bags are taken to the runway, and we are walking after them when we are called back. The ceiling is too low for Reeve to land. The plane returns to Anchorage with most of the second group aboard. To keep everyone's spirits up, there is an encore performance by the Murrelets:

> Our leader Larry, is faring well
> His well-laid plans are shot to hell
> He's been through this many times before
> But now we know why he says, "I'll do this no more!"

May 29 Memorial Day. Three people hike to the Japanese monument above east Massacre Valley. Clouds come down, and it starts raining from the east. We are working Casco Point and the runway ponds. Nothing turns up. But Aleutian Terns have been fishing in the bay, and one flies over with its catch, shivering its wings and calling. Several more terns materialize out of the fog. For more than an hour small groups of terns fly in and out of the fog, up and down the taxiways and over the bay. The terns start landing on the taxiway. There are at least thirty birds. They court—a little dance, raising both wings akimbo, bowing heads, and moving in little stiff steps clockwise. Then a pair copulates. On some you can see a hint of deep lavender gray on the breast.

Along a creek Steve points out a Wandering Tattler. I want a closer look. A small white eye line and all-dark bill are among the features that distinguish it from Gray-tailed Tattler. The ride home is very wet. The day room is full, including the new arrivals, who were on a small plane that was able to land (and left with two of our lightest murrelets). One of the newcomers collects seaweeds—there are 300 species here (and indeed, I have never seen such colors and variety); this is his third trip, and he brings his own plant press. Activities include rousing games of Scrabble, quieter chess, and intricate jigsaw puzzles.

May 30 Had lunch with Carol and Linda at Puffin Island when two shorebirds dropped out of the fog, calling. Wood Sandpiper and Long-toed Stint! We rushed over to where they landed. Had good looks at the sandpiper, but the stint (a life bird) flew almost immediately high and out of sight. A frustrating miss.

May 31 Storm from the southwest. Winds too strong for bike riding. Walk to Murder Point. We are blowing all over the place, hanging on to each other's scope legs. The seas are wild, but we see a sea otter holding her young on her stomach, eiders, murrelets, murres, cormorants. A Fish and Wildlife Service boat is anchored in Casco Bay waiting to go out tomorrow to Buldir Island. Wind blows down the drying tent. Al puts heavier weights on the front door. Murrelets perform for the third time.

June 1 We are now delayed five days, but a plane is due. We're about to ride our bikes to Casco Bay with Steve when a group at Upper Base spots five Hawfinches. They fly between bicycles. One lands by a small willow, and we have marvelous close scope looks. Then a second Hawfinch flies in. They call. Lovely pewtery-blue bill: a female and a first-year male. On to the runway ponds. Steve's group is looking at something on the beach. Carol raises her arms straight up and parallel in the BBC "we are looking at the bird" salute. She has a life bird, her first for this trip: a Gray-tailed Tattler. We have superb views: light belly and fine breast streaking; overall dun-colored versus blue-gray of Wandering Tattler; white eyebrow line meets in front and flares behind; part of lower mandible appears yellow. We ride to the gathering spot as the runway lights go on. Two great new bonus birds.

Postscript. Back home at dinner one evening, Linda remarks, without rancor: "You know, I was on the second spring trip, but moved to the first when a place opened up. If I hadn't changed places I would have had ten more life birds." Meanwhile, Carol traveled a third time to Attu, joining the last fall tour and getting four new birds, including Baillon's Crake and a Fork-tailed Storm-Petrel that landed in the grass next to the hot tub (but that is another story).

REFERENCES

Baicich, P. J. Attu Reflections. *Birding* 2000a 32 (6): 488–489.

Baicich, P.J. An Attu Showcase. *Birding* 2000b 32 (6): 545–552.

Garfield. B. 1995. *The Thousand-Mile War: World War II in Alaska and the Aleutians*. Anchorage: University of Alaska Press Classic reprint series.

Ode to Camp Attu, Sung to the tune of *Camp Granada*, by Allan Sherman. Excerpts by permission of A.L.C.I.D. (Alliance of Lady Carolers for Intermittent Disasters).

Photo: Jerry Maisel

From left: Jerry Maisel, Ed Greaves, and Bart Whelton, June 1986

Everyday Life Among the Birders

Photo: John Fitchen

Joe Swertinski, "Mr. Bicycle", who kept everyone rolling. May 2000

Bob Berman (left) and Al Driscoll, "Attu Power & Light", with the Honda, May 2000

Photo: John Fitchen

Jean Cohen, "the voice of Attu", relays messages on the CB at Lower Base, May 2000

Photo: John Fitchen

Joe Swertinski, Paul Baicich, Walter Chuck (cook), and James Huntington serve a meal, May 2000.

Photo: John Fitchen

From left: Joyce North, Dona Coates, Claire Miller, Dixie Coleman, Cathy Caballero, and Jean Cohen, September 2000

Photo: Dixie Colema

Attour participants unloading the plane, September 2000

Photo: Lyndia Terre

Photo: John Fitchen

Room no. 9 at the "Attu Hilton",
May 2000

Eli Elder takes a drawing
lesson at Upper Base,
September 2000

Photo: Lyndia Terre

Photo: Lyndia Terre

Jerry Rosenband,
September 2000

John Fitchen burning the trash,
a daily chore, May 2000

Photo: Mike Ord

Photo: Lyndia Terre

Donna and Larry Balch,
September 2000

Steve Heinl, Mike Toochin, and
James Huntington conduct
evening bird count, May 2000

Photo: John Fitchen

Spoonbill Sandpiper, 30 May 1986

Red-necked Stint, September 1983

Finding the Spoonbill Sandpipers— A Dream Come True

Ed Greaves

Birding on Attu in late May of 1986 had already been good. On 30 May, we'd had a particularly fine day: we had seen a Siberian Rubythroat, and in my book that was outstanding. As dinner time approached, most of the people in our group were already at the main base. But because Red-necked Stints had been reported from Casco Beach earlier in the day, I decided to stop to photograph them on my way back.

On arriving at the beach, I found a small group of presumed stints and focused my camera on the birds. As I peered through the lens, I noticed that the stint I was looking at appeared to have a deformed bill tip. Suddenly the bird turned its head, presenting an incredible spoon-shaped bill to my surprised eyes. To be more accurate, I should describe the shape as spatulate.

Two more birds were present. One really was a Red-necked Stint; the other was a second Spoonbill. A surge of emotion tore through me like a bolt of lightning. This was a hugely important find, and the immediate task was to get everyone here to see these birds—provided they stayed in place. After finding a friend on the other side of Casco to guard the birds, I streaked to the main runway, where I encountered Jerry Rosenband. He quickly put out the word on his radio. Pandemonium ensued, as every birder on the island, panicky lest the birds leave before they could see them, came rushing toward Casco Beach from wherever they heard the news.

Fortunately, the birds stayed in place even into the next day, enabling the photographers in the group to burn up many rolls of film on that wonderful trio of two Spoonbills and one Red-necked Stint.

Finding the Spoonbills was undoubtedly the emotional peak of all my birding encounters during the past 44 years, and I suspect it was a high point for most of the other birders on Attu that year.

Photo: Ed Harper

Casco Cove from the Casco Road with Gilbert Ridge in the background, September 1983

An Eventual Extinction

Macklin Smith

> Below banked Questars, Balscopes, and the people queued
> Up (exultant, reverential, jocular, dulled, depending
> Both on personality and on time spent observing
> The bird), a Spoon-billed Sandpiper monodramatically
> Probes and swallows tiny aquatic organisms.

Eurynorhynchus pygmeus. Like a small calidrid but all ages including pullus have unique spatulate bill. Adult in alternate plumage closely resembles *Calidris ruficollis*. Neck and face suffused with chestnut and streaked brown. Cap and scapulars blackish with rich chestnut edges; mantle edges slightly paler. Coverts grey-brown, inners fringed white. Underparts white, breast with much brown spotting and faint reddish wash. White wingbar and sides to rump. Black bill and legs. Length 6 in., weight about 1 oz. During courtship flights on nesting grounds said to utter high-pitched cicadalike buzzing trill, *zee-e-e, zee-e-e, zee-e-e*. Nests along north shore of Chukotski Peninsula, NE Siberia; winters E Assam, Burma, SE China; extremely rare migrant; casual NW Alaska—two shot from a flock near Wainwright, Alaska, on 15 Aug 1914; suspected breeding in vicinity of Wainwright Inlet unsubstantiated.

> We make it nervous. It glances at us, pauses
> Longer than it usually does, and fears
> Enough to edge away from us, preferring
> The bayside rims of its smooth beach-stones
> Whenever we forget, for want of tact or awe,
> To keep ourselves subdued. Never before
> Has it seen a thing like us. The passing fear
> Conforms with nothing it can or should remember
> And it resumes its feeding, and we disappear.

According to a recent readership poll, the ABA's Most Wanted Bird is Spoon-billed Sandpiper, by a wide margin. (Excluded from the competition this year were Ivory-billed Woodpecker, Eskimo Curlew, and Bachman's Warbler, our three species believed either extinct or almost so.) Commenting on the surprising success of this seldom seen Siberian peep, the survey judges attributed the winning entry's popularity to its "unique combination of rarity and imaginative appeal" and to the membership's "increasingly cosmopolitan, or at least Alaskan, awareness". In point of fact, the Spoon-billed Sandpiper is next to impossible to locate on purpose anywhere in the world.

> The candid thoughts in this shot figure
> Battlefield despair, that religious instant
> When an anguished saint foretastes ecstacy;
>
> But it's Maisel, downed, Gortexed, bandoleered
> With thermos, lenses, CB, Questar, references,
> And—the photographer I think means to gloat—
>
> He's discomfited. Birds! Fatigue and zeal
> Irradiate in his adrenalin-eyes: the weight
> Of all of what he needs impedes his way.

This curious little shorebird has a remarkably restricted breeding range on the north shore of the Chuckchi Peninsula and probably on the Alaska coast between the Bering Strait and Point Barrow. It is reported to nest on dry spots near freshwater ponds in the low swampy tundra along the coast. Nest is a rounded hollow in tundra moss lined with willow leaves. The four eggs are greenish buff, blotched with small dark spots. After nesting, flocks feed in shallow freshwater lagoons as well as on sea beaches.

> But why the bill? Darwin
> Taught us to appreciate the definite fluidity
> Of soft parts. Finches' bills
> Thicken for husked nuts, curl for flowers,
> And a godwit or a curlew can outdig
> All other mudflat-specialists. Creatures
> Need advantages to live. All adaptations
> Must have a practical utility, or else,
> So that other forms may flourish, perish.

Another hypothesis, perhaps worth noting briefly, is that of a positive causal correlation between the species' bill and its range and population density. Against any such theory of convergent maladaption, however, it may be argued that the estimated population of c. 500, while low enough to indicate the possibility of an eventual extinction, appears stable notwithstanding interspecific feeding competition with *Calidris ruficolis*, discussed above. Alternatively, intraordinary convergent adaptation within ornithoforms may be posited: *Ajaia ajaja* (Roseate Spoonbill), a widespread and successful Nearctic threskiornithid, has also been observed to feed in shallow water by means of a continual, rhythmic sidelong motion of the bill. However, no behavioral or ecological studies exist yet in litt. such as, in conjunction with the known taxonomics of spatulism, would support this latter hypothesis. In conclusion, no convincing explanation to date accounts for this species' distinctive rostral adaptation, unique among the Scolopacidae.

"An Observation of Species-Adaptive Feeding Behavior
in *Eurynorhynchus pygmeus*."
On May 30, 1986,
Between 9:00 and 11:30 a.m., this observer recorded
An adult Spoon-billed Sandpiper consuming kelp flies
Along fresh kelp-line in the upper tidal zone
Of sandy beach at Casco Cove, Attu Island, Alaska.
A highly specialized adaptive feeding behavior,
Not characterized in the previous species accounts,
Was observed repeatedly at this time. Conditions
Were ideal for viewing, with visibility unlimited,
North winds light to calm, moderate temperatures
Warming from 55 to 65 degrees Fahrenheit. 71 flies
Were consumed, of which 29 (40.85%) were taken
On the run and 42 (59.15%) from a fixed position
By opportunistic snatching, rapid and spontaneous,
Yet seemingly casual, amidst the abundance of flies.
Observation through the author's 10x40 Leitz Trinovid
Binoculars revealed that all of the kelp flies
Were captured cleanly in the bill's anterior tip,
And that on 6 such occasions this spatulate portion
Was determined to exhibit, functionally independent
From the basal portion, a semi-elastic motility.

Author's Note

Until the moment Ed Greaves saw the Spoonbill Sandpipers through his camera lens, he imagined he was viewing Red-necked Stints. Many other shifts of perspective took place during this island-buster event. My piece juxtaposes different ways of reacting to, looking at, and writing about this bird. I follow Boethius, Dante, and the Japanese haibun tradition in alternating verse and prose, and I mingle diverse styles in order both to memorialize and to play with our lucky interaction with this species. My documentation of its peculiar feeding behavior is perhaps original.

Siddens Valley, 27 May 1997

Navy Town jail, 21 May 1993

Photo: Steve Heinl

Photo: Steve Heinl

Siberian Blue Robin

Macklin Smith

To find it takes no skill at all. I* walk my usual canyon, and at the third bend there it is. It could be I have a karmic sensibility to the lower orders of life; I find rare birds, or they find me. But this time I have no idea what it is, only that it's never been seen this side of Kamchatka.

From here on out it's walkie-talkie time. My eyes are lasers but my left hand is shaking so hard I have a major problem raising the antenna: "I have an unidentified passerine. It is feeding quietly fifteen feet from me. I do not have the Japanese guide, I will transmit what I'm seeing." Five seconds of silence, like a prayer or agony, then at Lower Base Benton Basham, concertizing Dolly Parton, is awakened to large offings. People struggle into boots, run for binoculars. Mass evacuation. Thede and Noble overhear it on the Alexai Road, about-face their bicycles with an "Oh Jesus", and ride on speculation for the next hour and a half, twelve miles.

I nestle myself in prone behind a knife-edge, watching it forage. The wind turns south. A mild drizzle begins. The bird is exhausted from the storm and seems to be having difficulty finding food. It is warbler-sized. Yellow eye ring. Pink legs. Overall olive-gray, with a buffy wash on the breast. It has a weird, incessantly vibrating tail, gray or blue-gray. No wing bars. A female thrush.

When Thede arrives, he identifies it with ease and expertise: a female, possibly a first-year male Siberian Blue Robin. My one and only find of a First North American Record. For the rest of the day, birders gather, exhausted but fervent. They ask, "Where is it? Is it still here?" After seeing it well enough to count, they describe it to each other and compare it with the picture in the Japanese bird book. Some try to photograph it awhile. Gradually a ho-hum feeling displaces the mood of exaltation, but compassion for the older, slower comers maintains in some an alert communal responsibility.

By late afternoon, the bird has settled high into the canyon past the far midden, becoming extremely difficult to observe, skulking in the willows, no longer feeding. Even if it had the stamina to try, it could never make it to its breeding range—Japan, Mongolia, and southeast Siberia. The miracle is that it flew as far as 3000 miles off course to this spot on the island, and everyone who really tried for it has had an identifying look. "A long day for a lot of lucky people," Larry says, and soon the group heads off to Upper Base for dinner.

Pete stays with the bird, and in the interlude improves his marksmanship. That evening we put the specimen in the freezer in the same package with the pratincole. I keep this Remington 410 shell as a personal souvenir, and you can read about it further in *American Birds*. 🐦

*In point of fact, Terry Savaloja and I found the Siberian Blue Robin together.

The Fall Experience

View toward the waterfall along
Gilbert Ridge, September 2000

Photo: Lyndia Terre

Looking toward
Chichagof Point

Photo: Lyndia Terre

Fall Birding Journal, September 2000

Roger Taylor

Any birder casually looking at some of the Eurasian vagrants to North America in books like the *National Geographic Field Guide to the Birds of North America* (Fourth Edition) will have noticed that many of them were sighted on Attu among other places in Alaska. The farthest west of the Aleutian Islands, Attu is so far west that it is actually east, 173° east to be precise. The numerous sightings of vagrants stem from the fact that Attour, Inc. has been running birding tours to Attu nearly every spring since the late seventies, as well as a couple of fall tours.

Early in 2000 we received a card in the mail informing us that this would definitely be the last year that Attour would run birding tours to Attu. I had never been but had often been tempted, only to be deterred by the cost. My partner, Lyndia Terre, took one look at the card and announced that I would be going. A brief discussion ensued as I pointed out the cost figures, but she prevailed. I signed up for the September 2–6 tour. As information flowed in by email and snail mail, Lyndia got more and more interested and finally, in July, decided to fill one of the last remaining vacancies on the tour. Thus began a truly interesting odyssey for me, the birder, and Lyndia, the artist and poet.

Our first task was to get equipped with the right clothing, windproof and waterproof from head to toe. Probably our best purchase was a pair each of lightweight and totally waterproof NEOS overshoes. We wore them every day as we sloshed through wet vegetation, over trails through muskeg, and through lots of just plain mud on deteriorating roads. It rains a lot there, and water was everywhere. We never did find satisfactory waterproof gloves. They would have been nice on several days, but we managed. September weather on Attu can range from comparatively warm sunshine with temperatures in the 15–20° C range, to winds with cold driving rain and temperatures in the 5–0° C range. The Aleutians form the barrier between the warm Pacific waters and the cold Bering Sea. In our two weeks there we saw all the extremes that that combination can generate.

We flew to Anchorage via Vancouver and Seattle. After a day of sightseeing and birding around Anchorage (very impressive scenery), we assembled the next morning at our hotel to be bused over to the airport at 6:10 a.m. We took off from Anchorage at 7:30 a.m. in our chartered Lockheed Electra, flown by Reeve Aleutian Airways, with about 60 people on board. Most of the tour staff and a few early participants had arrived on Attu about four days earlier. After a four-hour flight we landed in Adak to refuel and all hustled off the plane to find Lapland Longspur, Gray-crowned Rosy-Finch, Bald Eagle, and Glaucous-winged Gull. Our first attempt to land on Attu was thwarted by fog, necessitating a return to Adak, one-and-a-half hours away.

On the second try, we just managed to make it to Attu at about 3 p.m. local time (two hours later than Anchorage). At the 6,000-foot landing strip near the Coast Guard station containing the island's only inhabitants, we were assembled into a baggage brigade to unload the airplane. Bags were piled onto an open wooden trailer pulled by an all-terrain vehicle (ATV), the only motorized transport available. Dressed in our rain gear, in case it rained, we set off on the mile-and-a-half walk to our base camp, established in buildings abandoned by the Coast Guard many years before. We heard a roar of plane engines and watched our Lockheed Electra take off and disappear into the clouds. As it rose into the air, the reality sank in. We were here on this remote island for the next two weeks and there was no way off.

En route, I picked up my first lifers, Gray-tailed Tattler, Dusky Warbler, Tufted Puffin, and Red-faced Cormorant, as well as several Rock Sandpipers. Dusky Warbler! Yep, a real rarity for North America. This sighting was our first exposure to birding Attu-style. As we hiked along the muddy road, dating back to World War II, one of our leaders, Mike Toochin, identified a *chip* from the chest-high vegetation beside the road as Dusky Warbler. Wow! A quick radio call to base camp got the early participants in very quick order on their bikes. Then we assembled a line of people stretching between road and shoreline to walk through the vegetation until they put up the bird. A chunky, dark, warbler-like bird with a rounded tail shot up from the grass and dived back out of sight. Major distractions were the numerous Lapland Longspurs and Song Sparrows of the *maxima* race, huge chunky sparrows radically different from what we are used to seeing in Ontario. The sweep was repeated three more times before the bird finally made its escape across the road up the nearby mountainside.

Birding, Attu-style: Sweeping for Dusky Warbler, September 2000.

In the Attu common room, the mossy plant-life grew right out of the windowsill (September 2000)

As we approached the base camp, we could appreciate the warnings we'd had that its external appearance was distinctly unappealing. The interior was worse. Lyndia and I were better off than most. We shared a narrow decrepit room with another couple, really nice people from Florida. A shower curtain down the middle provided for very nominal privacy. We had a choice between bunk beds with grungy mattresses and bunk beds with really grungy mattresses for our sleeping bags. We tossed a coin and got grungy. The floor was perpetually damp, and with rain and a north wind the water ran across the floor. During the hours the power was on we kept a heater going to try to keep the damp at bay. Many other participants were eight to a room and had worse water problems than we did.

There was a communal day room where we assembled to go over each day's list and to read or play cards in bad weather. I played a lot of bridge on two rainy days. In that day room, a large sheet of plastic was attached to the ceiling to catch the leaks and pour them into a drain. On one windowsill a large patch of moss was growing. Stalactites were growing from the ceiling. There were a couple of showers, three wash basins and a washer and dryer in the building, but the toilets were smelly outhouses, the odor of which increased during our stay. We wonder how the following, and last, tour group made out.

Our meals, pretty darn good food, were served in two shifts in another building a five-minute walk away.

The spectacular scenery of Attu helped compensate for the shortcomings of the accommodation. Mountains rising almost directly from the sea provided a magnificent backdrop for our excursions close to the shore. Even in September some of the mountains had patches of snow on them.

There were no trees native to the island, but lush vegetation covered most of the landscape, providing some rich green coloration to the mountainsides. The island's dimensions of 40 miles long and 20 miles wide meant that we birded only a small segment.

Attu dining room with (from left) Larry and Donna Balch, Roger Taylor, Eli Elder, Al Driscoll, and Ken and Jane Gordon

We were all assigned fairly decent multi-speed mountain bikes that were essential to get to some of the really good birding sites. Each morning after breakfast we assembled to hear what day trips were planned and to decide on which we wished to go. Each leader was equipped with a radio and was required to check in with the base camp every half hour to report on progress, which enabled people to abandon one excursion and madly pedal their bikes to catch up with a rarity sighted elsewhere.

Day 2: On our first full day on Attu, a lot of us headed down to a nearby point to look for a Yellow-billed Loon. I didn't see it but instead got a lifer, Horned Puffin. We finally got going on our day excursion with Jerry Rosenband at 10 a.m., walking out past Murder Point where we got Yellow Wagtail (NA lifer), both tattlers, Rock Sandpiper and interesting views of Common Eider, also a beautiful blue wild flag iris and cottongrass. Very tired on our return at 4:30 p.m.

Day 3: Went with James Huntington to Alexai Point. Left at 9:07, at a nice leisurely pace. First half of trip on gravel road, then trail deteriorated to a muddy path taking us through chest-high vegetation. Birded on the way and ten miles later, arrived at bike park at lunchtime. Walked two miles farther to the point, which is T-shaped. Circled to east, flushed from pond a Long-toed Stint (lifer). Got to beach and got Parakeet Auklet (lifer) and then Pacific Golden Plover flew by. Continued west along beach and got Wood Sandpiper. Finally picked up two Common Sandpipers, their long wing stripe, high-pitched call, yellow legs, and longish tail distinguishing them from Spotted Sandpiper. Left Alexai Point at 5 p.m. Took 85 minutes to pedal back against a strong headwind.

Day 4: Went with James again, this time to Barbara Point. Picked up Slaty-backed Gull (lifer) on Peaceful River bridge. Good view of prominent white trailing edge of wing. Proceeded past Coast Guard station to Barbara Point—incredible collection of rusted-out WW II debris.

Spotted Black-backed Wagtail (lifer) on island, barely visible when it showed in binoculars. Was able to see white wings once. Poor looks. On down the beach to "warehouse" Not much other than cormorants, Glaucous-winged Gull, Tufted Puffin, Common Murre, and Common Eider. Got good look at Red-faced Cormorant—large pale bill. Looked for wagtail again. No luck. Down to Brambling Point. Sat in a foxhole and picked up Kittlitz's Murrelet (lifer). Good view of pepper-and-salt plumage and white face. Going over to winter plumage. Then someone spotted a Short-tailed Shearwater (lifer), which settled in a group of feeding gulls and puffins. Difficult to make out all features at first. But it flew around for a while, settled, flew some more, settled and so on, repeatedly, until it was so close we could see every detail in binoculars. Watched it for about an hour. Biked back to camp against very heavy headwind—40 minutes, hard going most of the time.

Day 5: Biked over to the Coast Guard station with James in steady rain to buy souvenirs (an Attu backpack for Lyndia, a sweatshirt for me and T-shirts for our kids). Rain continued all day. Paul Lehman gave a great lecture in the afternoon on aberrant migration. Played a few hands of bridge.

Day 6: Rain all day. Did not go out except for meals. Played bridge, the Chicago system, from 9 to 5 with David Narins, Jeff Stephens, and Denny Hodsdon. Came out the winner by wide margin. Lyndia covered a few walls with fantasy birds, one wearing NEOS overshoes.

Day 7: Still raining, fairly light rain for breakfast. Heater barely keeping water at bay on floor of room. Better off than most. West to Barbara Point with Paul Lehman. Heavy rain at first, tapered off to drizzle, eventually stopped. Some beautiful effects with fog clouds shrouding the mountains, patches of sun, and a rainbow. Got a good look at Black-backed Wagtail in flight, snow-white wings. Got Eurasian Wigeon on the wing. The Slaty-backed Gull flew in to the mouth of Peaceful River and fed immature gull. Hybrid? Got back for a hot lunch. There were 12 Rock Sandpipers and a Gray-tailed Tattler at Kingfisher Creek. Walked out to Pete's Beach with Jerry—3.5 hour walk. Nice scenery.

Day 8: Beautiful sunshine. Large numbers decided to go up into the mountains to the Japanese Monument. Mike and Jim led. Hard work getting up there. Got Rock Ptarmigan in the dip before final push to monument. Then tragedy! John LaVia had a massive heart attack and died. Efforts by Bill Johnson and Ruth Brooks to revive him failed. Coast Guard came promptly but not in time. Meanwhile Lyndia, at the bottom of the mountain, wrote a poem forecasting death. Wrote it at just about the moment he died without knowing what was going on.

You will not be coming back

You will not be coming back this way again
for this is the graveyard of all your futures
every falling pebble is a life lost
a memory not collected
stop now
feel the cold wind
the hot sun on your back
the secrets in your ear

know the sounds of the raven

are warnings

for they will remember

and tell your stories

but you will be gone

stop now

take the solitude

for you will not be back this way again

the gates are closed.

—*Lyndia Terre*

A despondent group walked the final half hour to the monument. Scenery spectacular. Lyndia arrived, walking, just as I was starting to head back. We eventually went back to my bike. Al Driscoll was there with the ATV. He gave her a ride back down and picked up her bike. I rode my bike. Stopped at Henderson Bridge—very clear visibility but nothing of interest. Got shown a Ruff at Kingfisher Creek. Then word of a Garganey (lifer) came in. Back to base camp for NEOS and return to east end of runway to join assembled crowd. Eventually flushed by Paul. Great views for four minutes in air. Back to base for dinner.

[Note: John LaVia's two sons accompanied him to Attu. One was with him when he died. Garganey was one of his target birds. Both sons turned out to see it for him. The entire time the Garganey was in the air above us it was accompanied by two Mallards.]

Day 9: Woke up feeling groggy and headachy. Decided not to go out in drizzle and rain. Read for a while and slept from 11 to 2.

Bright and sunny afternoon. Ate some lunch and meandered out to the point to the southeast of camp with travel scope (a 22x Bausch and Lomb Elite scope with small tripod, very portable). Got three Ancient Murrelets (lifer), eiders, puffins, gulls, Red-breasted Mergansers, cormorants, and more with scope. Wandered back satisfied. Day room at 8:30 p.m., call came in re Great Spotted Woodpecker (lifer) on telephone pole on way to Murder Point. Room emptied instantly. Bikes pedaled madly down to site. "It was here until three minutes ago and then flew over the ridge." Groan!! But then it was spotted on a distant pole. Acceptable sighting. We moved up for a better look. Eventually a scope was in place. Got a quick good look. Then it flew from one pole to another and back. Red was clearly visible. Third NA record.

Day 10: Alexai Point—leader: Mike. Reasonable, not too leisurely, pace out there. Got to the bike park at 11 a.m. Lyndia followed behind. We flushed a stint. Long-toed? Mike thought so. A Sky Lark flew by—glimpsed it and heard call. Picked up the controversial plover where we had lunch. Very cooperative bird. To my naïve thinking it was a very obvious Ringed Plover (NA lifer)—bill was much larger than Semipalm, no eye-ring, no white gape, orange legs, broad breast band, seemed larger. Call when flushed very confusing. Roger Foxall recorded it. Very, very cooperative bird. Webbing between toes, not much between outer and middle and essentially none between inner and middle. Before that we had flushed a Whimbrel. On the west tip got a very, very cooperative Sharp-tailed Sandpiper (lifer) along with two Pectorals. Buffy breast, prominent pale supercilium, rusty crown and overall orange hue—juvenile. Lovely bird. On way back flushed Whimbrel. Same bird? White up the back, pretty obvious. Overall gray but bill had only slight curvature at tip. Stopped to look at murrelets with James at Brambling Bluff. Nasty headwind on way back. Arrived 6:15 p.m.

[Note: The Ringed Plover was seen the day before, but there was not 100 percent agreement that it was definitely Ringed, could conceivably have been a Semipalmated. However the detractors caved in that evening and agreed that it had to be a Ringed.]

Day 11: Slept well but still felt listless in the morning. Did not go out and finally napped for an hour or so. Ate lunch and finally went out with Linda and Paul (our roommates) to look at murrelets. Got a good look at Ancient Murrelet. Probable Parakeet Auklet out there. As I returned word came in re a cuckoo sighting at Smew Pond. Pedaled furiously over there, joined in the search but no luck. Tomorrow?

Day 12: The day of the cuckoo chase. Went out to Henderson Valley to scour for cuckoo and Northern Harrier. Lots of looking but no birds. Beautiful, beautiful scenery. Got back at about 3 p.m. Played some bridge, and then word came in that cuckoo was sighted at Navy Town. Back out again. Again, no luck. Lots of Rock Sandpipers and a Snow Bunting. Pedaled hard to catch first dinner. Second cuckoo sighting questionable.

Day 13: Cool and windy in the a.m. Set out with Jerry to do Casco Point. It started to spit rain. We got a Common Redpoll. Then it rained harder and harder. Finally packed it in at about noon and took my sodden self back. A few Rock Sandpipers were our only shorebirds. Read and played bridge in the p.m. Paul Lehman got a Whiskered Auklet at Murder Point. Too tired and clothes too wet to go. Also developing a head cold.

Day 14: Our last full day on Attu. Alexai Point called, and I decided to go despite my cold. James was leader. Had a great day. We rode out in a mixture of rain and no rain. Path muddy, but not too bad. Plodded over to the west tip of Alexai. Peder Svingen spotted the Spectacled Eider (lifer) in the scope. Then while we looked at it he picked out a strange plover standing next to a Pacific Golden-Plover.

Mongolian! Another lifer, North American this time. As soon as it was in the scope it flew out over the sea possibly to circle back to east tip but we found it no more. Two quick lifers to bring trip total to 22. On the way back to the bike park had very good looks at the Sky Lark, both white on the tail and trailing edges of the wing. As I biked past Gilbert Ridge I picked up three Winter Wrens. The usual headwinds on the return journey. Exhausted when I arrived, but very satisfactory day in the field.

There end my notes. Lyndia saw many of the same birds but did not chase the rarities fanatically. She stopped to look at the flowers, absorb the atmosphere, draw the scenery, and write many poems.

She sometimes went on the same excursions as I, but more often went elsewhere at her own pace. Her experience is captured in her poems and drawings. It is quite different from mine but no less fulfilling.

There was no birding on the last day. It rained heavily. We packed our gear in anticipation of the plane arriving and then just hung around waiting to hear if it was actually going to be able to land. Finally the word came that we were to hike the mile and a half to the runway in the wind and rain. We took shelter in some storage huts until the plane actually landed and then hiked over to it to help the incoming group unload. After that we had to stand for more than an hour in heavy rain while cargo was loaded onto the plane. An unfortunate feature of a Lockheed Electra is that the cargo hold is between the pilots' cabin and the passenger compartment. The crew insisted on filling the cargo hold before letting us onto the plane for fear that the plane would tilt backward from our weight. We were not happy as we stood in that driving, drenching cold rain.

We stopped to refuel in Cold Bay in the late afternoon. As we cruised in for landing, we were treated to magnificent views of two spectacular snow-covered volcanoes, one of which was belching forth vapor periodically. It was a reminder that the Aleutians, as part of the Pacific Rim, are sitting on a very dynamic area geologically. It is a strikingly beautiful region, but it will treat you harshly if you fail to be prepared.

We flew home from Anchorage early the next morning, returning to a very different world. Despite the cost, the rigors, and the undesirable accommodation, we agreed that it had been a great trip and we had no regrets about doing it. After I got home, I checked my weight. I weighed exactly the same, but I had lost at least four centimeters off my waistline. It is impressive what two weeks of hard biking and hiking can do.

Our memories are vivid and wonderful. Attu is a very special place.

Some Attu Birds

Photo: Jim Burns

Red-faced Cormorant, May 1989

Photo: Jim Burns

Yellow-billed Loon, May 1989

Photo: Ed Harper

Eyebrowed Thrush, May 1988

Photo: Jim Burns

Terek Sandpiper, May 1999

Photo: Jim Burns

Common Cuckoo, June 1999

Photo: Jim Burns

Ancient Murrelet, May 1999

Black-headed Gull, June 1999

Photo: Jim Burns

Long-toed Stint, May 1999

Photo: Jim Burns

Red-flanked Bluetail, June 1999

Photo: Jim Burns

Brambling, May 1999

Photo: Jim Burns

Sharp-tailed Sandpiper, September 1983

Photo: Jerry Maisel

Little Stint, September 1983

Photo: Jerry Maisel

Wood Sandpiper, June 1973

Rock Ptarmigan, June 1980

Olive-backed Pipit, May 1988

Gray-tailed Tattler, June 1980

Black-tailed Godwit, June 1988

Hawfinch, 1 June 1997

Photo: Jerry Maisel
Photo: Jerry Maisel
Photo: Ed Harper
Photo: Jerry Maisel
Photo: Ed Harper
Photo: Steve Heinl

Behind Lower Base, 8 May 1998

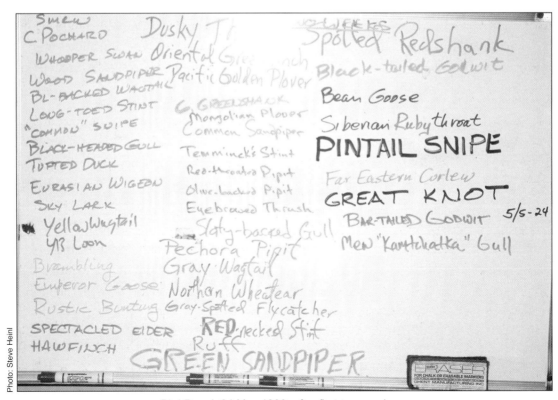

Bird Board, 24 May 1998, after first two weeks

1998: The Most Amazing Year

Steve Heinl

The main reason most birders went to Attu Island was to see Asian migrants. More to the point, most birders went to Attu Island to find shockingly rare Asian species to add to their life lists, perhaps even a bird never before recorded in North America. The 1997 spring trip to Attu Island was notable as one of the poorest years for finding Asian birds. We found only one shocker—a Eurasian Kestrel. A lucky group of 15 people saw the kestrel for five minutes after it was noticed sitting on a pole; then they watched it fly off, never to be seen again despite a full-day sweep of the area. (One of those giant sweeps that seemed less like birding, and more like a production from Monty Python's Flying Circus.) The 1997 trip was three long weeks of staggering around day after day after day, scouring, and pounding the island for birds. Days passed between interesting birds. Certainly, we enjoyed being in the Aleutians, and enjoyed the camaraderie, but wished we could see more rare Asian species to add to our life lists. The 1997 trip was fresh in our minds as a small group of us (16 people) flew out to Attu Island on 5 May 1998, to set up the facilities for another Attour trip. Never in our wildest birder-dreams could we have imagined what we were about to experience.

We dropped through the clouds over Shemya Island, and after flying low over Semichi Pass for a few minutes, we could see Attu Island. The island was completely covered with snow. As our plane made its approach into Massacre Bay we saw a swan flying toward Casco Cove. We landed, and as we unloaded the plane we saw another swan, clearly a Whooper Swan, fly past the runway toward Murder Point. This was an encouraging start.

There was more snow on the ground than anyone could remember seeing at the start of an Attour trip. Open ground was limited to the first 10 to 100 yards from the beach, and there was more than a foot of snow on the mile-long road to our base camp. The Coast Guard kindly plowed the road, and we began transporting all of our gear and food to camp. In the process, we saw a male Rustic Bunting along the road. The Rustic Bunting is a regular migrant to Attu Island, but this was the earliest record of the species in the Aleutians by five days. Our group had not encountered a single Rustic Bunting in 1997. Our advance-party worked like dogs mopping and squeegeeing water, dead rats, and "stuff" out of the two buildings that we used as a base camp. We dug the water lines out of four or five feet of snow, started up the generators, hooked up heating stoves, cleaned up the kitchen, and stored all the food. In the evening, exhausted, we had pizza and beer and ice cream.

James Huntington and I decided to walk over to the large pond called Big Lake. We hiked through the snow up the backside of a bluff at the edge of the lake, being careful to stay low so as not to flush any waterfowl that might be present. Peeking over the top of the bluff, we were astonished at what we saw. Among the Mallards, Common Goldeneyes, and Buffleheads, were an immature and three adult

Whooper Swans, three Common Pochards, four Smews, 35 Eurasian Wigeon, 15 Tufted Ducks, 10 Green-winged Teal (Eurasian *crecca*), and four Common Mergansers (Eurasian *merganser*). As we looked at this scene, we heard bugling calls from behind. We turned to see two adult Whooper Swans coast in low from the east and land right in front of us on the lake. For the next five minutes the swans called and displayed. We watched in awe. Normally we might see only a pair of Tufted Ducks and a few Mallards on Big Lake. This was like a winter scene from Hokkaido. Everyone from base came out to see the birds; some people even got out of bed to make the trip.

Terry Doyle sprucing the social room,
5 May 1998

We spent the next five days working—fixing the windows that had been blown out of the main building, attempting to cover the corner of the roof that had been ripped off the upper building, getting the bicycle fleet ready, brushing rust and mold and bits of building off the furniture and shelves and bunk frames in the rooms, mopping gallons of water out of the main building—really sprucing the place up nicely. We saw more Smews, Common Pochards, Common Snipe (*Gallinago gallinago*), Black-headed Gulls, Rustic Buntings, Yellow Wagtails, Sky Larks, Black-backed Wagtails, Bramblings, a Wood Sandpiper, and a Hawfinch. Some of these birds were very early too, and most were found in the course of work, as we had little time to actually look for birds. At the airport we saw clouds of Lapland Longspurs and Snow Buntings swirling around in the snow at the edges of the runway.

On 10 May, the first two-week group of 61 people arrived, and we showed them a slew of Asian birds. A Long-toed Stint was found, and we saw flocks of nine and three Whooper Swans fly in off the ocean and continue west over the island past Terrible Mountain and up the Peaceful River valley. That night, Joe Swertinski saw a pair of swans fly past the island in the light of the full moon. The next several days saw more of the same birds—in conditions of snow showers and mixed rain and snow. On 14 May, we woke to find that the night rain had frozen solid on the ground, and the airport runways were encrusted with a half-inch layer of ice. We saw our first great songbirds of the trip: a beautiful male Dusky Thrush and a female Oriental Greenfinch—both were the earliest records for the Aleutians. They were tired and easy to see. On 15 May, the wind howled out of the southwest all day at 25+ knots with higher gusts. We staggered around trying to "bird the lee", but we turned up nice birds throughout the day, including a Common Greenshank, and record counts of 158 Eurasian Wigeon, 250 Green-winged Teal, and 16 Smews. Everyday we bicycled past a Whooper Swan that sat on Savaloja Pond, a small body of water at Casco Cove. Everyone was having fun despite the poor weather and cold temperatures. In fact, as long as there were good birds—new birds—showing up daily, most people were more than happy to sleep in damp, clammy sleeping bags, and probably would have been happy to eat gruel every day, too, instead of the excellent meals that Attour provided. What's to worry about when you are adding rare Asian species to your life-list?

The wind was still out of the west on 16 May, and it rained and hailed off and on the entire day. We finally turned up a Slaty-backed Gull. Around mid-morning we discovered a Common Sandpiper, followed by an Eyebrowed Thrush, and an Olive-backed Pipit. Groups of people were dashing back and forth, trying to see these birds. A flock of Rustic Buntings landed right in front of a group of people eating lunch at Murder Point, followed shortly by a flock of Bramblings, and then a dozen Olive-backed Pipits. A single flock of 70 Wood Sandpipers was at Henderson Marsh. By mid-afternoon, we knew that a serious fallout of migrants was taking place, and the radio was crazy with people yelling bird findings almost non-stop. Paul Sykes had taken a group to the tip of Alexai Point, about 12 miles from camp. They had seen few birds on their way out to the point, but the reports coming in as they made their way back toward base were off the charts: 200 Wood Sandpipers, Mongolian Plovers, Common Greenshanks, Common Sandpipers, 20 Long-toed Stints, Hawfinches, Olive-backed and Red-throated Pipits, Eyebrowed Thrushes, Bramblings, Rustic Buntings, and Yellow Wagtails. Paul Sykes was shouting into his radio, "It's raining birds! It's raining birds!" And it really was. Small flocks of Wood Sandpipers, pipits, buntings, wagtails, and Bramblings were everywhere: overhead, on the roads, and on the beaches. The extensive snow cover concentrated these birds onto the limited open ground where they were easy to see, and the birds were tired and allowed close approach. Late in the day, we watched three Temminck's Stints that were hunkered-down on the beach at Casco Cove with a flock of Long-toed Stints.

The west winds and fallout continued through the night, and the next day, 17 May, was unbelievable. There were far more birds than had been present the evening before. Buntings and pipits were flying around the camp buildings, and there were seven Eyebrowed Thrushes hopping around behind the upper building. Buntings and pipits flushed from the sides of the roads and the airport runways as we biked out for the day. The air was filled with their call notes —throughout the day we heard constant call notes wherever we went. Wood Sandpipers and Long-toed Stints were on virtually every puddle; flocks of them flushed off the beaches. It was surreal. We floated around. Who would possibly believe this? There were so many birds that it made birding difficult—overwhelming, really. We were unable to cover much ground as we tried to sort through all of the birds, and tried to show new finds to everyone who wanted to see them.

Around mid-morning a Pechora Pipit was reported, then another, and I ended up at Gilbert Ridge trying to refind one of them. My group spent nearly the entire day working back and forth in just one quarter-mile section of trail on Gilbert Ridge known as the pyramid area. The open ground was crawling with birds; we estimated 30 Eyebrowed Thrushes, 30 Olive-backed Pipits, 30 Rustic Buntings, and 40 Bramblings in just this small area. We heard songs from all of these species—something that I had never experienced on Attu. We counted a dozen Eyebrowed Thrushes as they flushed out of a single pile of logs on the beach. We heard the two-note call of a Gray Wagtail, and looked up in time to see it fly in and land on the slope of the ridge above us. A flock of six Hawfinches landed on the ground right in front of us during a snow-squall. One of them hopped to within 15 feet of us before the flock took off, flashing white wing and tail patches as they bounded away. We happily rode our bikes back to camp that evening in a driving wet snowstorm. After chasing Pechora Pipits around all day, we found a Pechora Pipit in the grass between our two camp buildings after dinner, and everyone enjoyed close looks at the bird.

At the evening countdown at base, we tried to come up with a tally of the birds seen during the day. High counts included 17 Common Sandpipers, 35 Temminck's Stints, 58 Long-toed Stints, 50 Common Snipes, 180 Eyebrowed Thrushes, 29 Yellow Wagtails, 225 Olive-backed Pipits, 7 Pechora Pipits, 17 Red-throated Pipits, 193 Rustic Buntings, 366 Bramblings, and 18 Hawfinches. Some of these counts were several-fold higher than any previous counts in the Aleutians, yet most were underestimates. Accurate counts of buntings and pipits would have been impossible; they easily outnumbered Lapland Longspurs, normally the most constant and ubiquitous songbird on the island.

May 18 was more of the same. In the morning we added a Northern Wheatear, and a Gray-spotted Flycatcher to the trip list. Both of those birds provided the earliest Aleutian records, and there was only one prior spring record of the wheatear in the Aleutians. We also saw three Gray Wagtails together at Gilbert Ridge, the first Red-necked Stint and Whimbrel (Asian *variegatus*) of the trip, and a flashy Ruff. The Ruff was a large bird, with a well-developed black and white ruff, pink bill and face, and bright orange legs. It might have been a chicken. Three Spotted Redshanks were found in Henderson Marsh, the largest freshwater marsh in the Aleutians. In a normal year, it would take a coordinated sweep through the entire marsh to find the one or two Long-toed Stints that might be present. On this day, Wood Sandpipers filled the marsh (Paul Sykes estimated 500 Wood Sandpipers were in the marsh and West Massacre Valley). Wood Sandpipers were running up and down the road, singing, displaying, and copulating. The marsh rang with the calls and songs of Wood Sandpipers and Long-toed Stints. Temminck's Stints were scattered among them, and the shore of Smew Pond was peppered with Common Sandpipers. The marsh was alive with birds, as a marsh that size should be at the height of spring migration.

That evening, Mike Toochin radioed in a fly-by Green Sandpiper at Brambling Bluff. It was the first serious shocker of the trip; a bird that we had all dreamed of finding. There were only six Alaska records, and none in 15 years. The Green Sandpiper seemed an almost impossible bird. Toochin based his iden-tification primarily on hearing the bird's call notes as it flew by high in the sky, and he and the people he was with watched an already tiny speck disappear over Massacre Bay. After making such a brash report, he naturally spent the next hour in agony, praying that the bird would turn up again. We tracked it down, and, after a bit of a chase, the bird settled in on the beach at the mouth of the Henderson River. About half the birders on the island bicycled out to watch it after dinner. It was the first life bird of the trip for most of the staff and long-time Attuvians.

Great birds continued to trickle in over the next few days: a Siberian Rubythroat and three Black-tailed Godwits on 19 May; two Far Eastern Curlews and a Bean Goose on 20 May; and a Great Knot on 21 May (only the third Aleutian record). On 22 May, we tallied a record-high 35 Black-tailed Godwits, including a single flock of 23 birds. A single Bar-tailed Godwit on 23 May was followed by 130 on 24 May. On 19 May, Terry Doyle and Walter Chuck (the non-birding cook and self-proclaimed "anti-birder") kicked up an odd snipe in a large area of tall dry grass near camp. It turned out to be a Pin-tailed Snipe, only the second documented record for North America. Like most of the other birds we had seen, it was tired and did not fly far when flushed. We lined up nearly every birder on the island in a wide semi-circle, then slowly moved the bird through the grass toward the group and closed in. After about 45 min-utes, we were able to study the snipe at length through spotting scopes from as close as 15 feet as it fed and preened.

By 23 May, the numbers of songbirds had dropped considerably, but there were still more birds around than any of us had ever seen at one time. That evening we said good-bye to the participants of the first two-weeks. A high percentage of the people had never been to Attu before, and we jokingly told them that they should not think of coming back to Attu Island again. The island would seem devoid of birds to them, even in a good year.

Poor weather on 24 May delayed the flight until the next day. After a futile flight over Attu Island, the people on the second two-week trip (escorted out by Dave Sonneborn and Paul Baicich) were rerouted to the Pribilof Islands to spend the night. They saw a Wood Sandpiper there, and Red-legged Kittiwakes and thousands of auklets were a welcome bonus to their Attu trip. Larry Balch had been sending reports about the trip to these people over the Internet during the previous two weeks. The reports were one- or two-page rundowns of the incredible birding, updates of the total tally of Asian species, predictions that this would be the "best year ever," and included statements such as, "33 Asian species now, and the pace is not yet slowing," and, "we would not have fantasized the numbers of birds we are seeing," and, "absolutely phenomenal, unbelievable, unprecedented." It was Asian birds that the second group of birders wanted to see, and by the time they arrived at Attu Island they were crazed, they wanted to see Asian birds Right Now.

We split the new arrivals into several large groups and set out on foot to bird the rest of the day. The largest group headed to Henderson Marsh to look for the Bean Goose. Craig Roberts and a small group from our first group of participants found a Mew Gull (Asian *kamtschatschensis*) just before boarding the plane back to Anchorage.

After the luggage, gear, and two more weeks of food had been transported to base, Jim Fowler and I were given the task of running a four-wheeler and a cart full of food and beverages out to the birders who had hiked north of the airport. This was a chance for Jim and me to relax and not be very responsible. We ran into a small group of people with Paul Baicich at Warehouse Beach, so we stopped to dole out some food and chat. After only a short time, we saw people streaming back from Navy Town. Obviously, something was going on. The first person to reach us was racing forward, moving just short of a run. He had a look on his face commonly associated with news of a shocker—a look that says, "I'm going to see the bird or die trying." He grabbed some food and juice off the cart and bolted it down. When I asked him what was going on, he said, "Yellow-throated Bunting at Blue Robin Canyon," and was gone. We all looked at each other. None of us had any idea what that was. I got on the radio to find out what was going on, and couldn't raise anyone right away; another sign that something big was happening. Finally, someone confirmed that there was a Yellow-throated Bunting in Blue Robin Canyon. I asked, "Do you mean Yellow-breasted Bunting?" (also a very good bird). "No, Yellow-throated Bunting." We looked in the Japanese bird guide, and there it was on page 272: an exotic looking small bunting with a yellow throat, black mask, black triangular chest patch, and short crest. It was not a bird anyone I knew had even considered as a possible vagrant to Attu.

Blue Robin Canyon was seven miles from Henderson Marsh. Few people knew where Blue Robin Canyon was and we had to run around making sure everyone was headed in the right direction. A large chunk of the group, then, fresh off the plane, had hiked several miles to Henderson Marsh, then had to turn around and hike seven miles back to Blue Robin Canyon, as fast as they could—a grueling hike. More than 50 people were lined up in the bottom of the steep-sided canyon when I finally arrived. A few were positioned on the tops of the low canyon walls trying to keep track of the bunting. The bird was feeding along the edges of snow banks on the canyon walls, but it made short flights and occasionally disappeared for a couple minutes in a hole or behind a bank. When it popped back into view the crowd went nuts. The bird didn't seem to pay any attention to the wild shouting and laughing and crying. Someone yelled, "I'm goin' over the edge! I'm goin' over the edge!" Others continued to straggle in, sweat pouring down. "Is it still there?" They were ushered to spotting scopes. Some looked only briefly at the bird through a spotting scope, then collapsed on the tundra to recover from their hike. This scene was exactly what everyone had been hoping for.

The group who came for the second two weeks saw nearly all of the same species that were seen in the first two weeks, including a second Pin-tailed Snipe, discovered by Ted Robinson in the dry beach grass along Massacre Bay. (Ted's report over the radio: "I'm looking right at a Pin-tailed Snipe, and it's looking right at me.") We added Sharp-tailed and Terek Sandpipers to the trip list on 29 May, Arctic Loon on 30 May, and Red-flanked Bluetail on 31 May.

The total number of Asian species seen in 1998 was slightly higher than any previous trip to the island. (The total number depends on what one considers an "Asian" species, and I have listed all the possible species and identifiable subspecies here.) Migration was very early in 1998, and we saw new early arrival dates for many species. It was the fantastic number of Asian birds, though, that was most impressive. In a post-trip mailing, Larry Balch calculated that we tallied over 11,000 Asian bird days—that is, the sum of the total number of Asian birds seen per day—and about 80 percent of that total was seen in the first two weeks of the trip. For comparison: In 1982, a great year that had long been considered the finest trip to Attu, 2,000 total Asian bird days were recorded.

In a normal year at Attu, I would listen intently, day after day, for the call note of a Rustic Bunting or an Olive-backed Pipit. Some years, the entire trip would go by and I would not have seen either species, let alone heard their call notes. And if someone did find an Olive-backed Pipit or an Eyebrowed Thrush it could take all day long, and loads of patience and luck, to show the skittish bird to 70 people as it skulked in vast willow thickets, or rocketed from one canyon to the next. The pressure was on if the bird was a shocker, and I remember more than a few classic moments. Being a bird guide could not have been any easier than it was in 1998. At the nightly countdown on 16 May, the first day of the fall-out, a few people mentioned that they hadn't seen an Eyebrowed Thrush. "Well," I said, "let's go out behind the building after the countdown, and I'll show you one." And we did, as simple as that.

North American Life Lists

I look at all these numbers
scrawled
on the wall
by former birders
738, 727, 683
trophies of the birds seen
not killed
and I think about all
the rushing around
to count so high

I look at all these numbers
on the wall
and know that these
buildings on Attu
will soon be empty
and I will be the last
to see these numbers
on the wall
and I continue to sit
indoors
in the rain
and count
their numbers
on the walls.

—*Lyndia Terre*

White-tailed Eagle, photographed 4 June 1982 in the Temnac Valley on an all-day trip with
Paul Sykes and Davis Finch.

After Storm, Late May

Golden Plovers! Two
Flash through sun-filtering fog
Calling, veering north.

A White-tailed Sea Eagle
Glides
With torn meat of salmon.

The Lapland Longspur males
Arc high over nesting females' eggs, then
Wings spread, singing, float down.

—Macklin Smith

Poets in a Warriors' World

Jim Burns

When the Beringian east gales, which had driven the horizontal sleet/snow for eight continuous hours, blew Pete Isleib through the door into the common room, the clock on the wall said 5:45. The first dinner shift was 15 minutes away, but no one had moved. Louie Banker was slouched in his customary position beside the radio, but nothing had come in all day because no one was out there. Louie's sonorous snoring droned over the desultory banter of the card players. A few dogged scribes were scribbling in their journals held inches from their faces in the dim, murky light. The rest were either dozing or trying to read.

Pete Isleib is the embodiment of the term "indefatigable." His unexpected entrance from the jowls of the howling storm turned forty heads and his condition brought hope to forty faces. His full beard and mustache, like his heavy down parka, were totally encrusted with ice, his face the color of the coils on the space heater next to Louie's chair, which had long since lost the daily battle against the cold and damp.

Pete's physical endurance and intense enthusiasm were legendary throughout the birder's world. Those who knew him found it easier to picture him making the 12-mile trek to Alexai and back along the muddy traces euphemistically called roads than to imagine weather bad enough to confine the hardest core birders in North America to quarters all day.

My wife and I had spent the previous day, in the same weather, with Pete and Frank Jestrab, we the only four fools about outside. Frank was 73, and, though interested in birds, had come to Attu to remember—he had fought the Japanese here in 1943, the same year my father, Lieutenant-Colonel James P. Burns, Seventh Cavalry, was killed on Luzon. We had fought our way through the gales out to Murder Point, then on around to Krasni over rain soaked tundra and moss slicked boulders, scarcely able to see our feet beneath us, knowing at every step Frank was going to slip and break a leg. Pete and Frank, each lost in his own world, were having the time of their lives. And we had found a Mongolian Plover.

Today, the bad news was that Pete had turned up no Asian vagrants. That was the good news too. It is the essence of the Attu experience that the crackling of the radio on a bad weather day is accompanied by equal parts anticipation and dread, elation and foreboding. As Pete thawed out and it became known he had seen nothing more noteworthy than a Snowy Owl flying the ridge behind Navy Town, forty privately relieved minds slipped thankfully back from the precipice of a frenetic, bone-chilling forced march into the worst elements on the North American continent.

Typically an Attu sunup consists of a bright suffusion through the clouds or fog and the dawn chorus is simply a male Lapland Longspur serenading his lady from the top of a tundra umbel whipping in the gusts. The storm had diminished overnight, but since it had not come from the south and west there seemed little likelihood of Siberian breeders blown off course. The leaders met to discuss the feasibility of a hike into the Temnac Valley for the White-tailed Eagle.

The Temnac had long been the home of a nesting pair of these magnificent birds; rare, declining, and little known breeders of Greenland and far northern Eurasia. Most years the pilgrims on Attu would observe one flying over base camp on its way to the coast. If the days waned without an observation, a couple of leaders would attempt the arduous five-mile hike over the snowfields of South Pass into the eagles' valley home. One of the pair had not been seen for several years now and was presumed dead. Eagle anxiety in this year's group was running high. There had been no flyovers. The Temnac hike was never a given and it had been a winter of heavy snows.

Canvassing the faithful for the most hardy, with dire warnings to the less hardy not to be foolhardy, Jerry Rosenband and Paul Baicich collected thirteen of us to give it a go immediately after breakfast, to see how far we could negotiate the snowfields. In the best of times hiking over tundra is far from the trivial matter it might seem, a constant, thigh-burning maze of hummock and hole, which exhausts the unfit. Slick with rain and runoff, it becomes a serious aerobic exercise that exhausts even the fit. Covered with a thick snow crust that hides the holes, the terrain becomes a nightmare.

Unless you are an eagle, there is only one passable route into the Temnac, even in high summer after the snow is gone: follow the Peaceful River valley up over South Pass, slipslide 300 feet into the ravine of George's Creek on ropes secured by metal stakes driven by previous pilgrims, ford the icy creek, then negotiate one last rocky incline before slopping through the quagmire of the Temnac meadows.

Jerry and Paul knew the worst part of the hike would be the first miles, where the heaviest snowfall lingered. Once on the highlands toward the pass much of the snow would be scoured away by the winter winds. Half a mile out I took the group's first misstep, plunging to my armpits as a rotten snowbridge gave way over a river channel. Hurriedly I was extricated before Jerry and Paul noticed, for they might have turned us all around.

The bonding of total strangers, totally out of their element but isolated together and for a shared avocation, is one of the primary truths of Attu. By the time fourteen gentlemen waxing chivalrous had coaxed and half carried my lovely wife, elevationally terrified and the only woman on the Temnac tour, down the rope to the creek, we were unfazed to find it running knee deep. Some took the icy plunge across the slippery cobbles in bare feet, saving dry boots and socks for lunch and eagle. Some had fashioned gaiters from plastic garbage bags. Some waded through oblivious to the soaking, knowing/hoping body heat from the strenuous hike ahead would dry them inside out and preclude hypothermia.

As we sprawled across the damp grass for lunch in the lee of a tundra heave, speculation ranged from when the eagle would come to why no one had ever died on an Attu tour to just what we all were doing here. And then the eagle came. Some had it in their binocular field simultaneously with the Peregrine flying beneath it—and below that the flock of Aleutian Rosy-finches. Two of our three speculations having been answered, Gil Ewing produced from his pack a bottle of wine. The grueling hike back out of the Temnac had been trivialized.

Climbing down to George Creek on the approach to Temnac Valley, 1983

Photo: Jerry Maisel

As we crested South Pass and stopped for snacks and water, Louie's voice crackled over the radio telling us the eagle had flown over base camp this morning. Groans met this first announcement, replaced almost instantly with smirks and smiles of satisfaction. Their eagle had been just a passive fortuity on just another layabout camp day. Our eagle, actively sought, had been a lifetime-once experience replete with memories of camaraderie in shared hardships and solved problems.

Louie's second announcement was that Terry Savaloja had refound Pete's Snowy Owl and was sitting on it in case anyone wanted to see it. I was the only taker on the owl. No one comes to Attu for Snowy Owl. Though certainly an arctic specialty, it is not an Asian vagrant nor is it all that uncommon in the Lower 48 due to its periodic winter irruptions. Such was the experience of this year's Attu sojourners that it was not a lifer for any, and so jaded were they by thoughts of storm-tossed exotics from another continent, that none but I cared to detour the 2 miles or so to where Terry waited above Navy Town, for another glimpse at one of the most magnificent of raptors.

Snowies are the size of Great Horneds, smaller than Great Grays, but heavier of body. Powerful enough to take ptarmigan and geese, they prefer, on arctic breeding grounds, to prey on a rodent, the lemming. Older males are truly snow white, but females and younger birds, particularly those displaced to the States in winter, will have much dark spotting and barring. I had seen two Snowies prior to this, both winter birds in Washington state.

For birders with limited arctic experience but an appreciation for the mysteries of the more southerly and typical owls and how they live, the sight of a bird this size and color, hunting by day and so obviously a raptor, is fascination bordering on astonishment. When I found Terry he was hunkered down just below ridgeline, scope set up on the owl farther down the ridge. It was teed up on a tundra heave just like the pingaluks of the true arctic.

The bird was 100 yards away, what light left of this gray and misty day reflecting from the lemon yellow eyes, the heavily feathered lores giving every appearance of a neatly clipped mustache. For over an hour we watched as the bird, presumably a male with little barring, hunted the stark landscape. Though he made occasional graceful and deliberate forays (reminiscent of a Short-eared Owl) out over the grasses, he mostly sat waiting, seemingly indifferent. Apparently there were mice about. From time to time his head would snap alert or swivel completely to echolocate some rustling beneath his perch.

What followed then was a downward jump on half-raised wings askew for balance. Awkward but efficient on the ground, the owl would flop around for several seconds, splaying a taloned foot here and there amongst the hummocks, then return to his post with mouse in beak. Terry had seen a pair of Snowies in the area and presumed they would breed though no nest had been discovered.

The chance to spend quality time alone with another of our leaders had made small price of the additional time and miles after our Temnac tryst. Though he had seen hundreds of Snowy Owls in a still short lifetime begun as a birding prodigy in the wilds of northern Minnesota, Terry was as delighted with our extended observation as I and just as dismayed that no one else was there to enjoy this intimate visit with one of the most sought after of North America's nineteen owl species.

Quiet and reflective, Terry revealed his joy in birding all corners of the continent as he spoke of his travels and observations. Although Terry ranked among the top five listers in the country, his fellow travelers would never have known it from his helpful and unassuming personality. As we left the owl, sloshed down through Navy Town, and pedaled back along the darkening miles to base, Terry spoke of the ironies of Attu and his love of this wild and desolate place.

Navy Town itself is a moldering tract of flattened barracks and offices abandoned after the war with Japan and now being inexorably reclaimed by frost, wind, and willow bog. Somehow the rotting vestiges of civilization do not seem out of place against the vast treeless backdrop of tundra and mountain, weather and sky, the four verities of the far Aleutians. The island seems a symbol of wilderness prevailing. And for Terry, the Snowy Owl is the signature bird of this far northern wilderness.

The Rubythroats, the Bluethroats, even the eagle, are indeed spectacular additions to any life list, but they and all the other Eurasian birds are flukes of geography brought by the vagaries of the weather. Snowy Owl belongs here. Snowy Owl is native, a resident since before the Beringian land bridge, a survivor. Snowy Owls will roam the bogs and highlands long after the scars of Navy Town disappear into the tundra.

Terry and I were late for the dinner serving, and Pete was later still. While we ate I thanked Terry for waiting on the bird for me and I thanked them both for their insights and their passion, for guiding us pilgrims from the Lower 48 across the immense solitude of this breathtaking outpost, compressing the typical joys and frustrations of a birding lifetime into a three-week marathon of exhilaration and fatigue.

Black volcanic rocks, September 2000

Over a last cup of hot tea, I offered my allegiance to the gods of wilderness. I told Terry and Pete this day's highlight for me, the eagle encounter in the Temnac notwithstanding, had been the hunting Snowy. We were the only three on the island to have seen it. This we lamented. I told them we would be back, though I knew not when. We shook hands and embraced.

Three years removed from our once-in-a-lifetime journey to one of the last great places on this earth, the beckon stirs deep within us. We check vacation schedules and bank accounts. We cannot shake the feeling. With equal parts anticipation and dread, elation and foreboding, we know we must make the pilgrimage once again. The island calls. It cannot be denied.

News moves rapidly along the hotlines of the birding world. Usually it is the glad tidings of an unexpected bird or an expected bird in an unexpected place. But occasionally an old flame flickers out. Terry Savaloja has picked up an intestinal parasite in the jungles of South America. He is dead, not yet 40 years old. The birding world has lost a quiet force, a persistent voice for the joy of frontiers, adventures, discoveries. I see the windswept tundra ridge, Terrible Mountain rising up behind it, Navy Town below. I dream of the great white owl.

Another year passes, and arriving birding literature carries an obituary. Pete Isleib has had a forklift accident on one of his fishing boats. He is dead at 55. We birders have lost an intense force, a passionate voice for environmental integrity and sensible wilderness management. I see the moss-slicked rocks of Krasni Point, the horizontal sleet enshrouding four wayfarers on a desolate coastline of wrack and rubble. I dream of the great white owl.

The Records

Photo: Ed Harper

Coming off the plane in June 1998

The Attu Records: Comparing Some Alaskan Outposts

Thede G. Tobish

Almost 30 years ago Dan Gibson introduced me to Alaska's original list of projected "next possible species" when I first met him at the University of Alaska Museum. This was really his own private list since he was one of the original modern advocates of the Aleutians as an Asian species hotspot and source for new records. In the early 1970s, Aleutian birding was in its infancy, accomplished mainly by federal biologists doing seabird and Aleutian Canada Goose work. Asian fever had taken hold in the previous few years after first Aleutian and North American records brought attention to places like Adak, Amchitka, Buldir, Shemya, and Attu islands. We all know the history from there, especially after others followed Joe Taylor to Attu (in 1972). Once regular trips were initiated to Attu, the Pribilofs, and St. Lawrence Island in the mid-1970s, Asian fever was perpetuated as new North American records were added almost annually.

Of course, all of Gibson's original next-five list (Red-breasted Flycatcher, Siberian Flycatcher, Yellow-breasted Bunting, Lesser White-fronted Goose, and Red-flanked Bluetail) have since been documented (three by Gibson), and another 28 or so followed in between. In fact, in this past century alone, some 83 species have been added to the North American list from Alaska's outposts, mainly from the western Aleutians and the Bering Sea Islands (the Pribilofs and St. Lawrence). For details, you can see, for example, Kessel and Gibson (1978).

The accompanying table for particulars shows the new species for North America from Alaska since 1911. As for the "Attu contribution" to this list, fully 19 of those species were from Attu, and a baker's dozen since 1984 alone.

In addition to those first records, birders and field biologists also produced first Nearctic records of several Asian subspecies, including nominate Common Merganser, Kamchatka (Mew) Gull, *longipennis* Common Terns, *quarta* Rock Sandpipers, *coloratus* Lapland Longspurs, etc. Because of Alaska's proximity to northeast Asia and its location either within the ranges or at the termini of several East Asian flyways, new North American finds continue at a consistent rate. Concentrated birder coverage at Alaska's outposts—mainly Attu, the Pribilofs, and St. Lawrence Island's Gambell village, have been the source of guaranteed documentation of North American firsts for more than 20 years.

TABLE 1.

New species for the ABA Area from Alaska since 1911, presented in chronological order

SPECIES	DATE RECORDED	LOCATION
Tufted Duck	May 1911	St. Paul I., Pribilofs
Siberian Rubythroat	June 1911	Kiska I., Aleutians
Rustic Bunting	June 1911	Kiska I., Aleutians
Gray-tailed Tattler	October 1911	St. Paul I., Pribilofs
Hawfinch	November 1911	St. Paul I., Pribilofs
Black-backed Wagtail	May 1913	Attu I., Aleutians
Spoonbill Sandpiper	August 1914	Wainwright, NW Coast
Brambling	October 1914	St. Paul I., Pribilofs
Falcated Duck	April 1917	St. George I., Pribilofs
Jack Snipe	1919	St. Paul I., Pribilofs
Red-necked Stint	August 1920	St. Paul I., Pribilofs
Fork-tailed Swift	August 1920	St. George I., Pribilofs
Steller's Sea-Eagle	August 1921	Kodiak Island
Baikal Teal	September 1921	Wainwright, NW Coast
Great Knot	May 1922	Cape Prince of Wales, NW Coast
Black-tailed Godwit	May 1927	Little Diomede I.
Middendorff's Grasshopper-Warbler	September 1927	Nunivak I.
Siberian Accentor	October 1927	Nunivak I.
Cook's Petrel	August 1933	Off Adak I., Aleutians
Pechora Pipit	1937	Gambell, St. Lawrence I.
Eurasian Wryneck	September 1945	Cape Prince of Wales, NW Coast
Bean Goose	April 1946	St. Paul I., Pribilofs
Common Swift	June 1950	St. Paul I., Pribilofs
Eyebrowed Thrush	May 1956	Amchitka I., Aleutians
Gray-spotted Flycatcher	June 1956	Amchitka I., Aleutians
Far Eastern Curlew	June 1961	St. Paul I., Pribilofs
Spotted Redshank	September 1961	St. Paul I., Pribilofs
Little Stint	September 1961	St. Paul I., Pribilofs
Common Greenshank	May 1962	St. Paul I., Pribilofs
Olive-backed Pipit	June 1962	Gambell, St. Lawrence I.
Gray Wagtail	October 1962	St. Paul I., Pribilofs
Temminck's Stint	August 1965	St. George I., Pribilofs
Common Sandpiper	May 1966	St. George I., Pribilofs
Sky Lark	May 1967	St. George I., Pribilofs
Dusky Thrush	June 1967	Pt. Barrow, North Coast
Pallas's Bunting	June 1968	Pt. Barrow, North Coast
Spot-billed Duck	April 1970	Adak I., Aleutians
Little Bunting	September 1970	Chukchi Sea
Common Cuckoo	May 1971	Amchitka I., Aleutians
Common Rosefinch	June 1972	Old Kashunuk Village, Yukon Delta
Tree Pipit	June 1972	Cape Prince of Wales, NW Coast
Terek Sandpiper	May 1973	Cape Peirce, SW Coast

White-throated Needletail	May 1974	Shemya I., Aleutians
Common House-Martin	June 1974	Nome
Little Ringed Plover	June 1974	Buldir I., Aleutians
Chinese Egret	June 1974	Agattu I., Aleutians
Marsh Sandpiper	September 1974	Adak I., Aleutians
Reed Bunting	May 1975	Buldir I., Aleutians
Eurasian Hoopoe	September 1975	Old Chevak, Yukon Delta
Oriental Greenfinch	May 1976	Attu I., Aleutians
Gray Bunting	May 1977	Shemya I., Aleutians
Jungle Nightjar	May 1977	Buldir I., Aleutians
Red-breasted Flycatcher	June 1977	Shemya I., Aleutians
Brown Shrike	June 1977	Gambell, St. Lawrence I.
Oriental Scops-Owl	June 1977	Buldir I., Aleutians
Dusky Warbler	June 1977	Gambell, St. Lawrence I.
Broad-billed Sandpiper	August 1977	Adak I., Aleutians
Siberian Flycatcher	September 1977	Shemya I., Aleutians
Green Sandpiper	June 1978	Attu I., Aleutians
Eurasian Siskin	June 1978	Attu I., Aleutians
Yellow-breasted Bunting	June 1978	Gambell, St. Lawrence I.
Stonechat	June 1978	Gambell, St. Lawrence I.
Eurasian Kestrel	September 1978	Shemya I., Aleutians
Wood Warbler	October 1978	Shemya I., Aleutians
Red-flanked Bluetail	June 1982	Attu I., Aleutians
Eurasian Hobby	July 1982	Off Attu I., Aleutians
Black-winged Stilt	May 1983	Nizki I., Aleutians
Lanceolated Warbler	June 1984	Attu I., Aleutians
Oriental Turtle-Dove	June 1984	St. Paul I., Pribilofs
Oriental Pratincole	May 1985	Attu I., Aleutians
Siberian Blue Robin	May 1985	Attu I., Aleutians
Mugimaki Flycatcher*	May 1985	Shemya I., Aleutians
Asian Brown Flycatcher	May 1985	Attu I., Aleutians
Pine Bunting	November 1985	Attu I., Aleutians
Great Spotted Woodpecker	April 1986	Attu I., Aleutians
Yellow Bittern	May 1989	Attu I., Aleutians
Narcissus Flycatcher	May 1989	Attu I., Aleutians
Pin-tailed Snipe	May 1991	Attu I., Aleutians
Lesser White-fronted Goose	June 1994	Attu I., Aleutians
Chinese Pond-Heron	August 1996	St. Paul I., Pribilofs
Yellow-throated Bunting	May 1998	Attu I., Aleutians
Yellow-browed Warbler	October 1999	Gambell, St. Lawrence I.
Rufous-tailed Robin+	June 2000	Attu I., Aleutians
Baillon's Crake**	September 2000	Attu I. Aleutians

*Although officially on the A.O.U. and ABA Checklists, this record is not substantiated on the Alaska List.

+ Not on ABA Checklist yet. One appeared at Attu in June 2000 and was photographed.

** Not on ABA Checklist. Reported from Attu in September 2000, but no photograph or specimen.

New Species By Geographic Area:

Aleutian Islands	=	46% of total
Pribilof Islands	=	26%
Bering Strait Area*	=	18%
Other Sites	=	10 %

[* Includes St. Lawrence Island, Little Diomede Island, Nome, Wales, Wainwright, etc.]

In a relatively short time, we have contributed immensely to the knowledge about status and distribution of Asian species on this continent. Of the Roberson article's (1988) predictions, four have now been substantiated (Pin-tailed Snipe, Oriental Turtle-Dove, Yellow-browed Warbler, and Pine Bunting). Moreover, Roberson's earlier prognostications (1980) have produced a dozen correct guesses out of 35 made. Therefore, with most of the "expected" new species now documented, an entirely new mix of possibilities is recognized.

In the December 2000 issue of *Birding*, a panel of experts mused over the "next birds" to appear in Alaska. That panel consisted of five Alaskans—Dan Gibson, Steve Heinl, R. L. "Buzz" Scher, Dave Sonneborn, and myself—all of whom have extensive experience at the region's Asian outposts and are directly responsible for documentation of numerous first North American finds. The remaining panelists also share longstanding field experience from Alaska's periphery: Larry Balch is responsible for making Attu the signature Alaska site from which the majority of new records for the continent have come since he initiated tours there in 1979; Jon L. Dunn and Gary H. Rosenberg are St. Lawrence Island and Nome-area specialists, having led tours there since the early 1980s. Each of the panelists approached the voting in a different way, from Scher's "engineer" method that assigned points based on six criteria, to Sonneborn and Balch's "lust" factoring.

The top half-dozen vote getters were:

1. Eurasian Sparrowhawk (*Accipiter nisus*)
2. Black-faced Bunting (*Emberiza spodocephala*)
3. Gray Heron (*Ardea cinerea*)
4. Carrion Crow (*Corvus corone*)
5. Chinese Goshawk (*Accipiter soloensis*)
6. Eastern Crowned Leaf-Warbler (*Phylloscopus coronatus*)

The panel also identified another set of eleven species, a set of "honorable mentions." These include a host of species with breeding and winter ranges, migration routes, and vagrancy patterns similar to the six top species and to species already recorded from Alaska, mainly from the western Aleutians.

1. Daurian Redstart (*Phoenicurus auroreus*)
2. Brown-headed Thrush (*Turdus chrysolaus*)

3. Gray's Warbler (*Locustella fasciolata*)
4. Chestnut-cheeked Starling (*Sturnia philippensis*)
5. Oriental Reed-Warbler (*Acrocephalus orientalis*)
6. Siberian Thrush (*Zoothera sibirica*)
7. Black-browed Reed-Warbler (*Acrocephalus bistrigiceps*)
8. Blue-and-white Flycatcher (*Cyanoptila cyanomelana*)
9. Willow Warbler (*Phylloscopus trochilus*)
10. White-cheeked Starling (*Sturnus cineraceus*)
11. Japanese Sparrowhawk (*Accipiter gularis*)

The Final Considerations

So what chances are there to find these birds?

Observers should realize that although the spring migration traditionally produces most first Alaska records, the fall season remains underexplored among Alaskan outposts with few recognized rarity patterns. Autumn may ultimately produce an even greater list of potential first records, based on the wild list of those already recorded (Eurasian Hoopoe, Wood Warbler, Pine Bunting) and the greater wandering propensity of first-year birds.

Unfortunately, with the closing of Attu to birders, regular spring coverage there will virtually cease. And as for the fall, because of the extreme protraction of that migration, and the acute challenge of immature plumages, we may not realize many next new North America records from this season.

Still, the continent's birding frontier continually beckons further investigation.

LITERATURE CITED:

Gibson, D.D. 1981. *Migrant birds of Shemya Island, Aleutian Islands, Alaska*. Condor 83:65–77.
Kessel, B. and D. D. Gibson. 1978. *Status and Distribution of Alaskan Birds*. Allen Press.
Roberson, D. 1980. *Rare Birds of the West Coast*. Woodcock Publications, Pacific Grove, California
Tobish, Thede, 2000. The Next New ABA-Area Birds. *Birding 32*: 498-505.

Some Attu Vistas

Photo: Dixie Coleman

Waterfall along Gilbert Ridge, September 2000

The Stacks, September 2000

Fishing, September 2000

At the edge of a barrel dump, September 2000

Vestiges of earlier days

Photo: Lyndia Terre

Photo: Lyndia Terre

Vestiges of earlier days

142

Fall Birding at Attu and Other Western Alaska Outposts

Paul Lehman

The Aleutian Islands/Bering Sea region is well known to most North American birders as the place to go to find regular Asian migrants and vagrants, Alaska specialties, and spectacular seabird concentrations. Most observers who have visited Attu Island—as well as other sites, such as St. Paul Island (Pribilofs) and Gambell (Saint Lawrence Island)—have done so in spring. These sites have received annual birder coverage from mid-May through early June since about the mid-1970s. As is well known, many first records of Asian species for North America have been found on these islands during this period, and with the right weather conditions (e.g., storms characterized by prolonged southwesterly winds), major fallouts of vagrants may occur over a several-day period, particularly in the western Aleutians.

In contrast, these Alaskan outposts have been largely neglected by birders during the second half of June (a good time for late-spring mega-rarities), and coverage throughout the fall season has been sparse. One likely reason for the limited autumn coverage has been the protracted nature of the fall migration compared to the more concentrated, shorter "pulse" of birds in spring. To be assured of seeing a number of Asian strays during a single visit, a birder typically must make a longer commitment of time in autumn than is required in spring. Also, the spring vagrant seasons for waterfowl, shorebirds, and passerines all substantially overlap. Conversely, the peak southbound migration of shorebirds (between July and early September) is largely over before most vagrant passerines occur (late August to mid-October), which in turn is earlier than the period for many of the rare waterfowl (except for Garganey, which appears to be a rare but regular September visitor in the western Aleutians). Another factor may be that the relatively lush vegetation in early fall makes it more difficult to find low-density migrants and vagrants than to find spring migrants in the sparse cover characteristic of that season.

Fall birding in coastal western Alaska in general is still a pioneering effort, with much remaining to be learned. Although the logistics can, at times, be difficult, and the costs may be relatively high, birding there is one of the most interesting and exciting adventures possible in North America. An extended autumn trip provides the potential for the thrill of discovery. The composition of rarities in fall is somewhat different than in spring; thus birders with multiple spring trips under their belt may have better odds of seeing new birds with a fall visit.

Through 2000, autumn birding on Attu was limited primarily to three organized Attour trips (1983, 1993, and 2000), a visit by a small group of birders in 1979, and visits by one or a few researchers in at least 1985, 1997, and 1999.

On Attu, many southbound shorebirds likely pass through from July through early September—

Lyndia Terre, September 2000.
The relatively lush vegetation of early fall provides good cover for birds.

largely before the arrival dates of the few fall trips—although these September visits produced a number of sought-after species including moderate numbers of Sharp-tailed Sandpipers (which are regular migrants through western Alaska in fall), small numbers of Mongolian Plovers, Gray-tailed Tattlers, Wood and Common Sandpipers, "Eurasian" Whimbrels, Red-necked Stints, Ruffs, and Common Snipe, plus a number of other, rarer goodies including Eurasian Dotterel, Common Ringed Plover, Spotted Redshank, Green Sandpiper, and Little and Long-toed Stints. The two most mouth-watering autumn shorebirds to occur in the Aleutians did not occur on Attu, however. North America's only Marsh Sandpipers to date have been single juveniles on Buldir Island in September 1974 and at Adak in August 1998. Broad-billed Sandpipers were found on Adak in August 1977, Buldir in August 1989, and Shemya in September 1978 (five birds), September 1986, and September 2000. Shemya also has fall records of Eurasian Dotterel, Curlew Sandpiper, and multiple Temminck's Stints. Also, several North American mainland species have occurred on Attu and elsewhere in the western Aleutians more often in fall than in spring, including small numbers of Long-billed Dowitchers and multiple Buff-breasted Sandpipers. Another recent autumn waterbird highlight on Attu was a Whiskered Auklet in September 2000.

Vagrant landbirds, although likely trickling through beginning in late July or early August, probably don't really kick in until early September. The term "kick in" is a relative one. There simply are not the fallouts of passerines that occur periodically in spring. Fall storms from the west or southwest, including the remnants of tropical Pacific cyclones that generally move in a north or northwestward direction toward Japan before some recurve northeastward toward Alaska and become extra-tropical, likely increase the chances that strays reach Attu. Those storms that pass over or just north of the island, with resultant strong westerly or southwesterly winds and precipitation, are probably the most productive. Several intense storms—the remnants of tropical typhoons—struck Attu and western Alaska during the late summer of 1997. That fall a partial corpse of a Sooty Tern was found below the Loran tower, for a first, incredible record of that species in the state. It is hypothesized that one of these storms deposited the bird—which then flew into the tower's guy wires and died. It is anyone's guess, and fantasy, as to what other birds might have been found on Attu immediately after such storms have struck, if only birders had been present! An "unexceptional" storm that passed just north of the island, with moderate westerly winds and some rain, at the end of September 2000, resulted in a Reeve Aleutian flight delay and the final Attour group leaving the island three days late. It also was likely responsible for the appearance the following day of a Fork-tailed Swift, Dusky Thrush, and Rustic Bunting. Few of the participants complained further about the delay.

The search on many a day for the rare landbird vagrant may produce little more than good exercise on your bike and spying the local Lapland Longspurs, Snow Buntings, Winter Wrens, Song Sparrows, ravens, and perhaps a few redpolls. Digging up passerine strays in the fall at Attu really does require a small army out in the field. Most of those people find little to nothing, but then an individual or a small group stumbles onto those one or two great birds that make for the incredible excitement that is Attu. Finding such birds in the tall, luxuriant growth seems to be like trying to find the proverbial needle in a haystack. The thick cover that makes both the walking and the spotting of Asian passerines (which are shy and furtive to begin with!) rather difficult, has caused many a fall Attuvian to feel more than just a wee bit of frustration, especially those who are more accustomed to the larger number of landbirds and relatively scant vegetation present in spring. The payoff comes, however, with the finding of fall strays that include species never or very rarely seen in spring. Yes, there are some of the same rare-but-regular Sky Larks, Black-backed Wagtails, Red-throated (and perhaps Olive-backed) Pipits, Rustic Buntings, and Bramblings. But there have also been such Attu autumn gems as Eurasian Kestrel (1983), Oriental Cuckoo (1999), Fork-tailed Swift (2000), Great Spotted Woodpecker (1985 and 2000 [2]), Middendorff's Grasshopper-Warbler (6+ in 1979), Dusky Warbler (1983 and 2000), Dusky Thrush (1993 and 2000), Siberian Rubythroat (7+ in 1979), Red-flanked Bluetail (1993), Little Bunting (1983), Oriental Greenfinch (2 in 1993), and, perhaps rarest of all, single Pine Buntings in November 1985 and October 1993. September census work at Shemya in 1977 and 1978 produced a fine selection of Old World vagrants, including North America's one-and-only, truly exceptional Wood Warbler (*Phylloscopus sibilatrix*)—a European species that breeds no farther east than the Ural Mountains—as well as Eurasian Kestrel, Fork-tailed Swift (2), Siberian Flycatcher, Siberian Rubythroat (4+), Little Bunting, Oriental Greenfinch (6+), and Eurasian Bullfinch. September 2000 on Shemya hosted a Fork-tailed Swift and Great Spotted Woodpecker. August–September 2001 birders saw Eurasian Kestrel, Eurasian Hobby, and Fork-tailed Swift; the same time period in 2002 netted Bean Goose, Baikal Teal, two Falcated Ducks, Eurasian Hobby, and a European Starling. Unfortunately, as a result of increased military activity and security, Shemya is off-limits to birders who don't have military clearance.

The Wood Warbler is one of a number of examples of mega-rarities with single continental occurrences that have turned up in western Alaska during the fall. Other examples include the only North American records of Eurasian Wryneck and Eurasian Hoopoe, which come from the mainland Bering Sea coast, in September 1945 and September 1975, respectively; Willow Warbler in August 2002; Lesser Whitethroat and Spotted Flycatcher during September 2002; and the Yellow-browed Warblers mentioned below. Attu's autumn claim to fame in this department is the Baillon's Crake (*Porzana pusilla*) seen by all participants there during the second half of the September 2000 Attour trips; unfortunately this bird was not photographed, so it will likely remain on the North American hypothetical list.

North of the Aleutians, the limited number of early autumn visits to the Bering Sea islands between 1991 and 2002 has produced records of a variety of Asian landbirds. Several visits to Gambell have produced passerine records that include the first continental records of Willow Warbler, Lesser Whitethroat, and Spotted Flycatcher, the only two North American records of Yellow-browed Warbler in September 1999 and August 2002, and the third record of Tree Pipit as well as two Oriental Cuckoos, Fork-tailed Swift, two Middendorff's Grasshopper-Warblers, five Dusky Warblers, five Siberian Accentors, Reed Buntings, two Common Rosefinches, Siberian Rubythroat, Olive-backed Pipit, and four Little Buntings. There have been records of *Cuculus* cuckoo sp., Eyebrowed Thrush, and Siberian Accentor at this season from Nunivak Island. Nunivak also has older fall records of Middendorff's Grasshopper-Warbler, another Siberian Accentor, and multiple Eurasian Bullfinches. Farther south in the Bering Sea, St. Paul Island remains largely unchecked in fall after the beginning of September. Relatively good coverage during the past decade in late July and August has proven to be good for Asian shorebirds and other vagrants, with 1990s records of Chinese Pond-Heron and a sight-record of Grey Heron (the only records for both species in the USA), Eurasian Hobby, Fork-tailed Swift, and Common House-Martin. Several recent, but very brief, visits to St. Paul later in the autumn have produced Red-flanked Bluetail and good numbers of Bramblings, and there are older fall records of Baikal Teal and Eurasian Coot.

Excitement and discovery are not limited to the finding of Asian strays. Apparently a good number of mainland North American breeding species wander west out to the offshore islands in fall, much more so than they do in spring. In the western Aleutians, there are autumn records from Attu and Shemya of Violet-green Swallow, Ruby-crowned Kinglet, Yellow-rumped, Townsend's, and Wilson's Warblers, multiple Savannah and Golden-crowned Sparrows, Dark-eyed Junco, and Pine Siskin. Perhaps some enterprising Palearctic birders some day will be interested in breaking new ground and will explore the islands and mainland coast of eastern Siberia, searching for Nearctic vagrants in autumn. Someone stationed on the Commander Islands, just west of Attu, may turn up a number of first records of New World strays for Russia and the Old World. Attu birding in reverse!

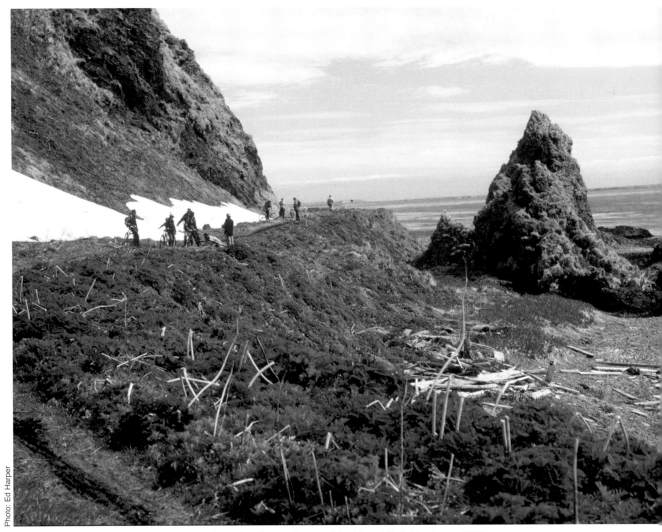

The Stacks on the road to Alexai Point in June 1998

Notes on the Birds Recorded on Attu Birding Trips

Larry Balch

The purpose of these notes is to provide a summary of all birding on Attu over the past 25 years or so. They are not meant as anything more than an informal presentation of the information gathered primarily on spring and fall birding trips that were organized either by me or (beginning in 1979) by my company, Attour, Inc. Any competent library search will locate a good number of articles in the ornithological literature that deal with the birds of the Aleutians, the Near Islands, and Attu in particular. (See especially works by Daniel D. Gibson.) Some of that literature refers to observations that we made and that are also reported below. The following annotated bird list makes use of a large database of Attu observations that others and I have assembled over the years, and of the annual trip lists that Attour prepared. (The trip lists for 1988 and later are posted at <www.attu.com>. I plan eventually to post trip lists for earlier trips.) Where I think it is interesting and credible, I have also included information that I have heard first- or second-hand from non-Attour people.

Spring trips took place in 23 years, from 1977 (one party) through 2000, with the exception of 1995. Group arrival dates ranged from 10 May to 20 May, with 16 May the median; departure dates ranged from 1 June to 17 June, with 7 June the median. After adjusting for days not spent in the field because of bad weather, the mean number of spring birding days for 23 years is 21.9. One to three people, primarily Attour advance staff, were usually on the island before or after the groups, particularly up to 1987.

Fall trips took place in four years: 13–22 September 1979 (only one party); 4–25 September 1983; 23 September–10 October 1993; and 29 August–3 October 2000. There were several individuals on the island before and/or after each of the last three trips.

There were usually four to six groups in the field daily, on bicycles. We tried to cover all areas still accessible by road. Beginning in 1979, on almost every day we covered the areas from South Beach to the beginning of Gilbert Ridge: Murder Point, Casco Cove, Navy Town, West Massacre Valley (which includes Henderson Marsh) up to Lake Elwood, and all associated coastline. Trips to Alexai Point were made every two to three days until about 1985, after which Gilbert Ridge and Alexai were covered almost every day. In most years, we also visited Temnac Valley. Krasni Point and Savage Island were visited one to three times per year. Occasionally, and usually when birding was slow elsewhere, small parties would hike as far as Holtz Bay or Chichagof Harbor, and two to three miles east of Alexai. Ocean watches for pelagic species such as tubenoses, jaegers, and certain gulls were done sporadically, again either when birding was slow generally, or (sometimes) when wind conditions made us believe such watches might be productive.

Data were collected each evening by our leaders, who were careful to avoid duplicate counts and were very strict about proper identification. The daily checklist produced by Attour leaders did not include single-observer sightings, even though many were undoubtedly accurate. We will note some of those here, since these notes are directed primarily at birders who are interested in what it was like to bird Attu.

Some of the records cited here are substantiated by specimens collected by a representative of the University of Alaska Museum, working under a U.S. Fish and Wildlife permit. Information on those records will be published elsewhere.

For some species of more-than-usual interest, I provide graphs to help clarify their occurrence patterns. Typically, the graphs give, for each date from about 10 May to 10 June, the total number of birds seen on that date in all years. The intention is to give an idea of when during the spring migration the species was most likely to be found. In some cases the numbers on each date are given separately for the year 1998, which turned out to be extraordinarily atypical, with numbers far beyond what we had ever dreamed possible. (For more about this extraordinary year, see the article by Steve Heinl on p. 121 .)

Although we cannot cite specific meteorological data, it is clear to those who visited Attu every spring that the weather conditions were trending over the years in the direction of earlier warming and concomitant earlier greening of the vegetation. In the late 1970s and early 1980s, we invariably had significant snow cover near the coastal roadways and along the runways when we arrived. We noted a gradual decline in that arrival snow cover over the following years. (A notable exception was 1998, when we arrived to find more snow and colder weather than we could ever remember.) Since we had often used the snow near our buildings to keep things cold, we were quite aware of the changes. In fact, a lack of any snow near the roads and our buildings became the norm by the time we stopped birding Attu. In the 1990s, from our plane we often saw green vegetation along Gilbert Ridge as we were arriving, something that we never saw in the early years.

These weather changes are just one of many factors, of course, which affected our birding results. In earlier years, we had fewer leaders and participants, but passerines were concentrated near the roads by the snow cover. In later years, we had many more eyes, but we had to spread out over a lot more snow-free tundra. I know of no way to account for such factors in order to produce meaningful, comparable data, so the narrative that follows is, of necessity, largely anecdotal.

N.B.: *When a record date is listed, it is for a single bird, unless noted otherwise.*

Red-throated Loon (*Gavia stellata*) Resident breeding bird. Usually seen flying, in pairs; the maximum of ten individuals was seen on 21 May 2000.

Arctic/Pacific Loon (*Gavia arctica/pacifica*) We did not distinguish these species until after 1991, when they were split, and identification criteria were better understood. Analysis of records since then shows that Pacific outnumbered Arctic by about two to one. Maximum annual numbers were eight Pacific individual birds in 1998 and four Arctic in 1992. No Pacific Loons were seen in 1994 and 1995, and no Arctics in 1993 through 1995.

Common Loon (*Gavia immer*) This species was seen every year, usually fewer than a half-dozen per day. However, unusual numbers were seen in 1985, with a maximum of 19 on 27 May. It probably breeds on larger lakes.

Yellow-billed Loon (*Gavia adamsii*) We saw this species every year. Very few birds were in adult breeding plumage. When present, we typically saw one or two birds a day; the peak number was nine on 19 May 2000. Fall records were mostly one or two a day, beginning 3 September.

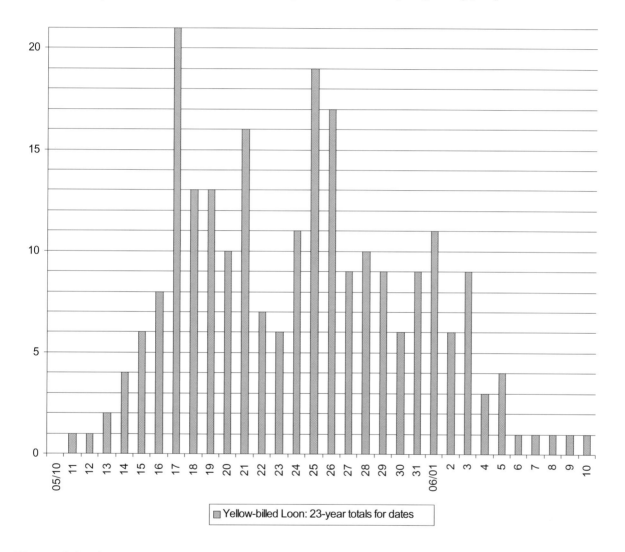

Horned Grebe (*Podiceps auritus*) This species was seen on 11 of our 23 spring trips, but never more than three a day. It was seen every fall, with the only record of more than three birds in a day being eight on 23 September 2000.

Red-necked Grebe (*Podiceps grisegena*) We saw this species on almost every trip, spring and fall. Numbers were about the same as the previous species. Notable exceptions were ten birds on 23 May 1977, and 32 birds on 18 May 1978. Both grebe species were usually seen in Massacre Bay.

Laysan Albatross (*Phoebastria immutabilis*) This species passes by the Near Islands in large numbers every summer. For example, from a fishing boat one day in August, 1999, about 2000 were seen resting on the water at Stalemate Bank, about 50 miles west of Cape Wrangell, Attu. More than once, biologists on the U.S. Fish & Wildlife boat *Tiglax* reported good numbers passing Krasni Point near shore, although we never had much luck spotting them there. Our most productive viewing spot was at Murder Point. While most daily counts were less than a dozen birds, occasionally wind conditions produced higher counts, with the maximum being 75 birds on 26 May 2000. They were usually seen at quite a distance, but sometimes individuals would come quite close to shore.

Short-tailed Albatross (*Phoebastria albatrus*) We never officially recorded this species, but it is occasionally seen from ships near Attu. On the August day noted above, 6 of these albatrosses were seen among the large number of Laysan Albatrosses.

Northern Fulmar (*Fulmarus glacialis*) Although this species was not recorded every year, it occurs in large numbers annually offshore, as it breeds in the Aleutians. From Murder Point, this and the following species (Sooty Shearwater) were often so far out that distinguishing them was not possible. The maximum recorded was 800 on 26 May 1993. We should note that while we were watching these birds, which were at a great distance, we thought they were shearwaters. Then we saw Pete Isleib head out to where the birds were in his Zodiac. When he returned, he told us that nearly every "shearwater" was in fact this species.

Sooty Shearwater (*Puffinus griseus*) This migrant shearwater is recorded from ships in Attu waters, but it is usually outnumbered by the next species listed. Separation is difficult enough with close looks at sea, and it would be foolish to try to identify this species from land, so we have never recorded it on our Attour trip lists.

Short-tailed Shearwater (*Puffinus tenuirostris*) This was the "default" shearwater when seabirds were counted from Murder Point. More than 10,000 were recorded on 6 September 1983. See Northern Fulmar above.

Fork-tailed Storm-Petrel (*Oceanodroma furcata*) We recorded this once in the fall and seven times in the spring. Most records were lone birds injured at night by flying into the Loran station antenna guy wires. However, five individuals were seen flying over land on 31 May 1997, and six were also seen on 31 May 1992. Most surprising, however, was the fall bird we saw. Just after dark on 29 September 2000, several people were relaxing in our outdoor hot tub when it landed in the grass next to the tub!

Leach's Storm-Petrel (*Oceanodroma leucorhoa*) A lone bird was seen from a small sailboat on the only pelagic trip we were able to make (4 June 1982), and five others were found on shore, most killed from having hit the Loran tower guy wires.

Red-faced Cormorant (*Phalacrocorax urile*) A common resident, these cormorants are often seen west of South Beach.

Pelagic Cormorant (*Phalacrocorax pelagicus*) Most of the cormorants nesting on the cliffs and rocks around Massacre Bay, and formerly on the abandoned docks (now mostly collapsed) in front of the Coast Guard property, belonged to this common resident species.

Yellow Bittern (*Ixobrychus sinensis*) North America's only record of this species is a bird seen around the small lakes on Murder Point, 17–22 May 1989.

Black-crowned Night-Heron (*Nycticorax nycticorax*) Our advance-party leaders once recorded this species flying in off the Pacific when they were waiting on Shemya Island to cross over to Attu. After our organized trips ceased, the species was reported on Attu in May 2002 by biologists working for the University of Alaska Museum.

Grey Heron (*Ardea cinerea*) In April, 1986, a lone observer saw a bird thought to be of this species standing near the runway ponds. His attempt to collect it failed, and the bird flew off.

Bean Goose (*Anser fabalis*) In 10 of the 14 years it was recorded, only a single bird was seen. Often it was standing on the ground in Massacre Valley or on Alexai Point. In 1979, however, 25 were observed: 9 near the Loran Station on 11 May; 2 near Peaceful River on 20 May; and a total of 14 in three flocks passing Murder Point going west on 21 May.

*This drawing and all bird illustrations used in this chapter are by George West and are used with permission.

Pelagic Cormorant*

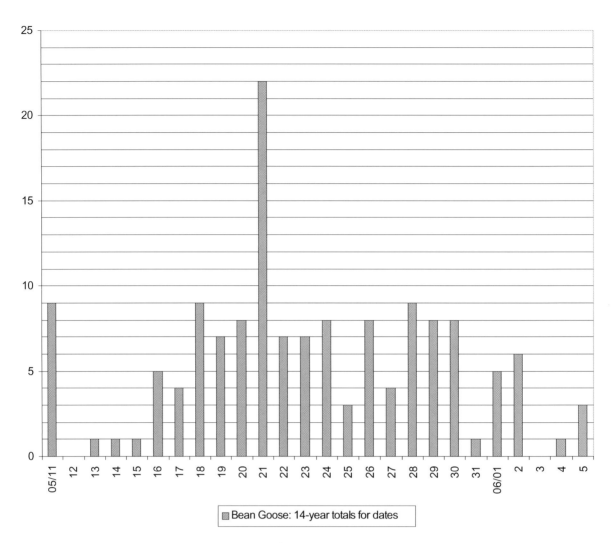

Bean Goose: 14-year totals for dates

Greater White-fronted Goose (*Anser albifrons*) Three spring records: single birds 24 May to 3 June 1981 and 17 May 2000; two birds on 21 May 1987. One fall record: two birds on 21 September 1983.

Lesser White-fronted Goose (*Anser erythropus*) The only North American record is of a bird seen at Barbara Point, 5 June 1994.

Emperor Goose (*Chen canagica*) This species winters on Attu, and in 18 years, a few remained until we arrived. In most years, there were only one or two, but on 14 May 1988, we saw 18. They were primarily found on rocky islets near shore. Our limited fall experience indicated that the first birds would return to Attu in mid-September, with numbers picking up in early October (e.g., there were 61 individuals on 3 October 1993.)

Snow Goose (*Chen caerulescens*) Four records: 5 and 20 May 1979; 2, 20–21 June 1982; and 28 May–7 June 1988.

Canada Goose (*Branta canadensis leucopareia*) When we first arrived at Attu in 1977, the Aleutian Canada Goose project to restore the species to its former breeding sites was under way at Buldir. Gradually, the foxes introduced by fur traders were removed from various islands, and geese were released. However, we did not see any Canada Geese at Attu until 1982. When foxes were removed from the nearby island of Agattu over a period of years in the early 1990s, we began noting flying geese at Attu more frequently and in ever-greater numbers. Eventually, we found them in flocks on the ground. Foxes were removed from Attu in 1999, and by then we saw geese every day, in large numbers (see the graph below). On 23 May of both 1999 and 2000, for example, we saw more than 300 birds. In those two final Attour years, we saw geese that were paired off, suggesting the possibility of nesting on Attu.

Canada Goose sightings by year

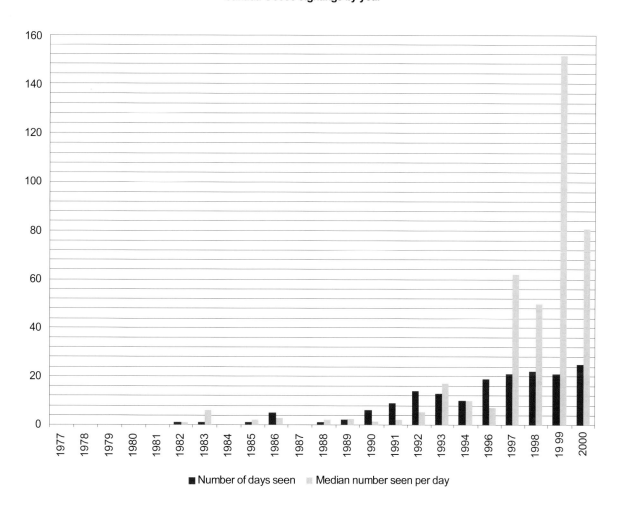

Brant (*Branta bernicla*) Four records: 26 May–1 June 1981; 31 May–8 June 1988; 2 on 20 May 1989; and 21 May 1996.

Whooper Swan (*Cygnus cygnus*) Leaders in our advance party saw a pair in 1981 and a lone bird in 1982, all the first week of May before our groups arrived. These were thought to be birds returning to Asia from wintering grounds in the Aleutians. However, on 17 May 1996, Dave Trochlell and Richard Wilt made a trip to the small ponds southeast of Lake Nicholas in Siddens Valley, an area where we did not regularly bird. They found two adult swans and what appeared to be a nest. When we returned on 5 June, the adults and five cygnets were seen swimming on one of the ponds, and the nest was confirmed three days later. Nesting was confirmed again in 1997; these are the only nesting records for North America.

In 1998, we saw small flocks of three and nine on 10 May that flew in off the ocean and continued west up the Peaceful River valley. It was a cold spring, so migration was later than usual for swans. These birds were probably migrating back to Asia. In 1999, swans were seen in the Massacre-Casco area frequently in the second and third weeks of May, and we began to wonder if they might perhaps nest in other areas. Unfortunately, on 22 May 1999, along the high-tide line of Massacre Beach between Brambling Bluff and the Henderson River, we also discovered the carcasses of two swans that had been shot. No swans were seen in 2000.

Gadwall (*Anas strepera*) First recorded in 1991, and seen in ones and twos most years after that.

Falcated Duck (*Anas falcata*) Seen in seven springs: 4 seen on 27–29 May 1980; up to 5 birds per day 20 May to 5 June, 1982; 21 May–3 June 1984; 6–8 June 1985; 2 on 20 May 1987; 12–31 May 1991; and 16–27 May 1994.

Eurasian Wigeon (*Anas penelope*) This fairly common migrant was seen mostly on small lakes. Numbers fluctuated from a daily maximum of a dozen or so (most frequently) up to four or five dozen. In 1998, there was a large influx of this species, with more than 100 individuals seen on several days between 11 and 21 May. The peak was 158 on 15 May. The species was seen during each fall trip, with a few arriving early in September and building up to spring numbers by early October.

Northern Shoveler

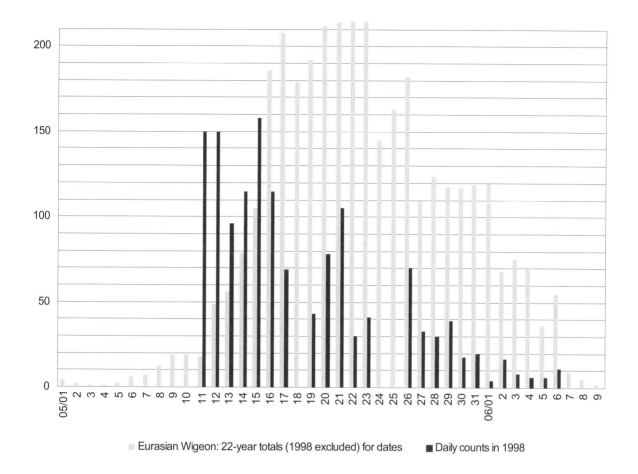

Eurasian Wigeon: 22-year totals (1998 excluded) for dates ■ Daily counts in 1998

American Wigeon (*Anas americana*) One to three birds were seen in spring in each of seven years.

Mallard (*Anas platyrhynchos*) Peak daily numbers of this common resident were 83 for spring, on 23 May 1998, and 150 for fall, on 22 September 2000.

Spot-billed Duck (*Anas poecilorhyncha*) One (the fourth record for North America) was found on the west shore of Krasni Point on 18 May 1993. The bird stayed at Attu for over a year. It was seen near the runway ponds in the fall and was last seen 19 May 1994.

Northern Shoveler (*Anas clypeata*) This migrant was seen in small numbers (usually fewer than ten per day) each fall and every spring except 1977, 1987, and 1996. In 1990, there were up to 24 birds present daily.

Northern Pintail (*Anas acuta*) The spring daily peak for this common resident was 75 on 15 May 1998; the fall daily peak was 185 on 8 October 1993.

Garganey (*Anas querquedula*) One to three birds were seen each fall. We have scattered records of one or two birds in May of 1977, 1980, 1984, 1989, and 1994. In 1987, five individuals were present when we arrived on 17 May; some of them were still there on 5 June, just before we left.

Green-winged Teal (*Anas crecca crecca*) We saw up to 250 of this species per day. As I recall, in the 1990s we had a male of the *carolinensis* form almost every year, but no priority was placed on recording this subspecies.

Canvasback (*Aythya valisineria*) The only records are single birds seen 19–26 May 1980, 17–20 May 1989, and 20 May 1990.

Common Pochard (*Aythya ferina*) This species was recorded in 14 springs, with a maximum of seven individuals on 9–11 May 1982. There are no fall records.

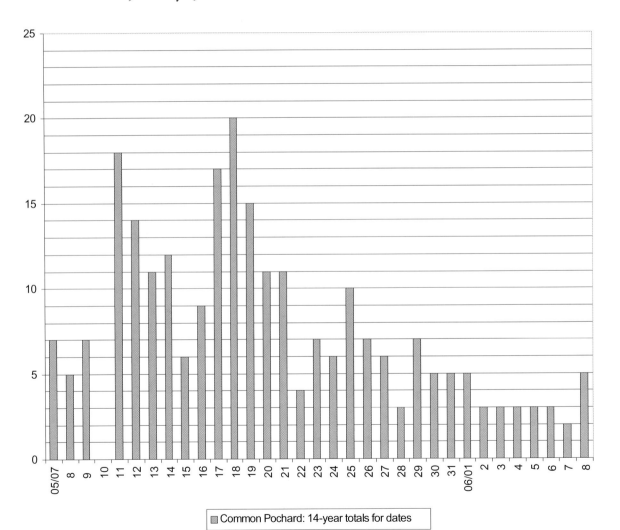

Common Pochard: 14-year totals for dates

Tufted Duck (*Aythya fuligula*) This common migrant was missed completely in 1981.

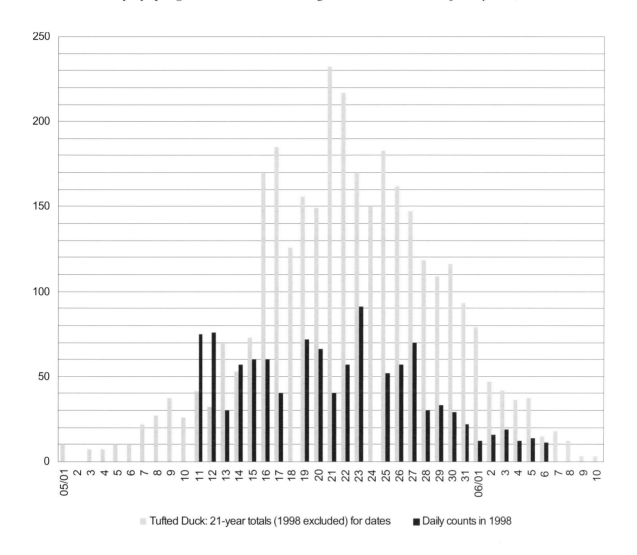

Tufted Duck: 21-year totals (1998 excluded) for dates   Daily counts in 1998

Greater Scaup (*Aythya marila*) This fairly common migrant was seen every spring, but it was more numerous in the fall. While fewer than one or two dozen individuals was the daily norm in most springs, it was not uncommon to see four or five dozen a day in 1984, 1989, 1993, 1997, and 1998. The fall peak was 182 birds recorded on 6 October 1993, as compared to a spring peak of 62 on 23 May 1984.

Steller's Eider (*Polysticta stelleri*) This wintering species was almost always gone by the time we arrived, so we recorded it in only seven springs and never in fall. Usually we would see a lone bird, but in 1977, 1980, and 1992, we saw small flocks of 5, 7, and 11 birds, respectively. We never saw an adult male.

Spectacled Eider (*Somateria fischeri*) An adult male of this species was found at Alexai Point on 17 May 1993. It was seen on every one of our trips after that, either at Alexai or near Barbara Point. University of Alaska researchers who visited Attu in May and June of 2002 reported that the bird was still there. No other individuals of this species were recorded.

King Eider (*Somateria spectabilis*) This eider species was seen in spring in all but four years, usually one or two birds a year. Exceptions were four individuals seen on 1 June 1977, and four on 25 May 1996. We regularly found adult males.

Common Eider (*Somateria mollissima v-nigra*) This is a common resident species. In the late 1970s, as many as 23 dogs were kept at the Coast Guard station, and presumably because of them, foxes were scarce in our birding area. We frequently came across eider nests near the roads and shores. By the early 1980s the dogs had been removed, the foxes had returned, and eider nests were hard to find. We occasionally made actual counts of the eiders to be seen along the shore of Massacre Bay, and these numbers tell the same story: 600-plus in 1977, 275 in 1996, 250 in 1997, 200 in 1998. Interestingly, in 2000, the first spring after foxes were removed from Attu, we again found nests along the beaches and also saw eiders standing around the runway and roads.

Harlequin Duck (*Histrionicus histrionicus*) Large numbers of this species summer on Attu, but do not appear to breed here. It was not uncommon to see 200 to 500 individuals in our birding area, poking about in flocks near shore. On 30 May 1977, we counted more than 1,000 individuals. Fall numbers did not appear to be as large, at least not in early fall.

White-winged Scoter (*Melanitta fusca*) This scoter was not as easy to find as the next-listed species, but we saw it on 15 spring trips, and every fall. More than ten were seen only twice: 12 on 20 May 1977, and 30 on 7 July 1977.

Black Scoter (*Melanitta nigra*) An uncommon migrant, we saw this bird on 21 spring trips. Most daily counts were less than a dozen individuals. In fact, counts ranged from only one in all of spring 2000 to 44 on 25 May 1982. One to three birds were often seen on fall trips.

Long-tailed Duck (*Clangula hyemalis*) Although our advance parties would often see hundreds of this wintering species in late April and very early May, by the time our birding groups arrived, most would be gone. We usually (19 years) recorded less than a half-dozen, although on 17 May 1983 we saw 55 individuals.

Bufflehead (*Bucephala albeola*) On five spring trips, we missed this uncommon migrant entirely. Rarely did we see more than half a dozen. Exceptions were counts of 22 on 12 May 1998 and 12 on 16 May 1999.

Common Goldeneye (*Bucephala clangula*) We missed this uncommon migrant only in 1978. Flocks of a dozen or more were seen in only a handful of years. In 1992, however, we saw 72 birds on 12 May.

Barrow's Goldeneye (*Bucephala islandica*) Single birds were seen the third and/or fourth week of May in 5 years: 1986, 1992, 1993, 1997, and 1999.

Smew (*Mergellus albellus*) We saw Smews on the small lakes on Murder Point and in lower West Massacre Valley on Smew Pond (naturally). The typical number in the 17 years in which we saw the species was of one or two birds. In 1998, however, we had significantly larger daily counts, with a peak of 16 individuals on 15 May. We often saw adult males.

Common Merganser (*Mergus merganser merganser*) A half-dozen or fewer birds were recorded in most years. Exceptions were 1984, 1998, and 2000, when our maximum number of 25 birds was recorded on 16 May. All males that we examined carefully were of the nominate Palearctic race.

Red-breasted Merganser (*Mergus serrator*) This species is common on Attu, where it nests. We noticed an upward trend in our maximum daily counts beginning soon after we started birding Attu in 1977. The median maximum daily count for 1977 through 1984, for example, was 14.5 birds, but for the 15 years after that, it was 50, and in every one of those 15 years, we had a higher daily count than in all the years before 1985. This is a conspicuous species, and it is difficult to attribute this increase simply to more intensive coverage.

Osprey (*Pandion haliaetus*) Single birds on 4 June 1985 and 19 May 1988 are the only records.

Bald Eagle (*Haliaeetus leucocephalus*) An adult, well-observed on 27 May 1994 is the only record.

White-tailed Eagle (*Haliaeetus albicilla*) We observed a pair in courtship flight on 27 May 1977 in lower West Massacre Valley. There were occasional sightings of adults in the following years. A year-old bird was seen in 1979; the 2-year-old bird seen in 1980 was probably this same bird.

We suspected that the eagles nested in Temnac Valley, and in fact, we found their nest site there on 25 May 1982. A chick was seen in the nest on 31 May and again on 4 June. In 1983, the nest had another chick in it, and the bird into which it fledged was seen feeding with its parents along the Temnac River in September of that year. That same bird could have accounted for our sightings of a 2-year-old bird in 1985 and a 3-year-old bird in 1986. These are the only nesting records for North America.

Two adults were never seen after 1983; we believe one of them died before we returned in 1984. With one exception—an immature that was believed to be a wanderer from elsewhere—every record after 1986 was of an adult. Our last sighting of what we presumed was the surviving bird of the pair was in 1996.

It is interesting to note that George Miksch Sutton and R.S. Wilson reported seeing two adults flying out of Temnac Valley on 15 March 1945. Given the long life span of the species, it seems possible that our two adults were the same birds he saw. For three summers (1983–1985), the U.S. Fish and Wildlife Service sponsored a search by one person for eagles elsewhere on Attu. All major river valleys were covered, but no other eagles were found.

Steller's Sea-Eagle (*Haliaeetus pelagicus*) We used to send one or two leaders to Attu early, sometimes in late April, to make quarters ready for our groups. They recorded this species twice: a pair of adult birds in late April and another bird on 9 May 1980. From 16 May to 2 June 1994, the rest of us were happy to watch a subadult bird that once perched on a phone pole near our base for two hours.

Northern Harrier (*Circus cyaneus*) Lone birds were recorded 18–20 May 1982, 18–22 September 1983, 12–13 September 2000, and 19 September–2 October 2000. In the first week of June, 2000, a harrier was seen on Murder Point that could not be identified, as it was in a plumage not shown in any of our several field guides. While some observers felt, after examining museum specimens later, that it could have been a Pied Harrier (*C. melanoleucos*), the lack of photographs and convincing descriptions leaves it simply a harrier.

Accipiter species On 26 September 2000, an accipiter was holding its position in a stiff wind several hundred (?) feet above our base. Then it slowly drifted away to the north over Casco Cove. While apparently of near-goshawk size, its tail shape, narrow from base to tip, ruled out that species. Its shape and plumage were correct for a Eurasian Sparrowhawk, *A. nisus*, probably a juvenile female. That is certainly the accipiter species most to be expected at Attu, based on range considerations. Again, the lack of acceptable documentation would make this at best a hypothetical record. In early October 1983, one of our leaders felt that an accipiter that flew by when he was walking alone on the Casco Cove road was also *A. nisus*.

Rough-legged Hawk (*Buteo lagopus*) Single birds were seen on almost every spring date, but only in 12 years. In 1997, one seemed to be lingering on the island for three weeks beginning 17 May.

Eurasian Kestrel (*Falco tinnunculus*) Three records: one bird on 4 and 7 May 1981; one showing devotion to a cliff site on the south side of West Massacre Valley 3–4 June 1984; and one on 22 May 1997. People who saw the 1984 bird at different times disagreed as to its sex, thereby raising the possibility that there were two birds.

Merlin (*Falco columbarius*) One, seen on 27 and 28 September 2000, is the only record.

Eurasian Hobby (*Falco subbuteo*) Five out of the first six North American records (there are now ten) are from Attu or the surrounding waters. The hobby that flew over Murder Point on 20 May 1983 was the second record, and the first seen on land. Another perched briefly near Brambling Bluff on 28 May 1994. Three more records are of birds coming aboard ships within 100 miles of Attu between 2 July 1982 and 25 June 1983. Also, feathers from a bird of this species that had died the year before were found on Attu in May 1987.

Gyrfalcon (*Falco rusticolus*) On 22 May 1978, Davis Finch and I saw a very high-flying Gyrfalcon flying north over the Coast Guard station. It appeared to be a passage bird. There are no other records.

Peregrine Falcon (*Falco peregrinus pealei*) This is a fairly common breeding species. We saw as many as six in a day. This race is very dark, causing some to initially mistake it for a Gyrfalcon until they take a more considered look.

Rock Ptarmigan (*Lagopus mutus evermanni*) This race is found only on Attu. It is arguably the most handsome of all the Rock Ptarmigans, the male being a rich fuscous and white. Until nesting commenced and the birds moved higher up the slopes, they were often seen (and heard giving their risible call) on the roads, around the buildings, even landing occasionally on an occupied outhouse. In 2000, the first year after foxes were removed from Attu, we saw many more ptarmigan, and in places (e.g., Alexai Point) where we had never seen them before. On 9 June, we recorded the completely unprecedented total of 365, greater than any previous count by a factor of more than 10.

Baillon's Crake (*Porzana pusilla*) On 20 and 21 September 2000, many of us got several good looks, in excellent light, at an immature bird of this species as it flew several times around a small marshy area near Barbara Point. Unfortunately, attempts to photograph it failed. There are no other reports of its possible occurrence in North America.

Sandhill Crane (*Grus canadensis*) Lone birds and small flocks (up to 20 in 1982) were seen between 10 May and 6 June in eight years from 1979 to 1994. I do not recall that any were ever seen on the ground. Most interestingly, we saw three birds during the summer of 1977, on 17 July and 5 August. We never saw any in fall.

Black-bellied Plover (*Pluvialis squatarola*) Altogether, 7 solitary birds were seen in 5 different springs. Lone birds were also recorded on 3 of the 4 fall trips.

Peregrine Falcon

163

Pacific Golden-Plover (*Pluvialis fulva*) This species, seen every year, was our second-most common migrant shorebird, after Wood Sandpiper. In about half the years, we'd count less than 10 a day, but in other years our peak daily count would be 2 to 4 dozen. Many more individuals than usual were seen in 1999, with a peak of 65 birds on 21 May. It was also seen every fall, in numbers comparable to spring.

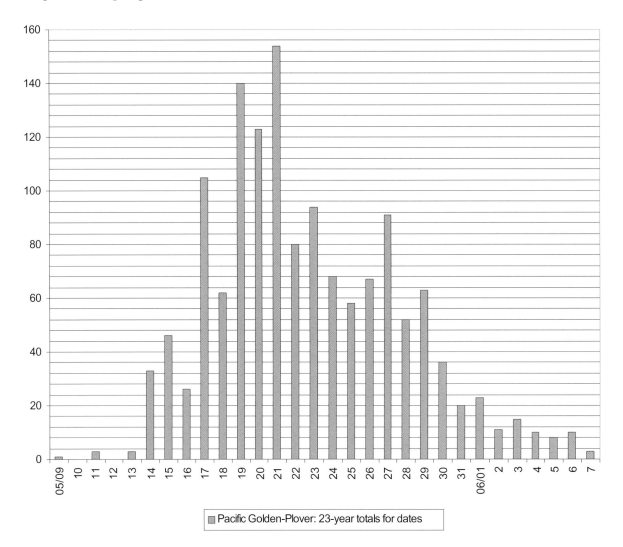

Pacific Golden-Plover: 23-year totals for dates

Mongolian Plover (*Charadrius mongolus*) In every spring except 1977, 1978, and 1984, we could find small numbers on the sandy beaches. Our maximum was 10 birds counted on 19 May 1983. Only 3 individuals in all were seen during our four fall trips.

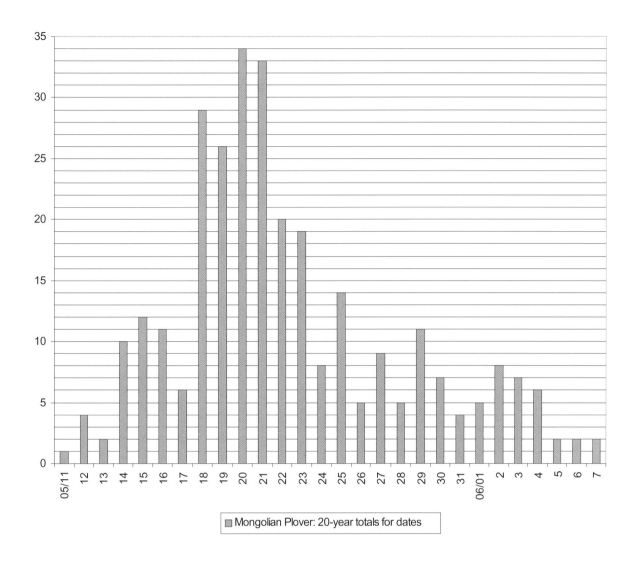

Mongolian Plover: 20-year totals for dates

Common Ringed Plover (*Charadrius hiaticula*) Only 1 spring record: 16–26 May 1982. We had 3 fall records: 11–13 September 1983; 30 September 1993; 1 on 11 September and 2 on 13 September, 2000.

Semipalmated Plover (*Charadrius semipalmatus*) 27 May 1992; 1–2 June 1998; 13 June 2000.

Little Ringed Plover (*Charadrius dubius*) The second (out of 3) North American record was on Alexai Point from 19 to 29 May 1986.

Common Greenshank (*Tringa nebularia*) This species was seen on 17 spring trips, up to 6 in a day (22 May 1981). It was never seen in fall.

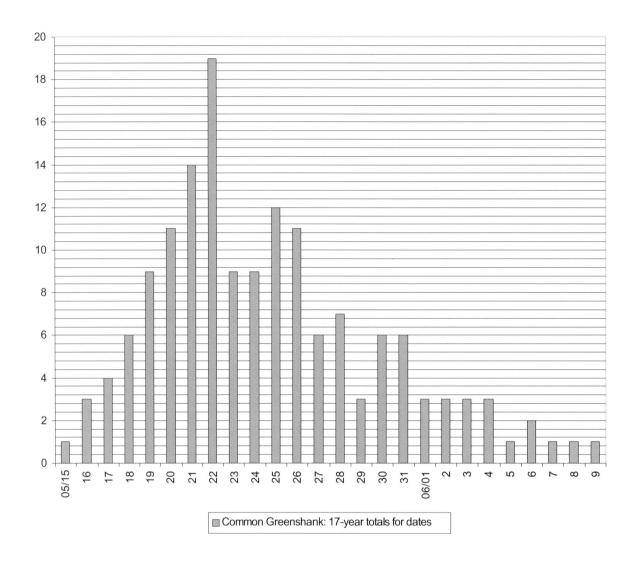

Common Greenshank: 17-year totals for dates

Lesser Yellowlegs (*Tringa flavipes*) A single bird present 4–7 June 1988 is the only record.

Spotted Redshank (*Tringa erythropus*) With one exception (4 birds on 18 May 1998), this species was seen in ones and twos between 18 May and 31 May, on seven spring trips. There is one fall record: 26 September 2000.

Wood Sandpiper (*Tringa glareola*) Found nesting on Attu in 1973, Wood Sandpipers were seen on every trip except the 1993 fall trip. Numbers could fluctuate greatly. For example, in 1996, we saw only 1 bird the whole trip, while we recorded 109 on both 20 May 1983 and 18 May 1987. (The 1998 maximum of 700 on 18 May was another example of how exceptional that year was.)

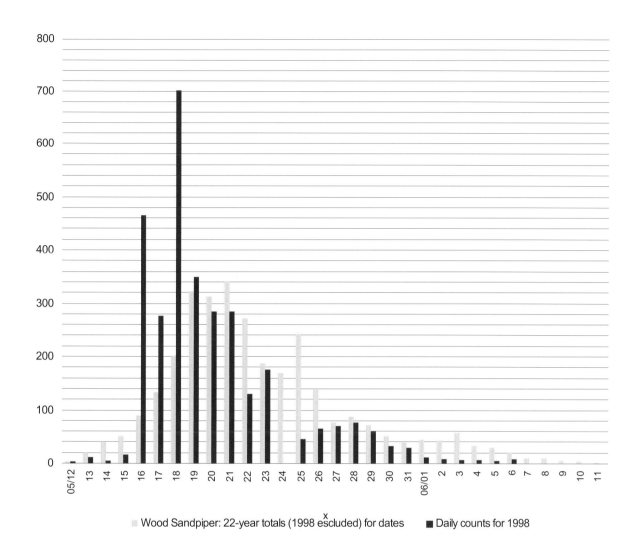

Wood Sandpiper: 22-year totals (1998 escluded) for dates ▪ Daily counts for 1998

Green Sandpiper (*Tringa ochropus*) Only 3 records of this species within the ABA Area are not from Attu, and two of those were from nearby Nizki and Shemya Islands. Our spring records are: 13 June 1978, 22 May 1979, 18 May 1982, 21 May 1989, and 18 May 1998. We also have the only fall record, 16–18 August 1983. All were lone birds.

Lesser Yellowlegs

Wandering Tattler (*Heteroscelus incanus*) The numbers seen of this species and the next were comparable—rarely did we see more than 4 of either species in a day. (Since most birds called, there were few identification problems.) In 15 of the 22 years (no tattlers were seen in 1977), we recorded more individuals of this species, but 7 was the maximum for any one day, on 4 June 1987.

Gray-tailed Tattler (*Heteroscelus brevipes*) On 30 May 1983, we saw a single flock of 35 birds fly over Alexai Point, and we recorded a total of 77 birds on that day. The next highest total was 11 birds on 30 May 1986. Interestingly, we did not record this species in 1998.

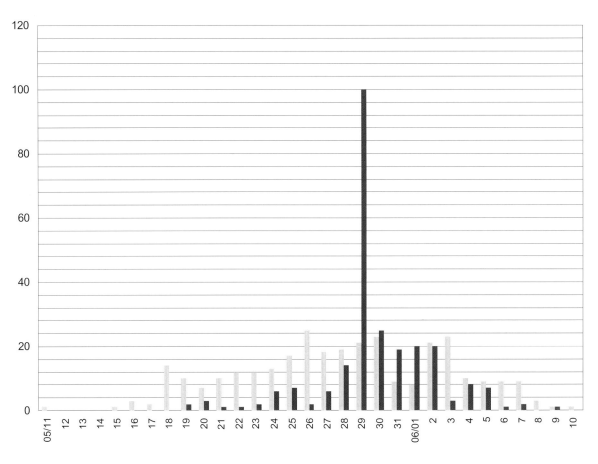

23-year Tattler Totals for Dates

Wandering Tattler   Gray-tailed Tattler

Common Sandpiper (*Actitis hypoleucos*) The usual daily count was less than half a dozen, but occasionally we would see more than 10 in a day, with a maximum count of 20 on 1 June 1999. We missed this species only in 1977 and 1978. Our only fall record was 2 birds seen on 4 September 2000.

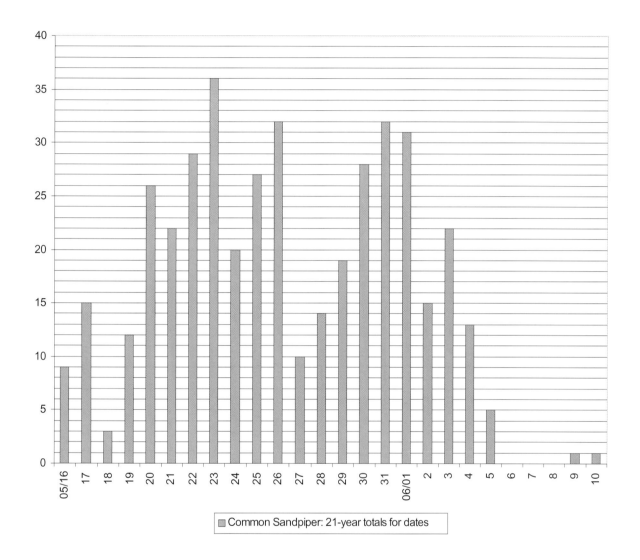

Terek Sandpiper (*Xenus cinereus*) A highlight of our observations was a flock of 14 of these charming birds at Smew Pond on 30 May 1983 (there were 3 others elsewhere that day). Yet on 25 May 1980, we recorded an even higher total, 21. Otherwise, we rarely saw more than 2 in a day, all the last week of May and the first week of June, on 9 spring trips. I estimate that apart from the groups of 17 and 21 noted already, we recorded a total of about 20 other individuals.

Whimbrel (*Numenius phaeopus variegatus*) We saw this Asian form in every year but 1992, although in 1988 we saw only one. Rarely did we see as many as 4 in a day, but saw a notable total of 25 on 21 May 1981. Fall records: 18 September 1979; 13–14 September 1983.

Bristle-thighed Curlew (*Numenius tahitiensis*) Four birds flew over us on 29 May 1986. The other records were all of lone birds on the ground on Murder Point: 17 May 1984; 2–4 June 1993; 16 May 1999; and 22 May 1999.

Far Eastern Curlew (*Numenius madagascariensis*) On only one day, 21 May 1998, did we record as many as 2 birds. The 16 individuals we recorded on 10 spring trips were seen mostly in the last week of May and the first week of June.

Black-tailed Godwit (*Limosa limosa*) We saw this species between 19 May and 10 June on 12 of the 20 spring trips before 1998, but never more than 3 birds per trip. Then in 1998 we had an unusual influx of birds beginning with 3 on 19 May, peaking at 35 on 22 May, and tapering off until the last one was seen on 6 June.

Bar-tailed Godwit (*Limosa lapponica*) We recorded this species every year, occasionally seeing good-sized flocks of more than 40 birds. However, the numbers were highly variable. Thus, we saw only 1 individual in each of the years 1988 and 1994, but recorded at least 145 altogether in 1998, 130 of them on 24 May. I estimate that we saw a total of 620 to 670 individuals on the 23 spring trips, with the distribution centered around 23 May.

Ruddy Turnstone (*Arenaria interpres*) This species was seen every spring and on every fall trip. In the spring, daily counts were usually under 10, but sometimes we had larger numbers (*e.g.*, 107 on 3 June 1987, 50 on 21 May 1999). We saw larger numbers, on average, in the fall. Our largest fall total was 121 birds on 27 September 1993.

Great Knot (*Calidris tenuirostris*) There are two records of single birds on Alexai Point: 21–22 May 1998 and 4 June 2000.

Red Knot (*Calidris canutus*) On 20 and 22 May 1979, we saw one bird in Henderson Marsh. We never recorded the species again.

Sanderling (*Calidris alba*) Spring records: 16 May 1982; 30 May 1982; 18–21 May 1994. Fall records: 18 September 1983; 4–8 October 1993; in 2000: 1 on 19 September, 26–28 September, and 2 on 1–2 October.

Semipalmated Sandpiper (*Calidris pusilla*) One bird on 27 May 1980 is the only record.

Western Sandpiper (*Calidris mauri*) There are three spring records: 20 May 1982; 3–4 June 1984; 6 June 1998. In the fall of 1983, we counted 1–3 on 13 days between 18 August and 24 September, inclusive. There was also a fall record of 1 bird on 8 September 2000.

Red-necked Stint (*Calidris ruficollis*) We did not see this species in 1985, 1989, 1993, 2000, or the fall of 1993. In most years, we saw only a few individuals, but in 1983, we recorded our largest number, with 47 individuals present on 30 May. Then again in 1991, numbers were large, with over 30 birds arriving on 22 May.

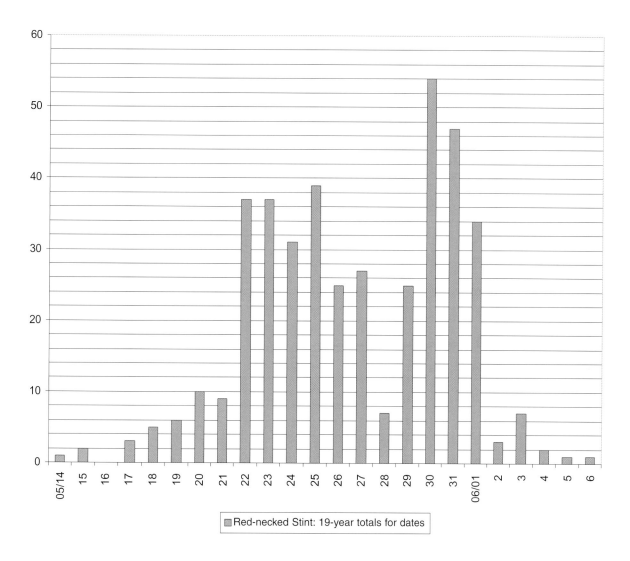

Red-necked Stint: 19-year totals for dates

Little Stint (*Calidris minuta*) A bird on 23–25 May 1991 was our only spring record. We saw 1 to 3 individuals each day 5–7 September 1983.

Temminck's Stint (*Calidris temminckii*) In 1979, 1982, 1984, and 1999, we had a total of 7 individuals, recording the species on 7 different dates. In 1981, however, there were as many as 14 in a day, from 22 to 31 May. On 22 May 1991, 40+ birds arrived, and some stayed through 30 May. Another large group was present 16–26 May 1998, with a maximum of 35 on 17 May. A lone bird 3–6 June 1998 was the latest spring record. In the fall of 1983, we saw 2 birds: one present for 3 days beginning 30 August, and another present 13–17 September.

Long-toed Stint (*Calidris subminuta*) This is the one stint that never failed to appear each spring. We never saw more than 20 in a day (and usually less than half a dozen) until the flood of birds of many species in 1998. Our only fall records were single birds on 3–4 and 11 September 2000.

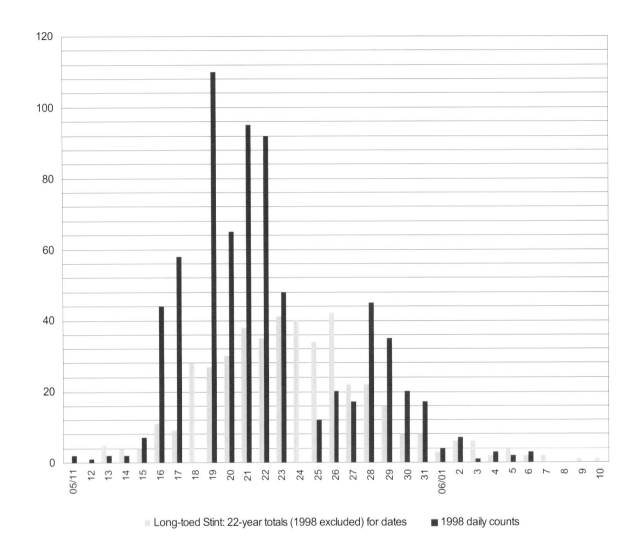

Long-toed Stint: 22-year totals (1998 excluded) for dates ■ 1998 daily counts

Baird's Sandpiper (*Calidris bairdii*) One bird on 1–2 June 1985 was the only spring record. Fall records are: 25 and 29 August 1983; 2 on 31 August 1983, with 1 the next day; 24–25 September 1993; 30 September–1 October 1993.

Pectoral Sandpiper (*Calidris melanotos*) This species was uncommon in spring—we saw a grand total of 10 individuals in 8 different years, the dates ranging from 19 May to 6 June. It was very common in fall, however. We recorded it from 1 September to 9 October, with the largest numbers the third and fourth weeks of September. For example, we had maximums of 63 on 18 September 1979, 19 on 19 September 1983, and 37 on 24 September 1993. In September 2000 we recorded two waves of the largest numbers of all: 78 birds on the 18th dwindled away over a period of days, and then suddenly on the 23rd, we counted 466! The next day we could find only 8.

Sharp-tailed Sandpiper (*Calidris acuminata*) The pattern of occurrence of this species was quite like that of the Pectoral Sandpiper, but in much smaller numbers. Thus, fall daily maximums were 6 in 1979, 18 in 1983, 10 in 1993, and 16 in 2000. In spring, we saw a total of 10 individuals on 6 trips, with dates ranging from 19 May to 7 June.

Rock Sandpiper (*Calidris ptilocnemis*) This very common breeder was found wherever we went. We even found a nest above the vegetation line near the top of 1,550-foot Weston Mountain!

Dunlin (*Calidris alpina*) We recorded Dunlins in fair numbers on every trip except spring 1992. Spring dates ranged from 16 May to 8 June, fall from 19 August to 27 September. Many more birds were observed in spring than in fall, when the maximum daily count was 9 birds on 17 September 2000. By contrast, the median high daily count for 23 spring trips was 10, with the three highest being 51 on 21 May 1987, 83 on 22 May 1998, and 115 on 22 May 1999.

Curlew Sandpiper (*Calidris ferruginea*) There are two records: a pair of birds on 20 May 1982, and one bird on 5 June 1996.

Spoonbill Sandpiper (*Eurynorhynchus pygmeus*) We saw three individuals in 1986, between 30 May and 3 June. Two birds were together on the north shore of Casco Cove, and at the same time, there was a third bird at Alexai Point. These represent the fourth North American record.

Buff-breasted Sandpiper (*Tryngites subruficollis*) Fall records only: 3 on 15 September 1979; 1 on 19 September 1983; and 1 from 3–8 September 2000, joined by a second bird on the last day.

Ruff (*Philomachus pugnax*) This species was seen on 14 spring trips, but never more than 3 birds in a day. Dates ranged from 14 May to 8 June. Similar low numbers were seen on 3 fall trips, with dates ranging from 22 August to 25 September.

Short-billed Dowitcher (*Limnodromus griseus*) There are two spring records: 22 May 1994 and 19–22 May 1997.

Long-billed Dowitcher (*Limnodromus scolopaceus*) In spring, we saw a total of 7 individuals on 4 trips, all between 19 May and 25 May. In fall, we saw these birds on every trip, between the dates of 13 September and 1 October, recording a grand total of 28 to 42 individuals on the four fall trips.

Common Snipe (*Gallinago gallinago gallinago*) This regular migrant was seen every spring, on dates ranging from 9 May to 10 June. Daily counts were usually in single digits, but ranged up to 35 in years other than 1998, when the count was 50 on 19 May 1998. This was deemed to be a distinct species from Wilson's Snipe *G. delicata* by the AOU in 2002. We often saw birds engaging in courtship flights.

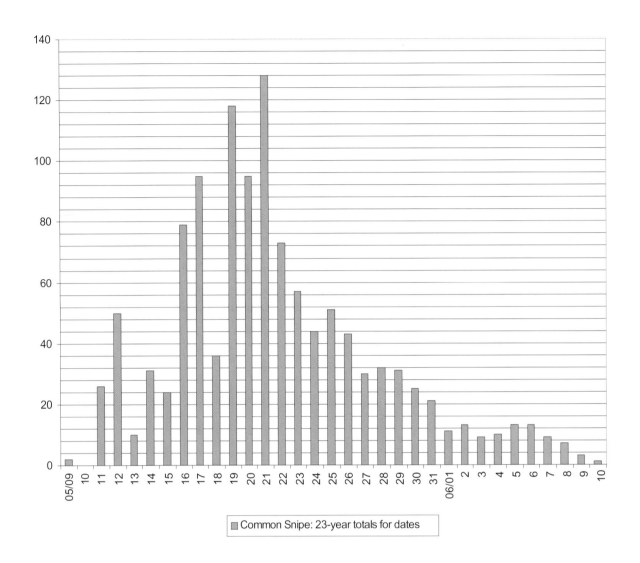

Common Snipe: 23-year totals for dates

Pin-tailed Snipe (*Gallinago stenura*) Both of the ABA Checklist "certain" records for North America are of specimens from Attu: 25 May 1991 and 19 May 1998. However, we also have sight records on 25–26 May 1984 and 30 May 1998. The calls, behavior, and microhabitat preferences of the latter two birds were identical to those of the specimen birds.

Red-necked Phalarope (*Phalaropus lobatus*) These were seen on 14 spring trips, all before 1993. Except for 9 birds on 4–5 June 1981, all daily counts were under 5. In fall, a total of 5 individuals was seen throughout September 1983, and the same number throughout September 2000. A juvenile was seen 14 September 1979.

Red Phalarope (*Phalaropus fulicaria*) Records of 11 individuals were distributed over eight springs, between 25 May and 11 June. Our chances of seeing this species in fall were much greater—we saw it on every trip, on more days per trip, and in greater numbers. Maximum daily counts for the four fall trips were 125 on 24 September 1979, 21 on 19 September 1983, 157 on 3 October 1993, and 10 on 26 September 2000.

Oriental Pratincole (*Glareola maldivarum*) The one we saw on 19–20 May 1985 accounts for the first North American record.

Pomarine Jaeger (*Stercorarius pomarinus*) Occasionally we would see jaegers flying over land, particularly the next two species, but most of them were observed from the Murder Point sea watch site. Not surprisingly, the order of decreasing abundance seemed to be Parasitic, Pomarine, and Long-tailed. Excluding 27 May 1987 (see below), the total numbers of individuals recorded on all our trips for these species are 378, 249, and 149, respectively, and the numbers of days on which each was recorded are 118, 58, and 34, respectively. On particular days, or course, any one of the three species might turn out to be most common. For Pomarine Jaegers, the peak count was 27 on 27 May 1987. Skimming our daily counts, it is quite evident that the likelihood of seeing jaegers dropped noticeably beginning in 1991: in the 10 years beginning in 1981, 182 individual Pomarines were seen, but in the next 10 years, only 45 were seen despite the fact that the number of people watching was often higher during the latter period.

Parasitic Jaeger (*Stercorarius parasiticus*) The peak count of this species was 46 on 27 May 1987. The 1980s/1990s numbers are 273 and 83 respectively.

Long-tailed Jaeger (*Stercorarius longicaudus*) The peak count of this species was 212 (!) on 27 May 1987. The 1980s/1990s numbers (with 27 May 1987 excluded) are 132/16.

Black-headed Gull (*Larus ridibundus*) Except in 1979, daily counts were usually less than half a dozen. In 1979, we had a flock of 22 visit on 21 May. In the spring, the species seemed as likely to appear on one date as on any other. The only fall record was a bird present 22–28 September 2000.

Black-tailed Gull (*Larus crassirostris*) The first North American record that did not bear the stigma of possibly being ship-assisted was a bird off South Beach on 29 May 1980. Our second record was near Barbara Point on 14 May 2000.

Mew (Kamchatka) Gull (*Larus canus kamtschatschensis*) A grand total of 12 individuals was seen in 9 years in spring; 1 was seen on the fall trips of both 1993 and 2000.

Herring Gull (*Larus argentatus*) Lone birds were seen on 18 spring trips, and in fall in both 1979 and 1993. We never saw more than 3 in a day; they were likely to occur on almost any date. Some of these birds were identified as *L. a. vegae*, and it is likely that they all are.

Slaty-backed Gull (*Larus schistisagus*) Occasionally, we would see two of these in one day, and once (21 May 1992) we saw 4. We missed the species on only two spring trips—1978 and 1980—and in the fall of 1979 and 1993. It was likely to occur on any date. Most birds seen were adults, but a juvenile was seen in the fall of 1983. From about 1986 until we left in 2000, an adult could regularly be seen on Puffin Island. That suggests that many of our records in those years were of the same individual. After considering the dates on which we recorded more than one bird, it appears that a minimum of 13 other individuals was seen in that period.

Glaucous-winged Gull (*Larus glaucescens*) Common breeding species.

Glaucous Gull (*Larus hyperboreus*) Lone birds were seen on 19 spring trips, and in fall in both 1983 and 1993. Never more than 3 present in a day, they were likely to occur on almost any date.

Sabine's Gull (*Xema sabini*) We saw 6 individuals during sea watches on 5 dates (one fall) in 1989, 1991, and 1993.

Black-legged Kittiwake (*Rissa tridactyla*) In addition to being seen during sea watches, this species often gathered by the hundreds just off the mouth of the Peaceful River, particularly in the fall.

Red-legged Kittiwake (*Rissa brevirostris*) Except for one adult bird that was standing on an Alexai beach, these birds were seen during sea watches in the spring. Most were immatures. At the distances involved, they were the easiest to distinguish. A grand total of 57 individuals was recorded during the 20 years in which they were seen, with a maximum count of 11 on 4 June 1981.

Ross's Gull (*Rhodostethia rosea*) On 20 May 1999, an adult bird floated for several hours just off the East Massacre Valley beach. This is our only record, but there is a spring record from nearby Nizki Island.

Common (River) Tern (*Sterna hirundo longipennis*) Up to 6 birds a day (30 May to 1 June, 1986) were seen on 8 different spring trips. I estimate that a grand total of 28 individual birds was sighted.

Arctic Tern (*Sterna paradisaea*) We used to see small numbers (1–5) of these every spring in the 1980s. In the 1990s, our only spring record was 27 May 1992. There are three fall records: 2 on 17 September 1983; 2 on 2 September 2000; and one on 14 September 2000.

Aleutian Tern (*Sterna aleutica*) The median arrival date of this resident species was 19 May. Their nesting site is around the runway ponds. In 1980, the large number of Coast Guard dogs disturbed the site frequently, which is why the number of dogs was reduced at first to 3, and then to 1. The birds returned, and we often saw them on the runway with minnows, in courtship displays. Our maximum daily counts for each year are shown below.

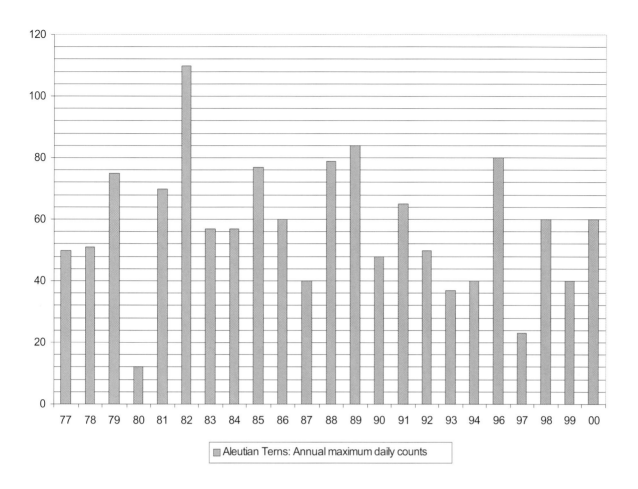

(chart x-axis labels) 77 78 79 80 81 82 83 84 85 86 87 88 89 90 91 92 93 94 96 97 98 99 00

Aleutian Terns: Annual maximum daily counts

White-winged Tern (*Chlidonias leucopterus*) One was on Alexai 19–21 May 1994. This is one of only 3 Alaska records.

Common Murre (*Uria aalge*) This common breeding species could be found every day in Massacre Bay. When birds were close enough to distinguish them from the next species, it was so unusual to find Thick-billed Murre that we counted all murre individuals as "Common" unless they were clearly Thick-billeds. Since it was such a common species, we often just checked it off instead of estimating the numbers for the day. However, when large numbers were present, we were often inspired to count them. The highest figures we obtained were, in spring, 1,400 on 6 June 1998, and in fall, 800 on 9 September 2000.

Thick-billed Murre (*Uria lomvia*) The largest number we saw in one day was 11 on 1 June 1997, and we could not always determine that this species was present in Massacre Bay.

Pigeon Guillemot (*Cepphus columba*) This species, along with Common Murre, was the most commonly seen. The typical maximum daily count for a year was around several dozen.

Marbled Murrelet (*Brachyramphus marmoratus*) This species was more likely to be seen in the vicinity of Murder Point than out in the middle of Massacre Bay, where the other murrelets were. It occurred in far fewer numbers as well. Our maximum daily count was 44 on 4 June 1996, and again on 17 September 2000. Usually, we saw fewer than 10 a day.

We once went by Zodiac to examine this species closely, as there was a question whether Long-billed Murrelet (*B. perdix*) might be found at Attu. We looked carefully enough from land to be confidant in saying that *perdix* does not regularly occur in the Massacre Bay-Krasni Point area.

Kittlitz's Murrelet (*Brachyramphus brevirostris*) These birds would often feed in Massacre Bay, at times in large numbers. Several times, we counted more than 200 individuals in the bay at once. Our grand total for all days, all years, is over 4 times as large as for Marbled Murrelets. Usually when we arrived at Attu, most Kittlitz's Murrelets were in transitional plumage, still with white faces that made identification easy at a distance.

Ancient Murrelet (*Synthliboramphus antiquus*) Our most common murrelet, this species was found not only well out in the bay, but also frequently very close to beaches. The daily count was often in the hundreds, our peak being 610 on 28 May 1998. For an idea of the relative abundance of the three murrelet species, the mean number seen per observation day, for all 23 years, for MM : KM : AM was 7.5 : 22.4 : 52.7.

Ancient Murrelet

Murrelet Numbers, Totals by Date, 23 Years

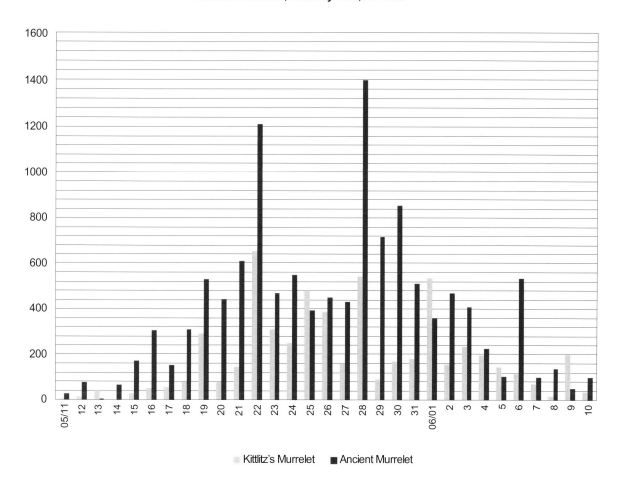

Kittlitz's Murrelet   ■ Ancient Murrelet

Parakeet Auklet (*Aethia psittacula*) Occasionally, auklets appeared near shore, anywhere from Barbara Point around to South Beach, and even in Casco Cove. Records for this species are: 2 on 25 May 1988; 4 June 1996; 4 September 2000; and 2 on 24 September 2000.

Least Auklet (*Aethia pusilla*) We had 6 records of an odd bird or two in the last week of May. Most interesting, however, were our sightings in the last two weeks of September, 2000, when we saw this species from sea watches on Murder Point on 6 occasions. Our two highest counts in that period were 250 on 22 September and 9,000 (!) on 23 September.

Whiskered Auklet (*Aethia pygmaea*) An immature bird was seen at close range in heavy waves breaking on shore (approximating this species' favored rip-tide habitat?) on the south side of Murder Point, 31 May 1982. Another bird was seen 14 September 2000 from the Murder Point sea watch.

Crested Auklet (*Aethia cristatella*) We saw this auklet on 31 spring days in 13 years, and on 10 fall days in 1993 and 2000. Most often, we saw lone birds, but on 9 September 2000, we saw 8.

Horned Puffin (*Fratercula corniculata*) The closest nesting colony of this species is at Savage Island, west of Krasni Point. Our daily counts were usually in single digits, but on sea watch days, those counts could move into double digits.

Tufted Puffin (*Fratercula cirrhata*) This common species—hundreds seen per day—nests on the small island next to Barbara Point that we named Puffin Island, and in spots along Gilbert Ridge. There were no noticeable fluctuations in numbers over the years.

Rock Dove (*Columba livia*) I mention this species only because it was so bizarre to be standing outside our dining hall on the sunny morning of 20 May 1989 and when I looked up, to see 2 Rock Doves headed toward me in rapid, direct flight. They flew over and disappeared, going north. Later, Pete Isleib saw them on the ground. He said they walked up to him. He identified them as racing pigeons. I think they lost the race, wherever it was.

Oriental Turtle-Dove (*Streptopelia orientalis*) Two records: 20 May to 10 June, 1989 (third North American record); 26 May to 3 June 1996 (sixth and most recent North American record).

Common Cuckoo (*Cuculus canorus*) We saw a grand total of at least 22 individuals on 10 of the spring trips. Only in 1988 were there more than 2 sighted in a day, the most being 8 on 9 June. Our earliest record was 21 May 1994, but almost all other records were in the first week of June. A few of the birds were hepatic phase. Note that any cuckoo counted simply as "cuckoo *sp*" is included, for counting purposes, with the positively-identified individuals of this species.

Oriental Cuckoo (*Cuculus saturatus*) There are three spring records of single birds: 4 June 1987, 27–30 May 1991, and 3–5 June 2000. The only fall record is one on 12 September 2000.

Snowy Owl (*Nyctea scandiaca*) When we began birding Attu, we could find this species regularly in three areas: up the Peaceful River Valley, up East Massacre Valley, and in the approaches to Alexai Pass. We once found a nest in the first location. We saw them every year through 1992, and then they suddenly became hard to find. In fact, after 1992, even though our coverage was more comprehensive than earlier, we saw only single birds in 1994, 1998, 1999, and 2000. On 28 May 2000 we flushed a Snowy Owl off the bluffs on South Beach and it headed straight out to sea until it was a tiny speck. The bird never veered off its flight path. Agattu was obscured by clouds, but the bird must have been headed in that direction.

Short-eared Owl (*Asio flammeus*) This migrant species was seen every year except 1999. Almost always, the sighting was of a single bird, although on six days we saw two, and once, three. The median arrival date was 20 May.

White-throated Needletail (*Hirundapus caudacutus*) A single bird was seen circling over the runway for almost an hour on 24 May 1978. Exactly six years later, two birds were found coursing back and forth off the tops of the cliffs on the west side of Krasni Point. We watched them all afternoon, and then at dusk, we saw them roosting on nearby cliffs. One bird was seen the next day, and finally, one on 27 May 1984. These are the second and third North American records.

Fork-tailed Swift (*Apus pacificus*) Spring records: 3–4 June 1987; 2 on14 May 1992. Fall record: 1 October 2000.

Great Spotted Woodpecker (*Dendrocopos major*) The first three North American records of this species are from Attu. The first bird was found by a lone observer on 9 October 1985, and it was still present when he left in November. He returned the next April to find a bird in the same location, and had no reason to believe it was not the same individual. It was collected on 27 April 1986. Our tours saw the next one on 21–22 May 1996. We saw different individuals on 10 September 2000 and 5 October 2000.

Brown Shrike (*Lanius cristatus*) One bird on 4 June 1984 was the fourth North American record.

Common Raven (*Corvus corax*) Common breeding species.

Sky Lark (*Alauda arvensis*) This is one of the earliest-arriving passerines, recorded as early as 28 April by our advance staff. We saw up to 10 in a day (17 May 1999), on 17 spring trips, and on every fall trip except 1979. Dates ranged from 28 April to 8 June in the spring, with the highest frequency of occurrences around 21 May. Fall dates were from 11 September to 6 October. On a couple of occasions we saw birds singing on territory as we left Attu in June, leading us to wonder if nesting might take place.

Bank Swallow (*Riparia riparia*) Single birds were seen in 4 years during the first week of June. Atypical was a bird seen 14 May 1977. The only fall record was on 22 September 1983.

Bank Swallow

Winter Wren (*Troglodytes troglodytes*) This species nests in rocky areas and cliff faces near shore, but not in large numbers. We most often saw them along Gilbert Ridge. We rarely recorded more than 10 on a spring day, though we did so frequently in the fall.

Middendorff's Grasshopper-Warbler (*Locustella ochotensis*) The third North American record was six birds, seen 18–25 September 1979. Our only spring record was a single bird seen 10–11 June 2000.

Lanceolated Warbler (*Locustella lanceolata*) A bird found near Barbara Point on 4 June 1984 was the first record for North America. We quickly realized, however, that it was just one of a large group that had strayed to Attu, as over the next 4 days we found them in many places, including as far west as Temnac Valley. There were clearly 25 or more individuals, although the most we counted on any one day was 11 on 8 June, just before we left Attu. Some singing males established territories, and on 9 June, a bird was observed carrying nesting material. Observers who remained on the island after we left last saw the species on 15 July. We had the third North American records in 2000: 2 June and 6 June.

Dusky Warbler (*Phylloscopus fuscatus*) There are two fall records: 21 September 1983 and 2 September 2000.

Arctic Warbler (*Phylloscopus borealis*) This species was recorded on 14 days (all in June) during 7 spring trips, usually more than one per day. Our high daily count was 19 on 3 June 1999. We also recorded one on 23 September 1983, and at least 3 on 21 to 25 September 1979. These birds were presumably *P. b. xanthrodryas*, since some were noticeably more yellowish than the form seen in western Alaska.

Narcissus Flycatcher (*Ficedula narcissina*) A black-backed male bird of the *F. n. narcissina* subspecies was seen on 20–21 May 1989, and another like it on 21 May 1994. They are the only North American records.

Red-breasted Flycatcher (*Ficedula parva*) A bird seen on 1 June 1982 was the third record for North America. Two were present 3 days later. In the following years, we recorded at least 25 individuals on 7 different occasions. Hardly any of these were adult males. On 4 June 1987, we counted 14 individuals, 10 more than we saw on any other day.

Siberian Flycatcher (*Muscicapa sibirica*) The second and third North American records are from Attu: 17 June 1986 and 20 May 1990. We also recorded at least 3 individuals on several days between 1 and 5 June 1999; it is possible that there were up to 7 present.

Gray-spotted Flycatcher (*Muscicapa griseisticta*) On the days when we saw this species (32 days in 11 springs), we usually saw 1–4 individuals. However, the following daily counts are of interest: 13 on 6 June 1986, and 27 on 2 June 1999 (dropping to 11 the next day).

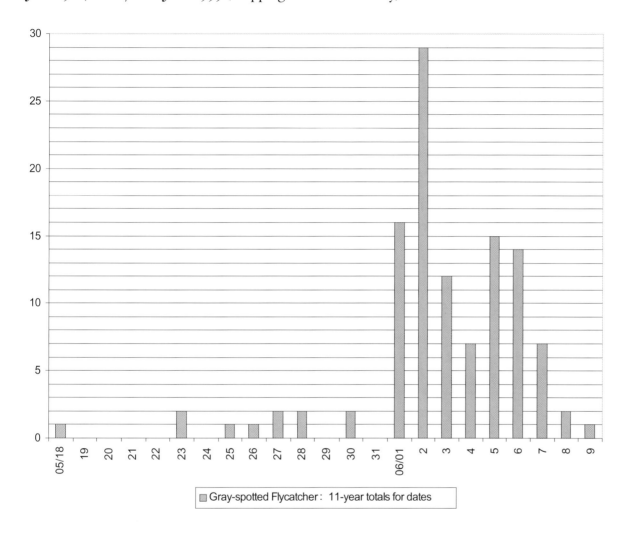

Gray-spotted Flycatcher : 11-year totals for dates

Asian Brown Flycatcher (*Muscicapa dauurica*) A bird at the base of Alexai Point on 25 May 1985 remains the first of only two North American records.

Siberian Rubythroat (*Luscinia calliope*) We missed this attractive species on 4 spring trips, but in the other years, a good fraction of the birds we saw were adult males. We would occasionally see double-digit numbers, such as 21 on 2 June 1999, and 27 (our maximum) on 1 June 1992. This is another species we thought might occasionally breed on Attu, since once, a singing bird was on what appeared to be a territory when we departed the island in early June.

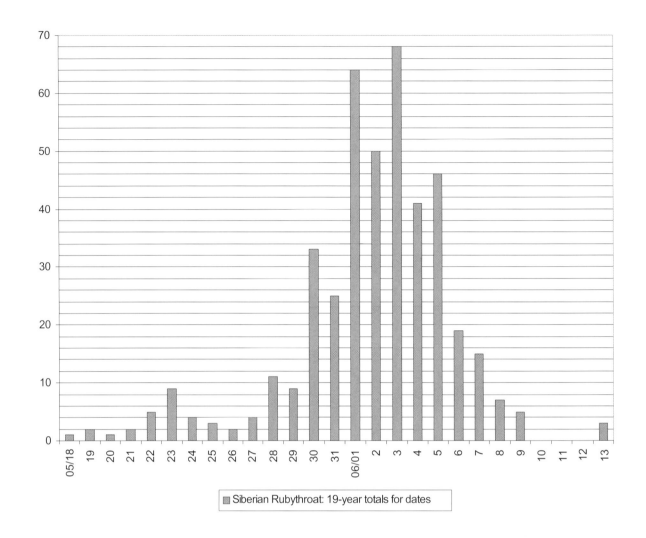

Siberian Rubythroat: 19-year totals for dates

Bluethroat (*Luscinia svecica*) We had not expected to see this species on Attu in the spring, so we were surprised when 4 appeared on 4 June 1987. There was a second record 30 May–1 June 1990, and there were 2 on 9 June 1996. We had two fall records: 1 on each of 2 September and 22 September 2000.

Siberian Blue Robin (*Luscinia cyane*) One bird sighted in a small canyon (since known as Blue Robin Canyon) west of South Beach on 21 May 1985 is the only North American record.

Rufous-tailed Robin (*Luscinia sibilans*) The first bird of this species seen in North America was found 4 June 2000 poking around the tundra at the base of Gilbert Ridge, where it also disappeared for short periods into cave-like spaces under rocks and snow banks. The bird was videotaped pumping its tail rapidly, behavior much like that we observed from the Siberian Blue Robin. Photographs can be seen at <http://www.attu.com/Robins.htm>.

Red-flanked Bluetail (*Tarsiger cyanurus*) Of all 10 North American records, the first was on Attu 5 June 1982. Of the 14 individuals seen in North America since then, 10 were also on Attu. Those records, all of single birds except where noted, are as follows. 1988: 22–23 May, 27 May, 30 May, and

6 June; 5–6 October 1993; 1996: 25 May (2 the next day), 20 May, and 7 June; 31 June 1998; and 2 June 1999.

Northern Wheatear (*Oenanthe oenanthe*) One spring and one fall record: 18 May 1998, and 19 September 1983.

Gray-cheeked Thrush (*Catharus minimus*) One bird on 20 September 1983 is the only record.

Eyebrowed Thrush (*Turdus obscurus*) We missed this species in 1989 and 1992. Our daily counts for the 19 non-1998 years were in single digits, with these exceptions: 10 on 19 May 1982; 12 on 25 May 1983; and 11 on 22 May 1985. Contrast these with the 1998 daily counts shown in the graph below! We had only one bird in fall, on 30 September 1993.

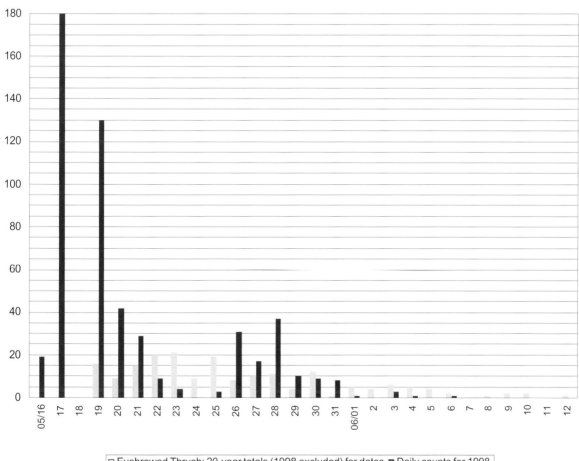

☐ Eyebrowed Thrush: 20-year totals (1998 excluded) for dates ■ Daily counts for 1998

Dusky Thrush (*Turdus naumanni*) Three birds were seen on 20 May 1983. All other spring day counts, on 8 trips, were of single birds, between 13 May and 4 June. It appears that a grand total of 12 individual birds were involved in these spring sightings. A bird seen 20–21 May 2000 was the second Alaska sighting of the nominate race *T. n. naumanni*. We saw 3 birds in the fall: 28 September 1993; 3–8 October 1993; and 1 October 2000.

American Robin (*Turdus migratorius*) On 25 May 1977, while alone near Barbara Point, I spotted a *Turdus* thrush on the ground a short distance ahead of me. I maneuvered to get a good look at it, feeling certain that it must be an Eyebrowed Thrush, which would be a life species for me. I studied it carefully at close range, but could only conclude, to my great disappointment, that it was a female American Robin. Knowing how much more unusual that species would be on Attu than an Eyebrowed Thrush, I documented the sighting and submitted it to regional authorities. They rejected the record, not because of any dissatisfaction with the description or the viewing conditions, but because of my inexperience with Eyebrowed Thrush, and because of the lack of spring records of North American passerine vagrants in the Near Islands. However, since my subsequent experience with many Eyebrowed Thrushes has never shown any of them to have the white corners to the tail that the bird in question showed (as do many American Robins), and since vagrant North American passerines are no longer unknown from Attu (see the warbler below), I think this record deserves mention here.

Yellow Wagtail (*Motacilla flava*) This regular spring migrant was recorded on several days of every spring trip. Daily counts were usually under 10, but occasionally as high as 21 (20 May 1982); in the unusual conditions of 1998, the peak was 29 on 17 May. In addition to the record dates shown below, we had early arrival of a single bird on 2 May 1981. This species was a very uncommon migrant in the fall—we recorded only 3 individuals.

Black-backed Wagtail

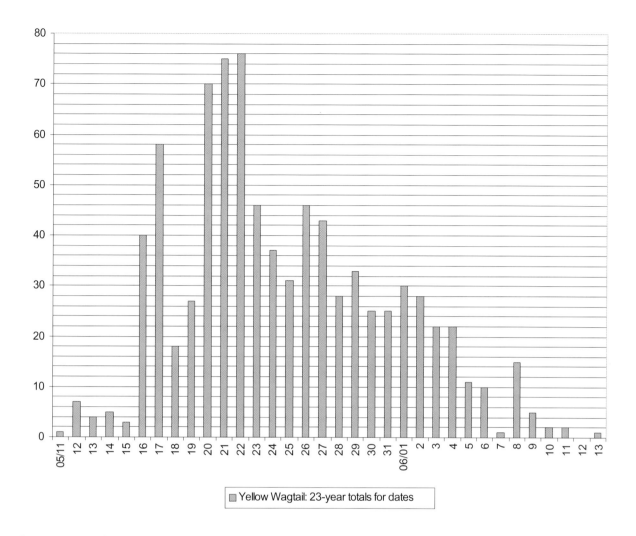

| Yellow Wagtail: 23-year totals for dates |

Gray Wagtail (*Motacilla cinerea*) On 48 days spread from 16 May to 6 June over 13 spring trips, we recorded a grand total of 25 individuals. The median arrival date for the species was 23 May.

White Wagtail (*Motacilla alba*) We have one spring record: 17 May 1988. There is also one fall record: 1 and 2 individuals, 4–8 October 1993.

Black-backed Wagtail (*Motacilla lugens*) A nest of this species was found under a bridge on the Peaceful River by a lone birder one summer in the mid-1980s. In all but three springs, we saw small numbers (up to 7 a day) of these birds in their favorite haunts along the shore from Peaceful River to the Coast Guard warehouse. We recorded it as early as 1 May (1981), but the median arrival date was 16 May. The latest we recorded it in fall was 1 October (2000). Note: the first North American record of this species was collected on Attu on 4 May 1913.

Olive-backed Pipit (*Anthus hodgsoni*) This was another regular Asian migrant, which we saw on 20 spring trips. We recorded more than 6 in a day only three times (setting 1998 aside for the moment): 15 on 17–18 May 1982, 10 on 1 June 1982, and 10 on 21 May 1985. Compare that to the graph below, and it is clear how extraordinary our results were in 1998.

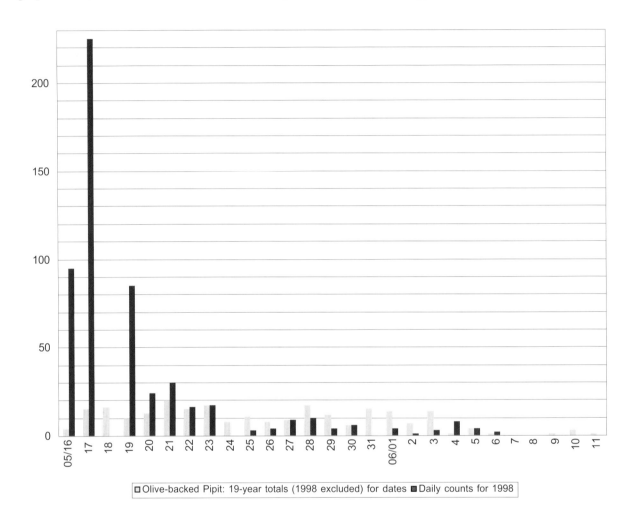

Olive-backed Pipit: 19-year totals (1998 excluded) for dates ▪ Daily counts for 1998

In fall, we saw a total of 4 individuals on three trips, all between 11 and 23 September.

Pechora Pipit (*Anthus gustavi*) Our first sighting of this species, 22 May 1979, was the third North American record. Over the next 12 years we saw 8 or 9 more individuals: single birds 19–21 May 1982 and 1 June 1982; 1–2 birds on 23–24 May and one from 31 May–12 June 1988; one on 25 May and 3 on 29 May 1991. Then with the flood of birds on 17 May 1998 came 7 individuals, some of which lingered on through 30 May.

Red-throated Pipit (*Anthus cervinus*) On 20 May 1979, the third morning of Attour's first official organized trip to Attu, we stepped out of our quarters before breakfast to find ourselves surrounded by these pipits. We counted over 55 that day, which led us to conclude that we were likely to see considerable numbers on future visits to Attu. As with so many predictions about Attu birding, that turned out not to be the case. In fact, we found that, excepting 1979 and 1998, the pattern of occurrence of this species—in counts, frequency of observation, and temporal distribution—was almost identical to that of Olive-backed Pipit. Even in the two exception years, the maximum daily counts for both species occurred on exactly the same day of May. They just differed significantly in size. They were (OBP/RTP): 3/55+ in 1979, and 225/17 in 1998. In fall, however, this species was the more numerous one, and we saw 22 or more individuals from 2 September through 8 October.

American Pipit (*Anthus rubescens*) This was our third-most-frequent pipit, with no wave years, and numbers that were about 80 percent of Olive-backed and Red-throated numbers. Our maximum daily counts were 13 on 21 May 1982, and 11 on "wave day" 17 May 1998. At other times we saw 4 or fewer. This pipit tended to arrive a day or two earlier than the others in spring. In 18 of the 21 years in which we recorded this species, some of the individuals were the distinctive Asian subspecies *A. r. japonicus*, seen in both spring and fall. Unfortunately, we weren't very assiduous in noting this form in our database, so I don't have firm data to cite. From reconstruction of other sources, however, I can at least say that somewhere between 10 and 30 percent of the birds we saw were this form.

Bohemian Waxwing (*Bombycilla garrulus*) Up to 5 birds were counted on 6 dates between 16 May and 1 June 1983. One was present 20–25 May 1989. The only other sighting was in the fall: 30 September–4 October 1993. The 1989 bird was confirmed as *B. g. centralasiae* (from Asia, of course!), and the others are also believed to be that form.

Yellow-rumped Warbler (*Dendroica coronata auduboni*) This was our only spring North American passerine vagrant, unless one also counts American Robin. This bright little jewel of a bird, an adult male, was foraging along the shore below Gilbert Ridge on 26 May 1980.

Savannah Sparrow (*Passerculus sandwichensis*) There are two fall records of single birds: 9 September 1983, and 21 September 2000.

Fox Sparrow (*Passerella iliaca*) One bird on 24 September 1993 is the only record.

Song Sparrow (*Melospiza melodia maxima*) This large, dark subspecies found from Attu east to Atka could be found everywhere along the shoreline, where it is a year-round resident. Unprepared birders seeing it for the first time might not recognize it immediately, but its identity would be clear as soon as it began to sing.

Golden-crowned Sparrow (*Zonotrichia atricapilla*) There were sightings of single birds on 19 September 1979, 23 September 1983, and 3 October 1993.

Lapland Longspur (*Calcarius lapponicus*) This is the most common land bird on Attu. Our advance staff recorded arrivals in the first week of May, when large flocks were often seen flying in from off shore. After the nesting season, they would begin to flock together late in September, peaking at about the end of the month before departing the island for their winter quarters. On our latest date, 10 October, some were still present, although numbers were declining noticeably at that time. In 1983, we first saw the subspecies *C. l. coloratus*, which is found on the Kamchatka Peninsula and Commander Islands. Its call note is different, and it has more black on the head than the Attu form. We saw this form on at least two other trips.

Pine Bunting (*Emberiza leucocephalos*) The only two North American records are single individuals from Attu: 18–19 November 1985, and one bird-of-the-year, 6 October 1983.

Little Bunting (*Emberiza pusilla*) There is a single-person report of this species by a respected observer (Pete Isleib), on 19–20 September 1983. Birding alone, he found it on the 19th. When we returned on the 20th, the bird was located again, but only a couple of people got marginal looks at it as it flushed and flew away.

Rustic Bunting (*Emberiza rustica*) A very reliable migrant, this species appeared in every year but 1997. However, the numbers were highly variable—in 13 springs we never saw more than 2 in a day, but in some years we had much larger numbers. Examples would be 64 on 18 May 1982; 37 on 18 May 1985; and 32 on 20 May 1988. Then there was 1998 (see below). We found Rustic Buntings only twice in the fall: 2 birds on 23 September 1983, and 1 on 1 October 2000.

Lapland Longspur

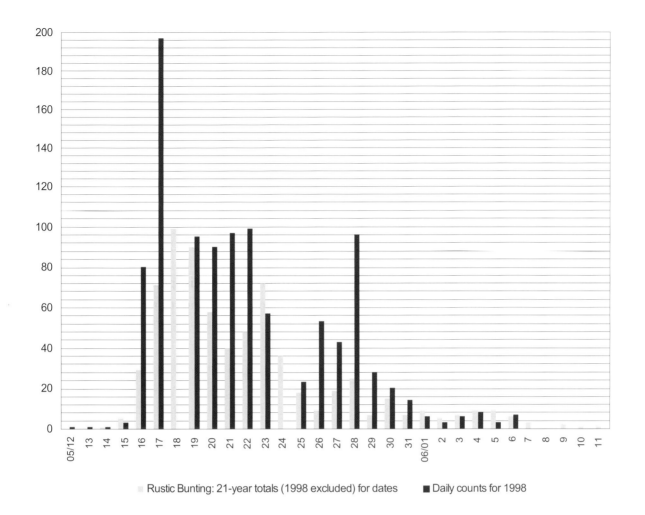

Rustic Bunting: 21-year totals (1998 excluded) for dates   Daily counts for 1998

Yellow-throated Bunting (*Emberiza elegans*) The only North American record is a male we saw in Blue Robin Canyon on 25 May 1998.

Yellow-breasted Bunting (*Emberiza aureola*) The second (first authenticated) North American record is of a male we saw near the airport on 26 May 1988. Another male was seen at South Beach on 27 May 1996.

Gray Bunting (*Emberiza variabilis*) The second of 2 North American records was a bird near Big Lake 29 May 1980.

Reed Bunting (*Emberiza schoeniclus*) Of 8 unquestioned Reed Buntings seen in North America, 6 were seen on Attu: 27 May 1977 (second N.A. record); 22–24 May 1987; 3 between 25 May and 1 June 1989; and 5 June 1992. The last record does not appear on the *ABA Checklist* for some reason. The bird was a well-marked immature male with rufous wing coverts, well seen at the tower ponds. At one point, it sat on top of the marsh grass and sang for half a minute. Only the first of these was a male in breeding plumage. While the Sixth Edition of the *ABA Checklist* claims that a bird seen well on Attu for a whole week at the end of May 1980 was a female of this species, I am not aware that the serious identification problems connected with this record have been satisfactorily resolved.

Snow Bunting (*Plectrophenax nivalis*) I would judge this to be the second-most-common land bird on Attu. In general, it would return from its winter quarters earlier than Lapland Longspur (e.g., 150+ recorded on 24 April 1979). Fall flocks would depart at about the same time as longspurs did.

Brambling (*Fringilla montifringilla*) Numbers could fluctuate wildly from year to year, with only one bird seen in 1984, hundreds in other years. Consider these high daily counts: 145+ on 20 May 1980; 122 seen on 17 May 1988. However, even these did not compare to 1998, as you can see below. In the fall, we recorded it between 11 September and 7 October, and in much smaller numbers, the peak being 20 on 23 September 1983. On 8 June, 1997. Paul Sykes, one of our leaders, discovered a male Brambling singing from territorial perches and interacting with a female. The next day he located a nest with 2 eggs, and on 10 June, the nest contained 3 eggs. Unfortunately, our scheduled departure on 11 June kept us from learning the fate of this only recorded North American nesting effort.

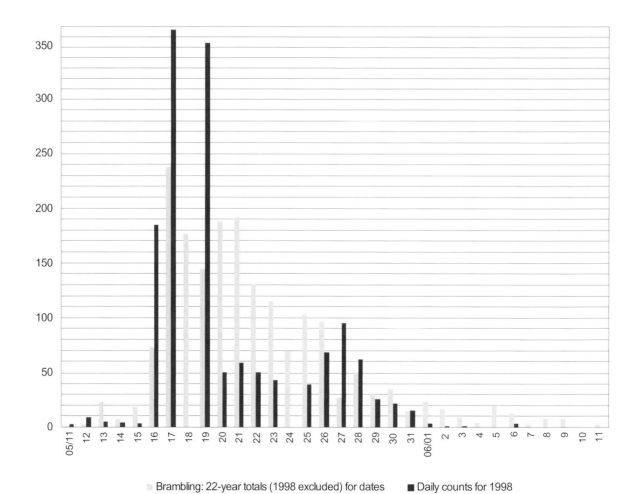

Brambling: 22-year totals (1998 excluded) for dates   ■ Daily counts for 1998

Gray-crowned Rosy-Finch (*Leucosticte tephrocotis*) This is a fairly common breeding bird on Attu. When abandoned Navy buildings were still standing, these birds often nested inside buildings. They would build new nests on top of the previous year's nest, until some structures would be 5 or 6 nests high. As the buildings collapsed, the species became less common near our base. We normally recorded up to two dozen a day. This species seemed to arrive at about the same time as the longspurs and Snow Buntings. Thus, advance staff noted 30 on 23 April 1979 and 50 on 4 May 1980. It seemed to flock and depart later in the fall. In 1993, for example, just before our latest-ever departure, we counted 95 rosy-finches on 8 October, but we saw only 11 longspurs and 24 buntings.

Pine Grosbeak (*Pinicola enucleator*) Two records, each of single birds sighted 22–28 May 1983; and 9–10 June 1989.

Common Rosefinch (*Carpodacus erythrinus*) We recorded a grand total of 14 individuals, from sightings on 14 days in 6 different years. The few that came all arrived 31 May or later. On 3 June 2000, we sighted 7 birds (our maximum count), which drifted away over the next 10 days.

White-winged Crossbill (*Loxia leucoptera*) A lone birder who spent three summers on Attu, roaming over the island, reported finding one of these far from our normal haunts.

Common Redpoll (*Carduelis flammea*) Both redpoll species presumably breed in small numbers on Attu. We normally found them in willow thickets well up West Massacre Valley, but we missed both species on about a third of our spring trips. We never recorded more than 7 of this species in a day, except in fall, when we saw up to 16 a day in 2000, and up to 80 in 1993. These high totals were both in the last week of September.

Hoary Redpoll (*Carduelis hornemanni*) Members of this species were more numerous than Common Redpolls. In the spring, we occasionally recorded daily counts of 1–2 dozen, with a peak of 50 on 23 May 1993. Fall counts ranged up to 50 per day. Almost all birds noted in October were Hoary Redpolls.

Eurasian Siskin (*Carduelis spinus*) Most records of this species in North America are suspect, because of questions about whether the birds are of wild origin. But there is no such question about our two Attu sightings: 1 bird on 4 June 1978, and 2 on 21 May 1993 (one bird remained on 22–23 May).

Oriental Greenfinch (*Carduelis sinica*) The first North American record was a flock of 6 seen on Attu by a group of three birders led by Paul Sykes. Our trips recorded a grand total of 18 individuals, seen on 8 spring trips with dates ranging from 14 May through 7 June. On 28 May 1991, we saw 5 individuals.

Eurasian Bullfinch (*Pyrrhula pyrrhula*) There are three records, all of single birds: 18–21 May 1978; 10 June 1996; and 14–15 May 2000.

Hawfinch (*Coccothraustes coccothraustes*) Finally, we come to the elusive Hawfinch—the bird that frustrated so many people by seemingly never staying put and that was the object of the infamous 1978 "Hawfinch Death March", when Northeast Birding's small group of people hoofed it at top speed all the way from West Massacre Valley to the south end of Casco Cove, only to be given the bad news from me: "The last time I saw it, it was gone."

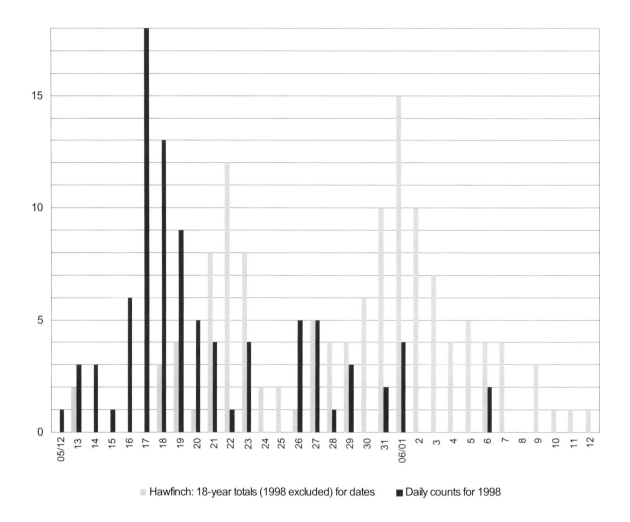

■ Hawfinch: 18-year totals (1998 excluded) for dates   ■ Daily counts for 1998

This graph tells most of the story of the approximately 60 individual Hawfinches seen in non-1998 years, and the 25–30+ birds we saw in 1998. Some additional information: the 5 years in which we did not see Hawfinches were all prior to 1986; except in 1998, we rarely saw more than 3 of them.

P.S.: Although our trips to Attu ended on 5 October 2000, we've managed to add one new species to the Attu list. On 26 August 2001, Thede Tobish and I, and about 25 ABA members, traveled by ship along the south side of Attu, perhaps 2–3 miles off shore. Even though we were in dense fog, we saw approximately 40 Mottled Petrels, *Pterodroma inexpectata.*

Near the Peaceful River, May 1988

Closing the Circle

Photo: Ed Harper

Where the battle raged

A Remembrance

Bill and Ruth Brooks

Bill and Ruth Brooks,
September 2000

Birding on Attu in the fall is quite different than in spring. The island is green, not brown, and the vegetation is a lot higher, giving the birds better cover. The migration season is longer, with lower numbers of birds arriving over a longer period of time. The generally warmer weather, with snowless ground, allows access to parts of the island that are inaccessible in the spring to both birders and birds, which in the spring tend to be concentrated near the coast. The pace of birding is, in general, less frenetic.

On 9 September 2000, a warm and generally birdless day, a group of twenty or so decided to take their bikes and head into the interior of the island to look for ptarmigan and Snowy Owls, which had been reported earlier. We also wanted to make the trek up to see the monument the Japanese had built in 1987 to commemorate the war dead in the North Pacific.

This was to be an unhurried all-day trip and we set out in high spirits under the leadership of Mike Toochin. The ride on gravel roads was not overly arduous for anyone who spent a lot of time on a bike but most of us chose to walk the significant hills, pushing our bikes some of the way.

Among the participants was Frank Brown from Seattle. An avid historian, Frank had spent a lot of time studying the war in the Aleutians. On this particular trip up Engineer Hill, Frank recounted the details of the battle of Attu, pointing out the various positions formerly held by both sides and describing the flow of the battle. He made our trek fascinating.

John LaVia and his two sons, Jay and Vernon, were among the 70 plus people on the fall Attu trip. The boys had given their father the trip as a retirement present and the trio were among the most enthusiastic of birders. On this particular day, John and Vernon had elected to join the trip to the monument while Jay chose to go to Alexai Point in the hopes of spotting some new bird that might have dropped in overnight.

The group had biked in a good distance and had stopped at the crest of a hill to rest. While the monument was not yet in sight, the long final hill in the approach was. Some folks set out across the tundra with Mike in search of birds while the rest of us relaxed, some standing, others sitting or lying in the grass beside the road. John LaVia lay down in the road on his back, which appeared a bit extreme and rather uncomfortable. Moments later he began making snoring type noises and I remember marveling at how quickly people can fall asleep in the strangest of places and feeling a bit envious of his apparent skill in this regard. I was about to comment to someone when Bill Johnson, a nurse, walked by and heard the sounds. He recognized something amiss and became alarmed. He called John by name and when there was no response, shook him gently. Again there was no response. To his credit, Bill knew that something was drastically wrong and asked if there were people who were skilled in CPR. Ruth Brooks volunteered and while Bill Johnson performed chest compressions Ruth gave mouth-to-mouth resuscitation. Ruth remembers it thusly:

"When Bill shouted, 'Who knows CPR'? I didn't stop to think, I just responded. I had my mouth full of granola bar, which I started spitting out as I ran to Bill, asking, "What do you want me to do?' It had been a few years since my last CPR training but I knew I would remember. Oddly, in the weeks before the trip, I had struggled with the thought that I really ought to take a refresher course in CPR before returning to Attu. Bill took charge and coordinated his chest compressions with my efforts with the mouth-to-mouth. It took all I had to concentrate on my breathing and timing. I remember being very concerned that my breath was going into John's stomach rather than into his lungs. Several people helped me to see his chest movement and removed some of my clothes as I worked up a sweat.

Vernon knelt beside his father praying and begging him to live. I had such a hard time hearing him thank me as I concentrated on my breath. I wanted to respond to him, comfort him, cry—something—but I didn't dare. At one point John vomited into my mouth. I spit it out, asked for some Kleenex and went back to the CPR. It felt like everyone was gone but John and me, that we were alone. I knew there were people around us; some were encouraging, praying, counting or offering to help. I had to keep my mind on John. Bill was completely professional. He appeared, to me, to have the situation in hand. He gave me the confidence that we were doing all we could."

Attempts to get help were agonizingly slow and frustrating. Mike was off on the tundra and it took some time for him to recognize that there was a serious problem and to get back to the scene. He took charge of trying to communicate with base camp. Unfortunately the area we were in was out of the line of sight range of the radios so Mike had to climb up a nearby hill to be able to communicate. There was considerable radio interference from the fishing fleet, which made it extremely difficult for base to hear.

Mike tried valiantly to convey the message that we had a man down, that it was an emergency and that we needed help immediately. The hope was that the Coast Guard could be summoned to provide assistance. At any rate the process of summoning aid was agonizingly slow and incredibly frustrating. People at base were under the impression that Mike was the man down and someone went off to check his medical form because Mike is apparently allergic to something. Eventually that confusion was cleared up and base began the process of summoning the Coast Guard as well as John's other son, Jay, who was several miles away.

Bill Johnson and Ruth continued to work tirelessly over John. Other participants, seeing that they could no longer help, began to move off, some to the monument, others to quiet spots to be alone with their thoughts.

Some forty or so minutes after the CPR process had begun, the Coast Guard arrived in a pickup truck. Ruth continues:

"I have no idea how long it took before the Coast Guard got there with the defibrillator. I was told to back off as they opened his shirt and put the paddles on his chest. After several attempts, it became clear that there was no heart rhythm. It was over, but I couldn't accept it.

We all threw our coats on the truck to pad John's ride back to the Coast Guard station. Bill eased a mask over his face, "bagging" him. The men placed him gently into the truck and drove off over the crest of the hill.

"I didn't know what to do, or where to go. As I looked around, I saw crystal blue skies and soft clouds smiling at me. The lupine and wild iris still bloomed in the tundra mosses. 'What happened here?' I wondered. John just died, and the world is still beautiful? Something is different. I guess it was I."

The Japanese monument took on a new significance for many. With its neighboring shrine, the memorial provided a welcome and comforting spot for many of us to sit and reflect and mourn a fallen comrade.

This monument, dedicated on 1 July 1987, is inscribed (in both Japanese and English) "In memory of all those who sacrificed their lives in the islands and seas of the North Pacific during World War II and in dedication to world peace."

And Just to Think That

Six months ago I was out doing
Extreme birding on Attu Island, Alaska,
Hiking twenty miles over a snowy pass
To see nesting Whooper Swans,
Then biking off to Alexai Point
For the Great Spotted Woodpecker:
Forty miles in one day,
And sure, I felt fatigued, but so did
Everyone else out there. And who

Could know, high up on Murder Point
Doing my open-eye sitting meditation
On the Minke Whales and Sea Otters,
The Tufted Puffins streaking past,
Surf pounding the black volcanic rocks
Below me, misted sunshine? Finding
Five-finger orchids and moonwort,
A Green Sandpiper. Having no idea.

                              —*Macklin Smith*

Closing the Circle

By Jim Burns

Attu Island—the last island in Alaska's Aleutian Island chain, the farthest birding outpost of the United States, is closer to Siberia than to Anchorage. You can get there from here, but just barely, and since Attour ran its last trip in the fall of 2000, Attu is likely to become only a fond and distant memory for a whole generation of North American birders.

Imagine seeing Siberian Rubythroat, Siberian Flycatcher, Gray-spotted Flycatcher, Common Cuckoo, and Hawfinch all on the same day, then waking up the next morning to Eyebrowed Thrush, Red-flanked Bluetail, and Gray Wagtail. Imagine being Larry Balch of Attour, running this birders' boot camp/focus group out of Chicago for more than 25 years, never knowing until the day before liftoff in Anchorage whether Reeve will find a replacement wing for that third Electra, or if fog will preclude the landing of 65 birders and a three-week supply of food and fuel.

When Deva and I made our first once-in-a-lifetime trip to Attu in May 1989 we barely knew what to expect and we did not even think about photography because of weather and weight restriction issues. When we returned a decade later, many things had changed—our birding skills and our knowledge and understanding of photography equipment had grown. But some things never change—Attu is still and always a cold, forbidding birding venue, rubble-strewn yet breathtakingly pristine, immense, and quiet, compressing all the typical joys and frustrations of a birding lifetime into a three-week marathon of exhilaration and fatigue.

For our '99 trip we had done our birding homework and prepared ourselves mentally for the physical challenge. Now we knew a *Tringa* meant greenshank or redshank, not yellowlegs, a *Calidris* with rusty scapulars would be Long-toed Stint, not Least Sandpiper, and a *Calidris* without rusty scapulars would be Temminck's, not Baird's. We also knew now that when the radio in base camp crackled with the report of an Olive-backed Pipit out on Alexai Point, 12 miles through the mud and horizontal rain, we would jump on our bikes and haul—no hesitation, no questions—no tomorrow. And I had room for the 300mm telephoto, ensconced in its Gore-Tex backpack, because I had left at home some of those little amenities like shaving cream, flashlight, and extra polar fleece to allow for the extra weight.

The Attu experience reads like a litany of good news/bad news jokes. The couple with whom you will share an 8- by 12-foot bunker euphemistically called a sleeping room turn out to be delightful people: Just your age and background, they both snore like dying banshees. The heating units in the "sleeping rooms" have been upgraded since '89 from kerosene to electricity, but the walls still ooze moisture so there is always two inches of water on the floor when you roll out of your bunk to urinate in the middle of the night. As you ride through base camp on your way from Alexai Point to the Gray-spotted

Flycatcher in Blue Robin Canyon, the two most widely separated birdable areas of the island, a stream of birders are riding hell-bent-for-glory in the opposite direction because a Gray Wagtail has just been located back on Alexai Point. The bikes have been upgraded since '89 from one-speed rust buckets to new 18-speed mountain bikes, which will be rust buckets at the end your three weeks because of the constant rain, blowing salt air, and derailleur-deep mud on the "trails".

In 1942 the Japanese invaded Attu, capturing it from the scattering of Aleuts and missionaries living there. In 1943 the U.S. Army and Navy collaborated in recapturing the island, subsequently building an extensive military presence. When the Army and Navy left decades ago, leaving the Coast Guard to maintain the runway and Loran station, they left behind several tracts of barracks and offices, both metal and wood, which have since fallen victim to wind, frost, and willow bog. Attour first prospected for Asian vagrants on the island in the spring of 1977. Fall 2000 was the last tour, and Reeve Aleutian Airways anticipates its Electras going the way of the old runways and Quonset huts.

The most resonant and jarring juxtaposition of natural beauty with military/industrial detritus on an island full of such strange contrasts is the mouth of the Peaceful River along the beach at Barbara Point. The Peaceful is born of snowmelt high in the cirques on Terrible Mountain behind base camp. And the water that flows down from a creek on Mount Weston is pure enough to be piped directly into base camp, without treatment, for drinking and cooking needs.

Barbara Point's beach is a long expanse of oceanfront, where the water's edge is littered with kelp and drift logs. The visitor's eye is drawn to spectacular views of the neighboring Aleutian Islands' snow-

The World War II debris that still clutters the beach at Barbara Point, May 2000

capped peaks, and tons of rusted, abandoned army and navy machinery and equipment. One day as our group sat on the overlooking bluff enjoying sack lunches in 40-degree rain mixed with snow, a Red-necked Stint dropped into the kelp and military litter, literally at our feet. My personal best-of-trip bird was the Terek Sandpiper. We recorded half a dozen during our stay, the most memorable the one I photographed atop a huge, brightly rusted cogwheel, a remnant of some giant conveyor system for moving implements in a long-past and largely forgotten war.

It is entirely fitting that southwest winds in spring blow us birds from our once and future rivals across the Pacific Rim. Were it not for the Japanese, the Chinese, and the Russians, the military would not have come here and created this odd habitat nor the access to it—no military presence, no runway, no birders—or certainly very few. One Attu leader, a veteran of many trips, searches for and indeed finds the tour's first Siberian Rubythroat almost every year in Navy Town. The barracks are proven rubythroat habitat now, at least on Attu. It makes you wonder where Rubythroats hang out in their native Siberia. Common Sandpiper: the tide pools along Gilbert Ridge; Black-tailed Godwit: the marshes along the runway.

But slip into the lee of a tundra heave and sit quietly on the soft tundra grass. The vestiges of war and civilization recede quickly. Ten yards away a male Lapland Longspur sings from the tallest tussock, impressing his female. Look to the northwest where the remnants of last night's storm linger on the peaks. A White-tailed Eagle climbs the spiral staircase of the day's first thermal. It wasn't so far north and west of here, after all, that our species first prospected this tundra and these beaches, seeking sustenance. Longspur and eagle were here then. Longspur and eagle will still be here when the debris is gone.

On Attu in '89 we met a midwestern woman who had made the trek here many times. She was not a lister. She was not even a birder. She brought neither binoculars nor daydreams of Asian vagrants. She brought books and poetry. She realized Attu was not the end of the earth but perhaps a beginning. Or perhaps a place where we birders come full circle, searching for some touchstone to a simpler place and time, seeking and finding a simpler, more elemental kind of sustenance. Even the "power listers," if only temporarily, seem becalmed and reflective when enveloped by the solitude and isolation that is Attu.

There are no jangling cell phones on Attu, no blaring vidiot boxes, no adrenaline-pumping decisions to be made. This place challenges us to ask whether being human depends on these modern implements so taken for granted in our society. Is our humanity so different now from that of our ancient ancestors who came across the land bridge accompanied by Tereks and rubythroats? Is the Terek still a Terek if it must perch on our abandoned litter? Is the rubythroat still a rubythroat if it must roost in our forgotten waste?

Attu will not reveal these answers, but it does help us understand the implications of our questions. Thank you, Larry for making Attu accessible and available to birders, to humans, for this past quarter century. We're glad we didn't miss this very special place. 🐦

Color-coded

I have color-coded
my blue book
of Checklist of Birds
Attu Island, Alaska
and I know which birds
I have yet to see

I have made a list
of wildflowers I've seen
bog candle, fireweed
wild geranium, lupine
and drawn pictures
of plants I cannot name

I have collected maps
to Barbara Point
and the mouth of the Peaceful River
so that I might see
the old abandoned bulldozer
on the road
and chains and boats
and war debris rusting
in the sea
and perhaps view
a black-backed wagtail

I have collected maps
to Alexai Point
so that I can see
the deep worn bluffs
and the Japanese bunker
buried in the ground
and maybe glimpse
the spectacled eider
and the red-necked juvenile stint

I have collected maps
to Chichagof Point
so that I can see
the grasses growing over
the burnt homes
of the last natives of Attu

and on my return perhaps see
a snowy owl
and rock ptarmigan
close to the Japanese
star monument

I have collected maps
to South Beach
where the ancient rocks
form stark primitive sculptures
and maybe catch a Laysan albatross
flying far out to sea

I would still want maps
of Henderson River
and Murder Point
and Terrible Mountain
and Jackass Pass
but we are leaving in four days
and no one will be allowed to return
as this Attu Island becomes
a Wildlife Refuge

A last refuge
between the North Pacific
and the Bering Sea
for the ghosts of old wars
the spring of ancient wildflowers
the nests of new generations

and the continuous wrestling match
between the cold Arctic air
and the warm Pacific
winds.

—*Lyndia Terre*

Etching by Lyndia Terre

Contributors

Paul J. Baicich is Director of Conservation and Public Policy for the ABA, and past editor of the organization's magazine, *Birding*. Paul was fortunate to have served as an Attu field-leader on 11 of his 12 trips to that magical island.

Larry Balch taught mathematics at Wilbur Wright College in Chicago for 31 years before retiring in December 1999. He started birding in 1962, an initially casual hobby that by 1967 had evolved (or devolved, depending on your point of view) into building as large an ABA life list as possible. He served as president of the ABA from 1983 to 1989. Since he stopped running Attour, Inc. trips at the end of 2000, he concentrates on more relaxing activities, including lots of travel.

Bill and Ruth Brooks from Delmar, New York, are avid birders who went to Attu three times—in 1998, 1999, and 2000. Prior to her retirement, Ruth was an early intervention specialist with the Burlington, Vermont, school system and Bill was a health planner and policy analyst with the New York State Health Department. They met on a birding trip in Arizona in 1994 and continue a rigorous travel schedule in pursuit of their birding interests.

Jim Burns is a teaching tennis professional who became hooked on birds while he and his wife were backpacking in college and trying to affix proper names to the fauna and flora they encountered on the trail. He has been photographing birds since 1993 and has completed a book, scheduled to be published by Willow Creek Press in 2004, recounting his personal experiences with North America's 19 owl species.

Eli Elder began birding in Cleveland, at first in her back yard, then across the city and around Lake Erie. Within a few years, she and two friends went to Adak. Then she heard about Attu. After her first visit, in 1980, she returned 21 times. Looking for birds up on the bluffs and out over the bay was exciting; soon she realized that looking down was exciting too. She began to pay closer attention to the flowers underfoot, to find friends who helped her identify them, and to take photographs, many of which are now in this Attu Memoir. Eli's complete collection can be found in *Some Flowers of Attu Island* (2000).

John Fitchen is a retired professor of medicine who lives in Portland, Oregon with his wife Ellen. He has been a serious birder since 1992.

Dan Gibson is on the staff of the University of Alaska Museum at Fairbanks and is co-author of the authoritative *Status and Distribution of Alaska Birds* (with Brina Kessel) Allen Press, Lawrence, Kansas (1978). He has spent many seasons on the Near Islands, including lengthy field seasons on Shemya and Attu.

Ed Greaves, an avid birder since 1958, was a pediatrician with the original not-for-profit health maintenance organization, Kaiser Permanente Group. He is now retired. Although interested in all of natural history, bird photography has become his prime interest. Alaska is his favorite location for pursuing this passion, and the place where he has had the most memorable adventures.

Ed Harper taught both mathematics and field ornithology courses at American River College in Sacramento, California before retiring in June 2003. He presently teaches part time at the college, where he continues doing field ornithology classes when not traveling or leading birding tours through his company, Sandpiper Journeys. Ed journeyed to Attu on three occasions: 1981, 1983, and 1988. In addition to a life-long interest in birds, Ed is a keen photographer and has photographed thousands of species of birds from every continent.

Steve Heinl lives in Ketchikan, Alaska. He served as an Attu field-leader for eight of Attour's trips to Attu.

Jennifer Jolis was born in New York City. She came to Alaska in 1966 as a VISTA Volunteer. After spending the last 20 years as cook and restaurateur in Fairbanks, Alaska, she now works for the Fairbanks Visitors and Convention Bureau. Her marriage to Dan Gibson put her in Attour's path, and it was as a cook for Attour that she first fell in love with Attu in 1987. Her contribution to this book is excerpted from a paper she wrote as a graduate student in the University of Alaska Fairbanks' Northern Studies Program. She is grateful beyond words for the opportunity Larry Balch gave her to know Attu.

Paul Lehman is the primary range-map consultant for the third and fourth editions of the *National Geographic Society Field Guide to the Birds of North America*, the second edition of the *Sibley Guide to Birds*, and the fifth edition of *Birds of Eastern and Central North America* by Roger Tory Peterson. He leads bird tours throughout North America for WINGS, Inc., and lectures on bird distribution, identification, and the effects of weather on bird migration. A former geography instructor at the University of California-Santa Barbara, he now lives in Cape May, New Jersey. He has a particular interest in underbirded areas and migration hot spots, including western Alaska. He made three trips to Attu, two in fall (1993, 2000) as a leader; and from 1997 to 2002 he made annual autumn trips to Gambell, St. Lawrence Island.

Cindy Lippincott is currently editor/mapmaker for the ABA Birdfinding Guide Series. She previously worked for ABA, starting in 1987, as founding editor of *Winging It*, manager of ABA Sales, and membership coordinator. Cindy's eight vacations on Attu since 1982 include four years on Attour's staff. She was the last Attour participant to tick a life bird on the island, Great Spotted Woodpecker

Jerry Maisel has been taking photographs as a hobby since 1936 and birding since the 1960s. He and his wife, Laurette, have birded every state in the United States, all the provinces of Canada, and many foreign countries, including most of the great birding meccas. He has been to Attu nine times (three trips with Laurette,) and, as he says, loves "the whole Gestalt of the experience: just BEING THERE—the exploring, never knowing what super bird would turn up," the "Death Marches" in response to a reported bird sighting, the bike rides up the runway into a stiff wind—"and always the tightening in the chest at the thought that the reported first-record Asiatic would disappear before I got there! Life doesn't get much sweeter than that!"

Randy Meyers lives in Kotzebue, Alaska and works for the Bureau of Land Management as a natural resource specialist. She has lived in Alaska for almost 28 years, and earned a masters degree in botany in 1985 from the University of Alaska—Fairbanks. Her first (and favorite) home in Alaska was at Cold Bay, where she botanized and birded for five glorious years. A latecomer to Attu, she birded there for two wonderful weeks in early September 2000.

Macklin Smith has been to Attu 20 times and has a long list of North American birds. After volunteering as a cook in 1981, he worked on staff in that capacity on most subsequent tours. He teaches English and creative writing at the University of Michigan. His most recent book of poems, *Transplant* (2003), deals with cancer and healing, birds and friendships, and is available from Shaman Drum Books.

Brooke Stevens, editor of *Bird Observer* (2000–2002), lives in Cambridge, Massachusetts with her husband, Tom McCorkle. "The Murrelets" was published in the June 2001 issue of *Bird Observer*. On 12 August 2002, she and Tom landed on Attu with an American Birding Association group traveling on the ship, *Clipper Odyssey*, from Nome, Alaska to Petropavlovsk, Russia. Both upper and lower base buildings were still standing, the rye grass was shoulder-high and wildflowers were everywhere. It was a beautiful day and the entire island was visible as the ship cruised slowly through tens of thousands of Short-tailed Shearwaters near Attu's westernmost tip.

Roger Taylor lives in Palgrave, Ontario. He is a physicist and network manager who has been actively birding for more than 30 years and is a life member of the ABA.

Lyndia Terre is a painter, printmaker and poet. Her work is in many public collections in the United States and in private collections all over the world. She is not a birder, but feels the presence of all elements in the natural landscape as a whole; whether on Attu, the Galapagos, Kiawah Island in South Carolina, or in her own wildflower gardens. Her studio and gallery are located in Alton, Ontario.

Thede Tobish is an Alaskan birder with experience at all of the vagrant outposts in the state. He is also the Alaska regional editor for *North American Birds*.

George C. West is an artist and professor emeritus of zoophysiology who retired as Vice President for Academic Affairs of the University of Alaska Statewide System in 1984. He and his wife, Ellen, then moved to Homer, Alaska where he was an active advocate for conserving habitat for migrating shorebirds. He started the Kachemak Bay birding telephone hotline, started and edited the *Kachemak Bay Bird Watch* newsletter for 10 years, and has written over 100 scientific papers as well as several guides to birds and birding, most recently *A Birder's Guide to Alaska* (2002 ABA). He and Ellen now live in Green Valley Arizona, where he continues to bird, conducts banding research on hummingbirds, and illustrates birding publications.

Index